THE BEST TEST PREPARATION FOR THE
SAT II: Subject Test

WRITING

Ellen Davis Conner, M.A.
Instructor of English
Clear Lake High School
Friendswood, Texas

Mamie Webb Hixon, M.A.
Director of the Writing Center
University of West Florida
Pensacola, Florida

Research & Education Association
61 Ethel Road West • Piscataway, New Jersey 08854

The Best Test Preparation for the
SAT II: SUBJECT TEST
IN WRITING

Revised Printing, 1995

Printed in the United States of America

Library of Congress Catalog Card Number 94-65497

International Standard Book Number 0-87891-935-X

Research & Education Association
61 Ethel Road West
Piscataway, New Jersey 08854

REA supports the effort to conserve and
protect environmental resources by
printing on recycled papers.

CONTENTS

About Research and Education Association

Research and Education Association (REA) is an organization of educators, scientists, and engineers specializing in various academic fields. Founded in 1959 with the purpose of disseminating the most recently developed scientific information to groups in industry, government, and universities, REA has become a successful and highly respected publisher of study aids, test preps, handbooks, and reference works.

Created to extensively prepare students and professionals with the information they need, REA's Test Preparation series includes study guides for the Tests of General Educational Development (GED), the Scholastic Assessment Tests (SAT I and SAT II), the Advanced Placement Exams (AP), the Test of English as a Foreign Language (TOEFL), as well as the Graduate Record Examinations (GRE), the Graduate Management Admission Test (GMAT), the Law School Admission Test (LSAT), and the Medical College Admission Test (MCAT).

Whereas most Test Preparation books present few practice tests which bear little resemblance to the actual exams, REA's series presents tests which accurately depict the official exams in both degree of difficulty and types of questions. REA's practice tests are always based on the most recently administered exams and include every type of question that can be expected on the actual exams.

REA's publications and educational materials are highly regarded and continually receive an unprecedented amount of praise from professionals, instructors, librarians, parents, and students. Our authors are as diverse as the subjects and fields represented in the books we publish. They are well-known in their respective fields and serve on the faculties of prestigious universities throughout the United States.

Acknowledgments

In addition to our authors, we would like to thank:

Dr. Max Fogiel, President, for his overall guidance which has brought this publication to its completion

Stacey A. Sporer, Managing Editor, for directing the editorial staff throughout each phase of the project

Wade Olsson, Project Editor, for coordinating the development of the book

Jeff Karnicky, for his editorial contributions

SAT II: Writing

Chapter 1
About the SAT II:
Writing Subject Test

Chapter 1

ABOUT THE SAT II: WRITING SUBJECT TEST

ABOUT THIS BOOK

This book will provide you with an accurate and complete representation of the SAT II: Writing Subject Test. Inside you will find reviews designed to provide you with the information and strategies needed to do well on the exam, as well as six practice tests based on the actual exam. The practice tests contain every type of question that you may expect to appear on the SAT II: Writing Test. Following each test, you will find an answer key and detailed explanations designed to help you more completely understand the test material. You will also find sample essays with scores and commentary.

ABOUT THE TEST

Who Takes the Test and What Is It Used For?

Students planning to attend college should take the SAT II: Writing Subject Test if:

(1) Any of the colleges they apply to require the test for admission;

   OR

(2) The student wishes to demonstrate proficiency in writing or ability to use standard written English.

Colleges place great emphasis on writing as an essential skill for academic success and use SAT II: Writing scores for both admission and placement purposes.

Who Administers the Test?

The SAT II: Writing Subject Test is developed by The College Board and administered by the Educational Testing Service (ETS). The test development process is designed and implemented to ensure that the content and difficulty level of the test are appropriate, and involves the assistance of educators throughout the country.

When Should the SAT II: Writing Subject Test Be Taken?

If you are applying to a college that requires SAT II: Subject Test scores as part of the admissions process, you should take the SAT II: Writing Subject Test by November or January of your senior year. If your scores are being used only for placement purposes, you may be able to take the test in the spring. Make sure to contact the colleges to which you are applying for more specific information.

When and Where Is the Test Given?

The SAT II: Writing Subject Test is administered five times a year, in November, December, January, May, and June, at many locations throughout the country, mostly high schools.

To receive information on upcoming administrations of the exam, consult the publication *Taking the SAT II: Subject Tests* which can be obtained from your guidance counselor or by contacting:

College Board Admissions Testing Program
P.O. Box 6200
Princeton, NJ 08541-6200
(609) 921-9000

Is There a Registration Fee?

To take the SAT II: Writing Test, you must pay a registration fee. For a fee schedule, consult the publication *Taking the SAT II: Subject Tests*. Financial assistance may be granted in certain situations. To find out if you qualify and to register for assistance, contact your academic advisor.

HOW TO USE THIS BOOK

What Do I Study First?

The SAT II: Writing Subject Test is designed to test knowledge that has been acquired throughout your education. Therefore, the best way to prepare yourself for the actual exam is by thoroughly studying our review material and test-taking tips and by taking the sample tests provided in this book. They will familiarize you with the types of questions, directions, and the format of the SAT II: Writing Subject Test.

To begin your studies, read over the reviews and the suggestions for test-taking, take one of the practice tests to determine your area(s) of weakness, and then study the review material, focusing on your specific problem areas. The reviews include the information you need to know when taking the exam. Make sure to take the remaining practice tests to further test yourself and become familiar with the format of the SAT II: Writing Subject Test.

When Should I Start Studying?

It is never too early to start studying for the SAT II: Writing Test. The earlier you begin, the more time you will have to sharpen your skills. Do not procrastinate! Last-minute studying and cramming is *not* an effective way to study, since it does not allow you the time needed to learn the test material. The sooner you learn the format of the exam, the more comfortable you will be when you take it.

FORMAT OF THE SAT II: WRITING SUBJECT TEST

The SAT II: Writing Test consists of 60 multiple-choice questions plus one 20-minute essay question. The total testing time is one hour.

Part A: Essay	**20 minutes**
Part B: Multiple-Choice	**40 minutes**
Usage	30 questions
Sentence Correction	18 questions
Revision-in-Context	12 questions

Usage Questions

These questions require you to identify errors in a given sentence. Four words or phrases are underlined; you must choose the underlined portion that is incorrect in the context of the sentence. If the sentence is correct as is, choose (E), "No error."

DIRECTIONS: Each of the following sentences may contain an error in diction, usage, idiom, or grammar. Some sentences are correct. Some sentences contain one error. No sentence contains more than one error.

If there is an error, it will appear in one of the underlined portions labeled A, B, C, or D. If there is no error, choose the portion labeled E. If there is an error, select the letter of the portion that must be changed in order to correct the sentence.

EXAMPLE:

The player was <u>so tired that</u> thoughts of <u>going to sleep</u> <u>was all</u> that
             A   **B**   **C**

<u>went through</u> her mind. <u>No error</u>.   (A) (B) ● (D) (E)
    D   **E**

The answer is (C). The sentence contains an error in verb agreement. "Thoughts" is plural, so the corresponding verb must be "were."

Sentence Correction Questions

This type of question asks you to examine an underlined portion of a sentence and choose from among five alternatives the best way of phrasing the underlined part. Choice (A) is always the same as the original; choose this alternative if you think the original sentence is correct as written.

DIRECTIONS: In each of the following sentences, some portion of the sentence is underlined. Under each sentence are five choices. The first choice has the same wording as the original. The other four choices are reworded. Sometimes the first choice containing the original wording is the best; sometimes one of the other choices is the best. Choose the letter of the best choice. Your choice should produce a sentence which is not ambiguous or awkward and which is correct, clear, and precise.

This is a test of correct and effective English expression. Keep in mind the standards of English usage, punctuation, grammar, word choice, and construction.

EXAMPLE:

The children swam in the lake all day <u>and that is because it was so hot.</u>

(A)   and that is because it was so hot.

(B)   when it was so hot.

(C)   which is why it was so hot.

(D)   since it was so hot.

(E)   at the time when it was so hot.

The original phrasing of the sentence is wordy and imprecise. Choice (D) corrects this error.

Revision-in-Context Questions

This type of question presents an early draft of a student's essay. Each sentence in the essay is numbered. You will then be asked a series of multiple-choice questions about errors in the essay. The errors may pertain to grammar, usage, mechanics, or organization. Some questions will pertain to errors in individual sentences, while others may ask you to consider transitions between sentences, or the organization and focus of the entire essay.

DIRECTIONS: The following passages are considered early draft efforts of a student. Some sentences need to be rewritten to make the ideas clearer and more precise.

Read each passage carefully and answer the questions that follow it. Some of the questions are about particular sentences or parts of sentences and ask you to make decisions about sentence structure, diction, and usage. Some of the questions refer to the entire essay or parts of the essay and ask you to make decisions about organization, development, appropriateness of language, audience, and logic. Choose the answer that most effectively makes the intended meaning clear and follows the requirements of standard written English. After you have chosen your answer, fill in the corresponding oval on your answer sheet.

EXAMPLE:

(1) Crime rates are rising alarmingly. (2) Newspapers and television newscasts report frightening situations in all of our major cities. (3) Young people form gangs, doing illegal activities and atrocities that were unheard of only a few years ago.

(4) HIV and AIDS are common terms, when we had never heard of this national health threat twenty years ago. (5) Many diseases were growing out of control, and threatening the health of our country.

Which choice is the best revision of Sentence 5?

(A) Many diseases were growing out of control, threatening the health of our country.

(B) Many diseases grow out of control, but threaten the health of our country.

(C) Many diseases are growing out of control, threatening the health of our country.

(D) Many diseases have grown out of control, and threatening the health of our country.

(E) Many diseases grew out of control; and overtook the health of our country.

Ⓐ Ⓑ ● Ⓓ Ⓔ

Choice (C) makes the most sense, both grammatically and in the context of the essay.

Essay Question

You will be asked to write a 20-minute essay about a given topic. You must write only on this topic. The essay topics often ask you to respond to famous quotations or well-known statements and ideas. Depending on the question, your response should be based on personal experience, reading, and current or historical events.

DIRECTIONS: You have 20 minutes to plan and write an essay on the topic below. You may write only on the assigned topic.

Make sure to give specific examples to support your thesis. Proofread your essay carefully and take care to express your ideas clearly and effectively.

ESSAY TOPIC:

Many schools group students by ability. Are you in favor of this practice?

ASSIGNMENT: Explain your position by discussing the positive and negative consequences of ability grouping for both students and teachers.

ABOUT THE REVIEW SECTIONS

The reviews in this book will teach you the skills and concepts needed to approach SAT II: Writing Subject Test questions and provide drills to help reinforce what you have learned. By using the reviews in conjunction with the practice tests, you will be able to sharpen your skills for the SAT II: Writing Subject Test.

English Language Skills Review

The English Language Skills Review covers grammar, usage, capitalization, and spelling. The concepts discussed in this review will help you to identify the kinds of errors which often appear in usage, sentence correction, and revision-in-context questions. Studying this review will also help you to write a clearer and more effective essay.

Essay Writing Review

This review shows you how to write a high-scoring essay within the 20-minute time limit of the exam. Topics discussed include thesis development, organization, and common writing errors. Sample essay topics and responses, along with analysis and commentary, will help you to sharpen your essay-writing skills.

SCORING THE SAT II: WRITING SUBJECT TEST

The SAT II: Writing Test, like all other Subject Tests, is scored on a 200-800 scale. The multiple-choice questions are machine-scored. Your writing sample counts for one-third of your total score and is read independently by two different scorers. If there is a discrepancy in their grades, a third reader reviews the essay to resolve the difference.

How Do I Score My Practice Tests?

Part A: Essay

Your essay score counts for one-third of your final score on the exam. Your essay will be evaluated by two scorers, so make sure to have two people (including yourself if necessary) read your practice essays. Since it is difficult to objectively judge your own writing, ask a teacher or friend to read your essay for a second opinion. The following chart summarizes the criteria that SAT II: Writing Test readers use when evaluating essays.

Score	Criteria
6	*Clear and Consistent Competence* An essay with a score of 6 is extremely well-organized. It is concise and easy to understand, displays an impressive range of vocabulary, and contains almost no errors in the use of language. The topic is effectively supported with examples that illustrate the thesis.
5	*Reasonably Consistent Competence* This essay is thoughtfully organized and presents adequate support for the main idea. Some errors in language may appear, but there is still variety in sentence structure and range of vocabulary.

4	*Adequate Competence* An essay with a score of 4 shows some lapses in quality, but still addresses the topic and uses appropriate examples to support the thesis. The use of language is adequate, but there may be problems in grammar and usage.
3	*Developing Competence* An essay in this category shows weaknesses in organization and development, as well as significant errors in grammar and usage.
2	*Some Incompetence* This essay shows flaws in organization, has thin development, and provides few details to support the thesis. In addition, there will be frequent errors in grammar and diction.
1	*Incompetence* An essay with a score of 1 is seriously flawed in every category. There will be virtually no structure or development of ideas, and numerous grammar and usage errors make the essay difficult to understand.

Part B: Multiple-Choice

Count the number of correct responses in Part B (Usage, Sentence Correction, and Revision-in-Context questions). Next, count the number of incorrect responses. Enter these numbers into the corresponding blanks on the scoring worksheet. Then, multiply the number of incorrect answers by one-fourth (this is the penalty for answering incorrectly). Subtract this product from the total number of correct answers. Fractions should be rounded off: round up for one-half or more and round down for less than one-half. This will yield your total score for the multiple-choice section. The score on the multiple-choice sections counts for two-thirds of your final score on the exam.

SCORING WORKSHEET

Multiple-Choice Raw Score

_____	−	_____ (x 4)	=	_____
number of correct answers		number of incorrect answers		Multiple-Choice Raw Score

Writing Sample Raw Score

_____	+	_____	=	_____
Score 1		Score 2		Writing Sample Raw Score

Composite Raw Score

_____	+	_____ (x 3)	=	_____
Multiple-Choice Raw Score		Writing Sample Raw Score		Composite Raw Score (round to nearest whole number)

Calculating Your Scaled Scores

To convert your composite raw score to a scaled score, consult the Score Conversion Table on the following page.

STUDYING FOR THE SAT II: WRITING SUBJECT TEST

It is very important for you to choose the time and place for studying that works best for you. Some students may set aside a certain number of hours every morning to study, while others may choose to study at night before going to sleep. Other students may study during the day, while waiting on a line, or even while eating lunch. Only you can determine when and where your study time will be most effective. Be consistent and use your time wisely. Work out a study routine and stick to it!

When you take the practice tests, try to make your testing conditions as much like the actual test as possible. Turn your television and radio off, and sit down at a quiet table free from distraction. Make sure to time yourself with a timer.

As you complete each practice test, score your test and thoroughly review the explanations to the questions you answered incorrectly; however, do not review too much at any one time. Concentrate on one problem area at a time by reviewing the questions and explanations, and by study-

SCORE CONVERSION TABLE

Raw Score	Scaled Score	Raw Score	Scaled Score
96	800	47	490
95	800	46	490
94	800	45	480
93	800	44	480
92	800	43	470
91	800	42	470
90	800	41	460
89	800	40	450
88	800	39	450
87	790	38	440
86	780	37	440
85	770	36	430
84	760	35	430
83	750	34	430
82	750	33	430
81	740	32	420
80	730	31	420
79	720	30	410
78	710	29	410
77	700	28	400
76	690	27	400
75	680	26	380
74	670	25	380
73	670	24	370
72	670	23	360
71	660	22	360
70	650	21	350
69	640	20	350
68	630	19	340
67	630	18	340
66	620	17	340
65	610	16	330
64	610	15	330
63	600	14	320
62	590	13	310
61	580	12	310
60	580	11	300
59	570	10	290
58	560	9	290
57	560	8	280
56	550	7	270
55	550	6	270
54	540	5	270
53	530	4	270
52	530	3	270
51	520	2	270
50	510	1	270
49	510	0	270
48	500	−1 through −14	270

ing our review until you are confident you completely understand the material.

Keep track of your scores. By doing so, you will be able to gauge your progress and discover general weaknesses in particular sections. You should carefully study the reviews that cover your areas of difficulty, as this will build your skills in those areas.

TEST-TAKING TIPS

Although you may be unfamiliar with standardized tests such as the SAT II: Writing Subject Test, there are many ways to acquaint yourself with this type of examination and help alleviate your test-taking anxieties. Listed below are ways to help you become accustomed to the SAT II: Writing Subject Test, some of which may apply to other standardized tests as well.

Become comfortable with the format of the SAT II: Writing Subject Test. When you are practicing to take the test, simulate the conditions under which you will be taking the actual test. Stay calm and pace yourself. After simulating the test only a couple of times, you will boost your chances of doing well, and you will be able to sit down for the actual exam much more confidently.

Know the directions and format for each section of the test. Familiarizing yourself with the directions and format of the different test sections will not only save you time, but will also ensure that you are familiar enough with the SAT II: Writing Subject Test to avoid nervousness (and the mistakes caused by being nervous).

Work on the easier questions first. Within each group of questions, the easier ones are usually at the beginning. If you find yourself working too long on one question, make a mark next to it in your test booklet and continue to the next question. After you answer all the questions you can, go back to the ones you have skipped.

If you are unsure of an answer, guess. However—if you do guess, guess wisely. Use the process of elimination by going through each answer to a question and eliminating as many of the answer choices as possible. By eliminating three answer choices, you give yourself a fifty-fifty chance of answering correctly, since there will only be two choices left from which to make your guess.

Mark your answers in the appropriate spaces on the answer sheet. Each numbered row will contain five ovals corresponding to each answer choice for that question. Fill in the circle that corresponds to your answer darkly, completely, and neatly. You can change your answer, but remember to completely erase your old answer. Any stray lines or unnecessary marks may cause the machine to score your answer incorrectly. When you have finished working on a section, you may want to go back and check to make sure your answers correspond to the correct questions. Marking one answer in the wrong space will throw off the rest of your test, whether it is graded by machine or by hand.

You don't have to answer every question. You are not penalized if you do not answer a question. The only penalty you receive is if you answer a question incorrectly. Try to use the guessing strategy, but if you are truly stumped by a question, you do not have to answer it.

Work quickly and steadily. You have a limited amount of time to work on each section, so you need to work quickly and steadily. Avoid focusing on one problem for too long. Taking the practice tests in this book will help you to learn how to budget your time.

Before the Test

Make sure you know exactly where your test center is well in advance of your test day so you do not get lost on the day of the test. On the night before the test, gather together the materials you will need the next day:

- Your admission ticket

- Two forms of identification (e.g., driver's license, student identification card, or current alien registration card)

- Two #2 pencils with erasers

- Directions to the test center

- A watch, if you wish, but not one that makes noise, as it may disturb other test-takers

On the day of the test, you should wake up early (hopefully after a decent night's rest) and have a good breakfast. Dress comfortably, so that you are not distracted by being too hot or too cold while taking the test. Also plan to arrive at the test center early. This will allow you to collect your thoughts and relax before the test, and will also spare you the stress of being late. If you arrive after the test begins, you will not be admitted or receive a refund.

During the Test

When you arrive at the test center, try to find a seat where you feel you will be comfortable. Follow all the rules and instructions given by the test supervisor. If you do not, you risk being dismissed from the test and having your scores canceled.

Once all the test materials are passed out, the test instructor will give you directions for filling out your answer sheet. Fill this sheet out carefully since this information will appear on your score report.

Remember—since no scratch paper will be provided, you can write in your test booklet.

After the Test

When you have completed the SAT II: Writing Subject Test, you may hand in your test materials and leave. Then, go home and relax!

YOUR SCORE REPORT

You should receive your score report about five weeks after you take the test. This report will include your scores, percentile ranks, and interpretive information. When you register for the test, you can also take advantage of two different reporting options: Score Choice and the Writing Sample Copy Service.

Score Choice allows you to review your scores before instructing the College Board to send them to the colleges you have chosen. If you decide your scores are too low, you can take the test again. Only you and your high school will know your original scores.

The *Writing Sample Copy Service* provides you with three copies of your graded essay, which you can send to colleges for admissions purposes. Additionally, if you plan to take the test again, a copy of your essay with graders' comments can be invaluable in assessing your strengths and weaknesses.

SAT II: Writing

Chapter 2
Question Types
and Strategies

Chapter 2

QUESTION TYPES AND STRATEGIES

There are four different types of questions on the SAT II: Writing Subject Test. This chapter will give you examples of each kind of question, along with strategies for solving them quickly.

USAGE QUESTIONS

These sentences will test your knowledge of word use, syntax, meaning, and grammar. The correct answers will follow the rules of standard written English. For each sentence in which you find an error, choose the one underlined part that must be changed to make the sentence correct and fill in the appropriate space on your answer sheet.

Be sure to read the sentence exactly as it is written:

Some people fail to realize that a twice-yearly dental cleaning
    A   **B**

and exam are a relatively painless way to avoid more serious
       C   **D**

complications later. No error.
                  E

If you determine that the sentence contains an error, proceed as follows:

Step 1 | Identify the incorrect part of the sentence. The incorrect part of the sentence is "a twice-yearly dental cleaning and exam are."

| Step 2 | Substitute the underlined answer that employs the correct usage. |

The word "are" is underlined; if it was changed to "is" the sentence would be correct.

| Step 3 | Re-read the sentence with your own usage substituted for the underlined part. |

Some people fail to realize that a twice-yearly dental cleaning and exam is a relatively painless way to avoid more serious complications later.

If you cannot find an error in the sentence, look for common errors first, such as subject-verb agreement and verb tense errors. Do not waste time looking for errors that are not there, since choice (E)—"No error" is sometimes the correct answer.

SENTENCE CORRECTION QUESTIONS

These questions test your ability to make appropriate revisions in accordance with the rules of standard written English. In the following sentences some part of the sentence, or all of the sentence, is underlined. Below each sentence you will find five ways of phrasing the underlined part. Choose the answer that most effectively expresses the meaning of the original sentence. The correct sentence should be clear and neither awkward nor ambiguous. Choice (A) is always exactly the same as the underlined part. Choose (A) if you think the original sentence needs no revision.

Read the sentence carefully:

<u>Intelligence is determined contrary to public opinion not by</u> the size of the brain but by the number and complexity of dendrites in the brain.

(A) Intelligence is determined contrary to public opinion by not

(B) Intelligence is contrary to public opinion and determined not by

(C) Contrary to public opinion, intelligence is determined not by

(D) Not by popular opinion is intelligence determined but by

(E) Contrary to public opinion, intelligence determines not by

If you determine that the sentence contains an error, proceed as follows:

Step 1 | Eliminate choice (A) since it restates exactly what is underlined in the sentence.

Step 2 | Eliminate the obviously incorrect choices.

(B) ELIMINATE — changes the meaning of the sentence

(C) Maybe

(D) Maybe

(E) ELIMINATE — awkward and unclear

Step 3 | Choose between the most likely answers.

(C) is clearer than (D). (C) directly links the phrase "Intelligence is determined not by" with the part of the sentence that logically follows this statement.

If you cannot find an error in the sentence, look over the answer choices and compare what is changed to the original sentence. If the original sentence seems best, choose answer choice (A), which is an exact restatement of the original sentence.

REVISION-IN-CONTEXT QUESTIONS

The passage below is the first draft of an essay written by a student. Following the essay are three questions based on the essay. The questions concern revisions that will make the essay clearer, more concise, and error-free.

The following essay was written by a student in response to an essay questions about how his/her use of language differs from proper English when speaking with a friend.

(1) The language I would use in talking to a friend would certainly differ from standard English. (2) In talking with a friend I would be prone to phrases drawn from popular culture that we are both aware of. (3) I would know that by employing certain phrases that my friends and I were members of a peer group, and thus friends.

(4) In talking with friends I would be more prone to use certain words and phrases, such as "hey," "like," and "you know," in ways that are both unconventional and grammatically incorrect. (5) This informal use of language implies the casualness and familiarity that I feel when among my friends.

(6) I would pepper my vocabulary with words that have no set meaning on their own, such as "like." (7) "Like" functions as an intensifier; "He was, like, so dumb," would imply that the person of whom I was speaking was quite stupid. (8) My friends would easily understand what I was saying.

1. Which of the following revisions most clearly states the meaning of sentence 3?

    (A) As it is now

    (B) I would know, by employing certain phrases, that my friends and I shared similar interests.

    (C) My friends and I would be peers by employing certain phrases that show we are friends.

    (D) I would know that my friends and I had things in common by our similar uses of language.

    (E) I would know, that by employing certain phrases and words, that my friends and I shared common interests and were, because of this knowledge, peers.

This type of question is very similar to the sentence correction questions. If you feel that the sentence is not in need of revision choose answer choice (A). If you determine that the sentence would benefit from revision, proceed as follows:

| Step 1 | Eliminate choice (A) since it makes no revision. |

| Step 2 | Eliminate the obviously incorrect choices. Choice (D) says something completely different that the idea implied by the |

original sentence, while (E) is a verbose and repetitive run-on sentence.

| Step 3 | Choose between the most likely answers. Choice (B) is clearer than (C) and (B) better expresses the thought that sentence (3) attempts to convey.

2.   Which sentence would best follow sentence 8?

   (A)   And that is all that matters.

   (B)   Furthermore, my friends and I would employ many more non-standard usages.

   (C)   The language I would use in talking to a friend would certainly be different from standard English.

   (D)   My friends and I have our own way of speaking.

   (E)   My use of language among friends would be casual, informal and idiosyncratic, reflecting these same qualities in our relationships.

This type of question tests your ability to write a good concluding sentence. Proceed as follows:

| Step 1 | Eliminate the obviously incorrect answer choices. (B) is not a concluding sentence, since it introduces a new idea. (C) merely restates the opening sentence.

| Step 2 | Eliminate the answers that fail to both organize and summarize the main idea of the essay.

Choice (A) does neither. Choice (D) restates one idea from the essay. Choice (E) both summarizes and organizes the main idea of the essay. (E) is the correct answer.

3.   How could the author make paragraph 1 stronger?

   (A)   By using concrete examples, as in the second and third paragraph.

   (B)   By combining sentences (2) and (3).

   (C)   By focusing on the meaning of "standard English."

   (D)   By switching the order of paragraph 1 and paragraph 2.

   (E)   By clearly stating a thesis in the paragraph.

This type of question deals with the essay as a whole. There are no simple steps to answering questions such as these; you must read the entire essay and then carefully, yet quickly, evaluate each answer choice. Answer choice (A) makes sense, since the opening paragraph lacks the concrete examples that help to strengthen the second and third paragraphs. (B) would serve no useful purpose; (C) is unnecessary; (D) would harm the essay, since the opening paragraph states the main idea of the essay. (E) is a poor choice because the opening paragraph already clearly states a thesis.

ESSAY QUESTION

The essay question will require you to write a 20-minute essay on a given topic. You may write only on the given topic.

ESSAY TOPIC:

Many leaders have suggested over the last few years that instead of a military draft we should require all young people to serve the public in some way for a period of time. The service could be military or any other reasonable form of public service.

ASSIGNMENT: Do you agree or disagree with the statement? Support your opinion with specific examples from history, current events, literature, or personal experience.

Before the test, you should:

- Study this review to be clear about essay writing strategies.

- Be familiar with the directions for the essay section of the exam.

During the test, you should:

- Take a stand on the issue presented and don't back down. You should acknowledge opposing viewpoints, but make sure your position is clearly and strongly stated.

- Take some time to brainstorm and organize your thoughts into lists, pictures, outlines, or whatever helps you make sense of your ideas.

After writing your essay, you should:

- Do a quick reading to make sure you have organized your ideas and presented them clearly. Make sure your essay clearly and strongly states your point of view, along with logical support and defense of your ideas.

- Quickly proofread your essay for grammar, spelling, and punctuation, and make any necessary corrections.

SAT II: Writing

Chapter 3
English Language Skills Review

Chapter 3

ENGLISH LANGUAGE SKILLS REVIEW

The requirements for informal spoken English are much more relaxed than the rigid rules for "standard written English." While slang, colloquialisms, and other informal expressions are acceptable and sometimes very appropriate in casual speech, they are inappropriate in academic and business writing. More often than not, writers, especially student writers, do not make a distinction between the two: they use the same words, grammar, and sentence structure from their everyday speech in their college papers, albeit unsuccessfully.

The SAT II: Writing Test does not require you to know grammatical terms such as *gerund, subject complement,* or *dependent clause,* although general familiarity with such terms may be helpful to you in determining whether a sentence or part of a sentence is correct or incorrect. You should watch for errors in grammar, spelling, punctuation, capitalization, sentence structure, and word choice. Remember: this is a test of written language skills; therefore, your responses should be based on what you know to be correct for written work, not what you know to be appropriate for a casual conversation. For instance, in informal speech, you might say "Who are you going to choose?" But in formal academic writing, you would write "Whom are you going to choose?" Your choices, then, should be dictated by requirements for *written,* not *conversational* English.

WORD CHOICE SKILLS

Connotative and Denotative Meanings

The denotative meaning of a word is its *literal,* dictionary definition: what the word denotes or "means." The connotative meaning of a word is what the word connotes or "suggests"; it is a meaning apart from what the word literally means. A writer should choose a word based on the tone and context of the sentence; this ensures that a word bears the appropriate connotation while still conveying some exactness in denotation. For example, a gift might be described as "cheap," but the directness of this word has a negative connotation—something cheap is something of little or no value. The word "inexpensive" has a more positive connotation, though "cheap" is a synonym for "inexpensive." Questions of this type require you to make a decision regarding the appropriateness of words and phrases for the context of a sentence.

Wordiness and Conciseness

Effective writing is concise. Wordiness, on the other hand, decreases the clarity of expression by cluttering sentences with unnecessary words.

Wordiness questions test your ability to detect redundancies (unnecessary repetitions), circumlocution (failure to get to the point), and padding with loose synonyms. Wordiness questions require you to choose sentences that use as few words as possible to convey a message clearly, economically, and effectively.

Notice the difference in impact between the first and second sentences in the following pairs:

INCORRECT: The medical exam that he gave me was entirely complete.

CORRECT: The medical exam he gave me was complete.

INCORRECT: Larry asked his friend John, who was a good, old friend, if he would join him and go along with him to see the foreign film made in Japan.

CORRECT: Larry asked his good, old friend John if he would join him in seeing the Japanese film.

INCORRECT: I was absolutely, totally happy with the present that my parents gave to me at 7 a.m. on the morning of my birthday.

CORRECT: I was happy with the present my parents gave me on the morning of my birthday.

☞ Drill: Word Choice Skills

<u>DIRECTIONS</u>: Choose the correct option.

1. His <u>principal</u> reasons for resigning were his <u>principles</u> of right and wrong.

    (A) principal . . . principals   (C) principle . . . principles

    (B) principle . . . principals   (D) No change is necessary.

2. The book tells about Alzheimer's disease—how it <u>affects</u> the patient and what <u>effect</u> it has on the patient's family.

    (A) effects . . . affect   (C) effects . . . effects

    (B) affects . . . affect   (D) No change is necessary.

3. The <u>amount</u> of homeless children we can help depends on the <u>number</u> of available shelters.

    (A) number . . . number   (C) number . . . amount

    (B) amount . . . amount   (D) No change is necessary.

4. All students are <u>suppose to</u> pass the test before <u>achieving</u> upper-division status.

    (A) suppose to . . . acheiving

    (B) suppose to . . . being achieved

    (C) supposed to . . . achieving

    (D) No change is necessary.

5. The reason he <u>succeeded</u> is <u>because</u> he worked hard.

    (A) succeeded . . . that   (C) succede . . . because of

    (B) seceded . . . that   (D) No change is necessary.

DIRECTIONS: Select the sentence that clearly and effectively states the idea and has no structural errors.

6. (A) South of Richmond, the two roads converge together to form a single highway.

   (B) South of Richmond, the two roads converge together to form an interstate highway.

   (C) South of Richmond, the two roads converge to form an interstate highway.

   (D) South of Richmond, the two roads converge to form a single interstate highway.

7. (A) The student depended on his parents for financial support.

   (B) The student lacked the ways and means to pay for his room and board, so he depended on his parents for this kind of money and support.

   (C) The student lacked the ways and means or the wherewithal to support himself, so his parents provided him with the financial support he needed.

   (D) The student lacked the means to pay for his room and board, so he depended on his parents for financial support.

8. (A) Vincent van Gogh and Paul Gaughin were close personal friends and companions who enjoyed each other's company and frequently worked together on their artwork.

   (B) Vincent van Gogh and Paul Gaughin were friends who frequently painted together.

   (C) Vincent van Gogh was a close personal friend of Paul Gaughin's, and the two of them often worked together on their artwork because they enjoyed each other's company.

   (D) Vincent van Gogh, a close personal friend of Paul Gaughin's, often worked with him on their artwork.

9. (A) A college education often involves putting away childish thoughts, which are characteristic of youngsters, and concentrating on the future, which lies ahead.

(B)   A college education involves putting away childish thoughts, which are characteristic of youngsters, and concentrating on the future.

(C)   A college education involves putting away childish thoughts and concentrating on the future.

(D)   A college education involves putting away childish thoughts and concentrating on the future which lies ahead.

10.   (A)   I had the occasion to visit an Oriental pagoda while I was a tourist on vacation and visiting in Kyoto, Japan.

(B)   I visited a Japanese pagoda in Kyoto.

(C)   I had occasion to visit a pagoda when I was vacationing in Kyoto, Japan.

(D)   On my vacation, I visited a Japanese pagoda in Kyoto.

SENTENCE STRUCTURE SKILLS

Parallelism

Parallel structure is used to express matching ideas. It refers to the grammatical balance of a series of any of the following:

Phrases:

The squirrel ran *along the fence, up the tree,* and *into his burrow* with a mouthful of acorns.

Adjectives:

The job market is flooded with *very talented, highly motivated,* and *well-educated* young people.

Nouns:

You will need a *notebook, pencil,* and *dictionary* for the test.

Clauses:

The children were told to decide which toy they would keep and which toy they would give away.

Verbs:

The farmer *plowed*, *planted*, and *harvested* his corn in record time.

Verbals:

Reading, *writing*, and *calculating* are fundamental skills that all of us should possess.

Correlative conjunctions:

Either you will do your homework *or* you will fail.

Repetition of structural signals:

(such as articles, auxiliaries, prepositions, and conjunctions)

> INCORRECT: I have quit my job, enrolled in school, and am looking for a reliable babysitter.

> CORRECT: I *have quit* my job, *have enrolled* in school, and *am looking* for a reliable babysitter.

Note: Repetition of prepositions is considered formal and is not necessary.

> You can travel *by car, by plane, or by train*; it's all up to you.

OR

> You can travel *by car, plane, or train*; it's all up to you.

When a sentence contains items in a series, check for both punctuation and sentence balance. When you check for punctuation, make sure the commas are used correctly. When you check for parallelism, make sure that the conjunctions connect similar grammatical constructions, such as all adjectives or all clauses.

Misplaced and Dangling Modifiers

A misplaced modifier is one that is in the wrong place in the sentence. Misplaced modifiers come in all forms—words, phrases, and clauses. Sentences containing misplaced modifiers are often very comical: *Mom made me eat the spinach instead of my brother*. Misplaced modifiers, like the one in this sentence, are usually too far away from the word or words they modify. This sentence should read: *Mom made me, instead of my brother, eat the spinach*.

Modifiers like *only*, *nearly*, and *almost* should be placed next to the word they modify and not in front of some other word, especially a verb, that they are not intended to modify.

A modifier is misplaced if it appears to modify the wrong part of the sentence or if we cannot be certain what part of the sentence the writer intended it to modify. To correct a misplaced modifier, move the modifier next to the word it describes.

> INCORRECT: She served hamburgers to the men on paper plates.

> CORRECT: She served hamburgers on paper plates to the men.

Split infinitives also result in misplaced modifiers. Infinitives consist of the marker *to* plus the plain form of the verb. The two parts of the infinitive make up a grammatical unit that should not be split. Splitting an infinitive is placing an adverb between the *to* and the verb.

> INCORRECT: The weather service expects temperatures to not rise.

> CORRECT: The weather service expects temperatures not to rise.

Sometimes a split infinitive may be natural and preferable, though it may still bother some readers.

> EX: Several U.S. industries expect *to* more than *triple* their use of robots within the next decade.

A squinting modifier is one that may refer to either a preceding or a following word, leaving the reader uncertain about what it is intended to modify. Correct a squinting modifier by moving it next to the word it is intended to modify.

> INCORRECT: Snipers who fired on the soldiers often escaped capture.

> CORRECT: Snipers who often fired on the soldiers escaped capture.

> OR   Snipers who fired on the soldiers escaped capture often.

A dangling modifier is a modifier or verb in search of a subject: the modifying phrase (usually an *-ing* word group, an *-ed* or *-en* word group, or a *to + a verb* word group—participle phrase or infinitive phrase respectively) either appears to modify the wrong word or has nothing to modify. It is literally dangling at the beginning or the end of a sentence. The sentences often look and sound correct: *To be a student government officer, your grades must be above average.* (However, the verbal modifier has nothing to describe. Who is *to be a student government officer?* Your grades?) Questions of this type require you to determine whether a modifier has a headword or whether it is dangling at the beginning or the end of the sentence.

To correct a dangling modifier, reword the sentence by either: 1) changing the modifying phrase to a clause with a subject, or 2) changing the subject of the sentence to the word that should be modified. The following are examples of a dangling gerund, a dangling infinitive, and a dangling participle:

INCORRECT: Shortly after leaving home, the accident occurred.

                  Who is <u>leaving home</u>, the accident?

CORRECT: Shortly after we left home, the accident occurred.

INCORRECT: To get up on time, a great effort was needed.

                  <u>To get up</u> needs a subject.

CORRECT: To get up on time, I made a great effort.

Fragments

A fragment is an incomplete construction which may or may not have a subject and a verb. Specifically, a fragment is a group of words pretending to be a sentence. Not all fragments appear as separate sentences, however. Often, fragments are separated by semicolons.

INCORRECT: Traffic was stalled for ten miles on the freeway. Because repairs were being made on potholes.

CORRECT: Traffic was stalled for ten miles on the freeway because repairs were being made on potholes.

INCORRECT: It was a funny story; one that I had never heard before.

CORRECT: It was a funny story, one that I had never heard before.

Run-on/Fused Sentences

A run-on/fused sentence is not necessarily a long sentence or a sentence that the reader considers too long; in fact, a run-on may be two short sentences: *Dry ice does not melt it evaporates.* A run-on results when the writer fuses or runs together two separate sentences without any correct mark of punctuation separating them.

> INCORRECT: Knowing how to use a dictionary is no problem each dictionary has a section in the front of the book telling how to use it.

> CORRECT: Knowing how to use a dictionary is no problem. Each dictionary has a section in the front of the book telling how to use it.

Even if one or both of the fused sentences contains internal punctuation, the sentence is still a run-on.

> INCORRECT: Bob bought dress shoes, a suit, and a nice shirt he needed them for his sister's wedding.

> CORRECT: Bob bought dress shoes, a suit, and a nice shirt. He needed them for his sister's wedding.

Comma Splices

A comma splice is the unjustifiable use of only a comma to combine what really is two separate sentences.

> INCORRECT: One common error in writing is incorrect spelling, the other is the occasional use of faulty diction.

> CORRECT: One common error in writing is incorrect spelling; the other is the occasional use of faulty diction.

Both run-on sentences and comma splices may be corrected in one of the following ways:

> RUN-ON: Neal won the award he had the highest score.

> COMMA SPLICE: Neal won the award, he had the highest score.

Separate the sentences with a period:

> Neal won the award. He had the highest score.

Separate the sentences with a comma and a coordinating conjunction *(and, but, or, nor, for, yet, so)*:

> Neal won the award for he had the highest score.

Separate the sentences with a semicolon:

> Neal won the award; he had the highest score.

Separate the sentences with a subordinating conjunction such as *although, because, since, if*:

> Neal won the award because he had the highest score.

Subordination, Coordination, and Predication

Suppose, for the sake of clarity, you wanted to combine the information in these two sentences to create one statement:

I studied a foreign language. I found English quite easy.

How you decide to combine this information should be determined by the relationship you'd like to show between the two facts. *I studied a foreign language, and I found English quite easy* seems rather illogical. The **coordination** of the two ideas (connecting them with the coordinating conjunction *and* is ineffective. Using **subordination** instead (connecting the sentences with a subordinating conjunction) clearly shows the degree of relative importance between the expressed ideas:

After I studied a foreign language, I found English quite easy.

When using a conjunction, be sure that the sentence parts you are joining are in agreement.

INCORRECT: She loved him dearly but not his dog.

CORRECT: She loved him dearly but she did not love his dog.

A common mistake that is made is to forget that each member of the pair must be followed by the same kind of construction.

INCORRECT: They complimented them both for their bravery and they thanked them for their kindness.

CORRECT: They both complimented them for their bravery and thanked them for their kindness.

While refers to time and should not be used as a substitute for *although, and,* or *but.*

INCORRECT: While I'm usually interested in Fellini movies, I'd rather not go tonight.

CORRECT: Although I'm usually interested in Fellini movies, I'd rather not go tonight.

Where refers to time and should not be used as a substitute for *that.*

INCORRECT: We read in the paper where they are making great strides in DNA research.

CORRECT: We read in the paper that they are making great strides in DNA research.

After words like reason and explanation, use that, not because.

INCORRECT: His explanation for his tardiness was because his alarm did not go off.

CORRECT: His explanation for his tardiness was that his alarm did not go off.

☞ Drill: Sentence Structure Skills

DIRECTIONS: Choose the sentence that expresses the thought most clearly and that has no error in structure.

1. (A) Many gases are invisible, odorless, and they have no taste.

    (B) Many gases are invisible, odorless, and have no taste.

    (C) Many gases are invisible, odorless, and tasteless.

2. (A) Everyone agreed that she had neither the voice or the skill to be a speaker.

    (B) Everyone agreed that she had neither the voice nor the skill to be a speaker.

    (C) Everyone agreed that she had either the voice nor the skill to be a speaker.

3. (A) The mayor will be remembered because he kept his campaign promises and because of his refusal to accept political favors.

    (B) The mayor will be remembered because he kept his campaign promises and because he refused to accept political favors.

    (C) The mayor will be remembered because of his refusal to accept political favors and he kept his campaign promises.

4. (A) While taking a shower, the doorbell rang.

    (B) While I was taking a shower, the doorbell rang.

    (C) While taking a shower, someone rang the doorbell.

5. (A) He swung the bat, while the runner stole second base.

    (B) The runner stole second base while he swung the bat.

    (C) While he was swinging the bat, the runner stole second base.

DIRECTIONS: Choose the correct option.

6. Nothing grows as well in Mississippi as <u>cotton. Cotton</u> being the state's principal crop.

   (A) cotton, cotton   (C) cotton cotton

   (B) cotton; cotton   (D) No change is necessary.

7. It was a heartwrenching <u>movie; one</u> that I had never seen before.

   (A) movie and   (C) movie. One

   (B) movie, one   (D) No change is necessary.

8. Traffic was stalled for three miles on the <u>bridge. Because</u> repairs were being made.

   (A) bridge because   (C) bridge, because

   (B) bridge; because   (D) No change is necessary.

9. The ability to write complete sentences comes with <u>practice writing</u> run-on sentences seems to occur naturally.

   (A) practice, writing   (C) practice and

   (B) practice. Writing   (D) No change is necessary.

10. Even though she had taken French classes, she could not understand native French <u>speakers they</u> all spoke too fast.

    (A) speakers, they   (C) speaking

    (B) speakers. They   (D) No change is necessary.

VERBS

Verb Forms

This section covers the principal parts of some irregular verbs including troublesome verbs like *lie* and *lay*. The use of regular verbs like *look* and *receive* poses no real problem to most writers since the past and past participle forms end in *-ed*; it is the irregular forms which pose the most serious problems—for example, *seen, written,* and *begun.*

...uence indicates a logical time sequence.

.sent tense

in statements of universal truth:

> I learned that the sun *is* ninety-million miles from the earth.

in statements about the contents of literature and other published works:

> In this book, Sandy *becomes* a nun and *writes* a book on psychology.

Use past tense

in statements concerning writing or publication of a book:

> He *wrote* his first book in 1949, and it *was published* in 1952.

Use present perfect tense

for an action that began in the past but continues into the future:

> I *have lived* here all my life.

Use past perfect tense

for an earlier action that is mentioned in a later action:

> Cindy ate the apple that she *had picked*.

(First she picked it, then she ate it.)

Use future perfect tense

for an action that will have been completed at a specific future time:

> By May, I shall have graduated.

Use a present participle

for action that occurs at the same time as the verb:

> *Speeding* down the interstate, I saw a cop's flashing lights.

Use a perfect participle

for action that occurred before the main verb:

> *Having read* the directions, I started the test.

Use the subjunctive mood

to express a wish or state a condition contrary to fact:

> *If it were not raining,* we could have a picnic.

in *that* clauses after verbs like *request, recommend, suggest, ask, require,* and *insist*; and after such expressions as *it is important* and *it is necessary*:

> It is necessary that all papers *be* submitted on time.

Subject-Verb Agreement

Agreement is the grammatical correspondence between the subject and the verb of a sentence: *I do, we do, they do, he, she, it does.*

Every English verb has five forms, two of which are the bare form (plural) and the *-s* form (singular). Simply put, singular verb forms end in *-s*; plural forms do not.

Study these rules governing subject-verb agreement:

A verb must agree with its subject, not with any additive phrase in the sentence such as a prepositional or verbal phrase. Ignore such phrases.

> Your *copy* of the rules *is* on the desk.

> Ms. Craig's *record* of community service and outstanding teaching *qualifies* her for promotion.

In an inverted sentence beginning with a prepositional phrase, the verb still agrees with its subject.

> At the end of the summer *come* the best *sales.*

> Under the house *are* some old Mason *jars.*

Prepositional phrases beginning with compound prepositions such as *along with, together with, in addition to,* and *as well as* should be ignored, for they do not affect subject-verb agreement.

> *Gladys Knight,* as well as the Pips, *is* riding the midnight train to Georgia.

A verb must agree with its subject, not its subject complement.

> *Taxes are* a problem.

> A *problem is* taxes.

> His main *source* of pleasure *is* food and women.

> *Food and women are* his main source of pleasure.

When a sentence begins with an expletive such as *there, here,* or *it,* the verb agrees with the subject, not the expletive.

> Surely, there *are* several *alumni* who would be interested in forming a group.

> There *are* 50 *students* in my English class.

> There *is* a horrifying *study* on child abuse in *Psychology Today.*

Indefinite pronouns such as *each, either, one, everyone, everybody,* and *everything* are singular.

> *Somebody* in Detroit *loves* me.

> *Does either* [one] of you have a pencil?

> *Neither* of my brothers *has* a car.

Indefinite pronouns such as *several, few, both,* and *many* are plural.

> *Both* of my sorority sisters *have* decided to live off campus.

> *Few seek* the enlightenment of transcendental meditation.

Indefinite pronouns such as *all, some, most,* and *none* may be singular or plural depending on their referents.

> *Some* of the food *is* cold.

> *Some* of the vegetables *are* cold.

> I can think of some retorts, but *none seem* appropriate.

> *None* of the children *is* as sweet as Sally.

Fractions such as *one-half* and *one-third* may be singular or plural depending on the referent.

> *Half* of the mail *has* been delivered.

> *Half* of the letters *have* been read.

Subjects joined by *and* take a plural verb unless the subjects are thought to be one item or unit.

> *Jim* and *Tammy were* televangelists.

> *Guns and Roses is* my favorite group.

In cases when the subjects are joined by *or, nor, either . . . or,* or *neither . . . nor,* the verb must agree with the subject closer to it.

> Either the teacher or the *students are* responsible.

> Neither the students nor the *teacher is* responsible.

Relative pronouns, such as *who, which,* or *that,* which refer to plural antecedents require plural verbs. However, when the relative pronoun refers to a singular subject, the pronoun takes a singular verb.

> She is one of the girls *who cheer* on Friday nights.

> She is the only cheerleader *who has* a broken leg.

Subjects preceded by *every, each,* and *many a* are singular.

> *Every* man, woman, and child *was* given a life preserver.

> *Each* undergraduate *is* required to pass a proficiency exam.

> *Many a* tear *has* to fall before one matures.

A collective noun, such as *audience, faculty, jury,* etc., requires a singular verb when the group is regarded as a whole, and a plural verb when the members of the group are regarded as individuals.

> The *jury has* made its decision.

> The *faculty are* preparing their grade rosters.

Subjects preceded by *the number of* or *the percentage of* are singular, while subjects preceded by *a number of* or *a percentage of* are plural.

> The *number of* vacationers in Florida *increases* every year.

> *A number of* vacationers *are* young couples.

Titles of books, companies, name brands, and groups are singular or plural depending on their meaning.

> *Great Expectations is* my favorite novel.

> The *Rolling Stones are* performing in the Super Dome.

Certain nouns of Latin and Greek origin have unusual singular and plural forms.

Singular	Plural
criterion	criteria
alumnus	alumni
datum	data
medium	media

> The *data are* available for inspection.

> The only *criterion* for membership *is* a high GPA.

Some nouns such as *deer, shrimp,* and *sheep* have the same spellings for both their singular and plural forms. In these cases, the meaning of the sentence will determine whether they are singular or plural.

> *Deer are* beautiful animals.

> The spotted *deer is* licking the sugar cube.

Some nouns like *scissors*, *jeans*, and *wages* have plural forms but no singular counterparts. These nouns almost always take plural verbs.

> The *scissors are* on the table.

> My new *jeans fit* me like a glove.

Words used as examples, not as grammatical parts of the sentence, require singular verbs.

> *Can't is* the contraction for "cannot."

> *Cats is* the plural form of "cat."

Mathematical expressions of subtraction and division require singular verbs, while expressions of addition and multiplication take either singular or plural verbs.

> Ten *divided* by two *equals* five.

> Five *times* two *equals* ten.

> OR Five *times* two *equal* ten.

Nouns expressing time, distance, weight, and measurement are singular when they refer to a unit and plural when they refer to separate items.

> *Fifty yards is* a short distance.

> *Ten years have* passed since I finished college.

Expressions of quantity are usually plural.

> *Nine out of ten* dentists *recommend* that their patients floss.

Some nouns ending in *-ics,* such as *economics* and *ethics*, take singular verbs when they refer to principles or a field of study; however, when they refer to individual practices, they usually take plural verbs.

> *Ethics is* being taught in the spring.

> His unusual business *ethics are* what got him into trouble.

Some nouns like *measles*, *news*, and *calculus* appear to be plural but are actually singular in number. These nouns require singular verbs.

> *Measles is* a very contagious disease.

> *Calculus requires* great skill in algebra.

A verbal noun (infinitive or gerund) serving as a subject is treated as singular, even if the object of the verbal phrase is plural.

> *Hiding* your mistakes *does* not make them go away.

> *To run* five miles *is* my goal.

A noun phrase or clause acting as the subject of a sentence requires a singular verb.

> What I need is to be loved.

> Whether there is any connection between them is unknown.

Clauses beginning with *what* may be singular or plural depending on the meaning, that is, whether *what* means "the thing" or "the things."

> What I want for Christmas is a new motorcycle.

> What matters are Clinton's ideas.

A plural subject followed by a singular appositive requires a plural verb; similarly, a singular subject followed by a plural appositive requires a singular verb.

> When the girls throw a party, *they* each bring a *gift*.

> The *board*, all ten members, *is* meeting today.

☞ Drill: Verbs

DIRECTIONS: Choose the correct option.

1. If you <u>had been concerned</u> about Marilyn, you <u>would have went</u> to greater lengths to ensure her safety.

   (A) had been concern . . . would have gone

   (B) was concerned . . . would have gone

   (C) had been concerned . . . would have gone

   (D) No change is necessary.

2. Susan <u>laid</u> in bed too long and missed her class.

   (A) lays   (C) lied

   (B) lay   (D) No change is necessary.

3. The Great Wall of China <u>is</u> fifteen hundred miles long; it <u>was built</u> in the third century B.C.

    (A) was . . . was built

    (B) is . . . is built

    (C) has been . . . was built

    (D) No change is necessary.

4. Joe stated that the class <u>began</u> at 10:30 a.m.

    (A) begins

    (B) had begun

    (C) was beginning

    (D) No change is necessary.

5. The ceiling of the Sistine Chapel <u>was</u> painted by Michelangelo; it <u>depicted</u> scenes from the Creation in the Old Testament.

    (A) was . . . depicts

    (B) is . . . depicts

    (C) has been . . . depicting

    (D) No change is necessary.

6. After Christmas <u>comes</u> the best sales.

    (A) has come

    (B) come

    (C) is coming

    (D) No change is necessary.

7. The bakery's specialty <u>are</u> wedding cakes.

    (A) is

    (B) were

    (C) be

    (D) No change is necessary.

8. Every man, woman, and child <u>were given</u> a life preserver.

    (A) have been given

    (B) had gave

    (C) was given

    (D) No change is necessary.

9. Hiding your mistakes <u>don't</u> make them go away.

    (A) doesn't

    (B) do not

    (C) have not

    (D) No change is necessary.

10. The Board of Regents <u>has recommended</u> a tuition increase.

    (A) have recommended

    (B) has recommend

    (C) had recommended

    (D) No change is necessary.

PRONOUNS

Pronoun Case

Pronoun case questions test your knowledge of the use of nominative and objective case pronouns:

Nominative Case	Objective Case
I	me
he	him
she	her
we	us
they	them
who	whom

This review section answers the most frequently asked grammar questions: when to use *I* and when to use *me*; when to use *who* and when to use *whom*. Some writers avoid *whom* altogether, and instead of distinguishing between *I* and *me*, many writers incorrectly use *myself*.

Use the nominative case (subject pronouns)

for the subject of a sentence:

> *We* students studied until early morning for the final.

> Alan and *I* "burned the midnight oil," too.

for pronouns in apposition to the subject:

> Only two students, Alex and *I*, were asked to report on the meeting.

for the predicate nominative/subject complement:

> The actors nominated for the award were *she* and *I*.

for the subject of an elliptical clause:

> Molly is more experienced than *he*.

for the subject of a subordinate clause:

> Robert is the driver *who* reported the accident.

for the complement of an infinitive with no expressed subject:

> I would not want to be *he*.

Use the objective case (object pronouns)

for the direct object of a sentence:

Mary invited *us* to her party.

for the object of a preposition:

The books that were torn belonged to *her*.

Just between you and *me*, I'm bored.

for the indirect object of a sentence:

Walter gave a dozen red roses to *her*.

for the appositive of a direct object:

The committee elected two delegates, Barbara and *me*.

for the object of an infinitive:

The young boy wanted to help *us* paint the fence.

for the object of a gerund:

Enlisting *him* was surprisingly easy.

for the object of a past participle:

Having called the other students and *us*, the secretary went home for the day.

for a pronoun that precedes an infinitive (the subject of an infinitive):

The supervisor told *him* to work late.

for the complement of an infinitive with an expressed subject:

The fans thought the best player to be *him*.

for the object of an elliptical clause:

Bill tackled Joe harder than *me*.

for the object of a verb in apposition:

Charles invited two extra people, Carmen and *me*, to the party.

When a conjunction connects two pronouns or a pronoun and a noun, remove the "and" and the other pronoun or noun to determine what the correct pronoun form should be:

Mom gave ~~Tom and~~ myself a piece of cake.

Mom gave ~~Tom and~~ I a piece of cake

Mom gave ~~Tom and~~ me a piece of cake.

Removal of these words reveals what the correct pronoun should be:

Mom gave *me* a piece of cake.

The only pronouns that are acceptable after *between* and other prepositions are: *me, her, him, them,* and *whom.* When deciding between *who* and *whom,* try substituting *he* for *who* and *him* for *whom;* then follow these easy transformation steps:

1. Isolate the *who* clause or the *whom* clause:

    whom we can trust

2. Invert the word order, if necessary. Place the words in the clause in the natural order of an English sentence, subject followed by the verb:

    we can trust whom

3. Read the final form with the *he* or *him* inserted:

    We can trust ~~whom~~ him.

When a pronoun follows a comparative conjunction like *than* or *as,* complete the elliptical construction to help you determine which pronoun is correct.

EX: She has more credit hours than me [do].

She has more credit hours than I [do].

Pronoun-Antecedent Agreement

These kinds of questions test your knowledge of using an appropriate pronoun to agree with its antecedent in number (singular or plural form) and gender (masculine, feminine, or neuter). An antecedent is a noun or pronoun to which another noun or pronoun refers.

Here are the two basic rules for pronoun reference-antecedent agreement:

1. Every pronoun must have a conspicuous antecedent.

2. Every pronoun must agree with its antecedent in number, gender, and person.

When an antecedent is one of dual gender like *student, singer, artist, person, citizen,* etc., use *his* or *her.* Some careful writers change the antecedent to a plural noun to avoid using the sexist, singular masculine pronoun his:

>   INCORRECT: Everyone hopes that he will win the lottery.

>   CORRECT: Most people hope that they will win the lottery.

Ordinarily, the relative pronoun *who* is used to refer to people, *which* to refer to things and places, *where* to refer to places, and *that* to refer to places or things. The distinction between *that* and *which* is a grammatical distinction (see the section on Word Choice Skills).

Many writers prefer to use *that* to refer to collective nouns.

>   EX: A family *that* traces its lineage is usually proud of its roots.

Many writers, especially students, are not sure when to use the reflexive case pronoun and when to use the possessive case pronoun. The rules governing the usage of the reflexive case and the possessive case are quite simple.

Use the possessive case

before a noun in a sentence:

>   *Our* friend moved during the semester break.

>   *My* dog has fleas, but *her* dog doesn't.

before a gerund in a sentence:

>   *Her* running helps to relieve stress.

>   *His* driving terrified her.

as a noun in a sentence:

>   *Mine* was the last test graded that day.

to indicate possession:

>   Karen never allows anyone else to drive *her* car.

>   Brad thought the book was *his,* but it was someone else's.

Use the reflexive case

as a direct object to rename the subject:

>   I kicked *myself.*

as an indirect object to rename the subject:

>   Henry bought *himself* a tie.

as an object of a prepositional phrase:

> Tom and Lillie baked the pie for *themselves.*

as a predicate pronoun:

> She hasn't been *herself* lately.

Do not use the reflexive in place of the nominative pronoun:

> INCORRECT: Both Randy and *myself* plan to go.
>
> CORRECT: Both Randy and *I* plan to go.

> _____

> INCORRECT: *Yourself* will take on the challenges of college.
>
> CORRECT: *You* will take on the challenges of college.

> _____

> INCORRECT: Either James or *yourself* will paint the mural.
>
> CORRECT: Either James or *you* will paint the mural.

Watch out for careless use of the pronoun form:

> INCORRECT: George *hisself* told me it was true.
>
> CORRECT: George *himself* told me it was true.

> _____

> INCORRECT: They washed the car *theirselves.*
>
> CORRECT: They washed the car *themselves.*

Notice that reflexive pronouns are not set off by commas:

> INCORRECT: Mary, *herself,* gave him the diploma.
>
> CORRECT: Mary *herself* gave him the diploma.

> _____

> INCORRECT: I will do it, *myself.*
>
> CORRECT: I will do it *myself.*

Pronoun Reference

Pronoun reference questions require you to determine whether the antecedent is conspicuously written in the sentence or whether it is remote, implied, ambiguous, or vague, none of which results in clear writing. Make sure that every italicized pronoun has a conspicuous antecedent and that one pronoun substitutes only for another noun or pronoun, not for an idea or a sentence.

Pronoun reference problems occur

when a pronoun refers to either of two antecedents:

INCORRECT: Joanna told Tim that *she* was getting fat.

CORRECT: Joanna told Tim, "I'm getting fat."

when a pronoun refers to a remote antecedent:

INCORRECT: A strange car followed us closely, and *he* kept blinking his lights at us.

CORRECT: A strange car followed us closely, and its driver kept blinking his lights at us.

when *this, that,* and *which* refer to the general idea of the preceding clause or sentence rather than the preceding word:

INCORRECT: The students could not understand the pronoun reference handout, which annoyed them very much.

CORRECT: The students could not understand the pronoun reference handout, a fact which annoyed them very much.

OR The students were annoyed because they could not understand the pronoun reference handout.

when a pronoun refers to an unexpressed but implied noun:

INCORRECT: My husband wants me to knit a blanket, but I'm not interested in it.

CORRECT: My husband wants me to knit a blanket, but I'm not interested in knitting.

when *it* is used as something other than an expletive to postpone a subject:

INCORRECT: It says in today's paper that the newest shipment of cars from Detroit, Michigan, seems to include outright imitations of European models.

CORRECT: Today's paper says that the newest shipment of cars from Detroit, Michigan, seems to include outright imitations of European models.

INCORRECT: The football game was canceled because it was bad weather.

CORRECT: The football game was canceled because the weather was bad.

when *they* or *it* is used to refer to something or someone indefinitely, and there is no definite antecedent:

INCORRECT: At the job placement office, they told me to stop wearing ripped jeans to my interviews.

CORRECT: At the job placement office, I was told to stop wearing ripped jeans to my interviews.

when the pronoun does not agree with its antecedent in number, gender, or person:

INCORRECT: Any graduate student, if they are interested, may attend the lecture.

CORRECT: Any graduate student, if he or she is interested, may attend the lecture.

OR All graduate students, if they are interested, may attend the lecture.

INCORRECT: Many Americans are concerned that the overuse of slang and colloquialisms is corrupting the language.

CORRECT: Many Americans are concerned that the overuse of slang and colloquialisms is corrupting their language.

INCORRECT: The Board of Regents will not make a decision about tuition increase until their March meeting.

CORRECT: The Board of Regents will not make a decision about tuition increase until its March meeting.

when a noun or pronoun has no expressed antecedent:

INCORRECT: In the President's address to the union, he promised no more taxes.

CORRECT: In his address to the union, the President promised no more taxes.

☞ Drill: Pronouns

<u>DIRECTIONS:</u> Choose the correct option.

1. My friend and <u>myself</u> bought tickets for *Cats*.

    (A) I   (C) us

    (B) me   (D) No change is necessary.

2. Alcohol and tobacco are harmful to <u>whomever</u> consumes them.

    (A) whom   (C) whoever

    (B) who   (D) No change is necessary.

3. Everyone is wondering <u>whom</u> her successor will be.

    (A) who   (C) who'll

    (B) whose   (D) No change is necessary.

4. Rosa Lee's parents discovered that it was <u>her who</u> wrecked the family car.

    (A) she who   (C) her whom

    (B) she whom   (D) No change is necessary.

5. A student <u>who</u> wishes to protest <u>his or her</u> grades must file a formal grievance in the Dean's office.

    (A) that . . . their   (C) whom . . . their

    (B) which . . . his   (D) No change is necessary.

6. One of the best things about working for this company is that <u>they pay</u> big bonuses.

    (A) it pays   (C) they paid

    (B) they always pay   (D) No change is necessary.

7. Every car owner should be sure that <u>their</u> automobile insurance is adequate.

    (A) your   (C) its

    (B) his or her   (D) No change is necessary.

8. My mother wants me to become a teacher, but I'm not interested in <u>it</u>.

    (A) this   (C) that

    (B) teaching   (D) No change is necessary.

9. Since I had not paid my electric bill, <u>they</u> sent me a delinquent notice.

    (A) the power company   (C) it

    (B) he   (D) No change is necessary.

10. Margaret seldom wrote to her sister when <u>she</u> was away at college.

(A)   who

(C)   her sister

(B)   her

(D)   No change is necessary.

ADJECTIVES AND ADVERBS

Correct Usage

Adjectives are words that modify nouns or pronouns by defining, describing, limiting, or qualifying those nouns or pronouns.

Adverbs are words that modify verbs, adjectives, or other adverbs and that express such ideas as time, place, manner, cause, and degree. Use adjectives as subject complements with linking verbs; use adverbs with action verbs.

EX: The old man's speech was *eloquent*.	ADJECTIVE
Mr. Brown speaks *eloquently*.	ADVERB
Please be *careful*.	ADJECTIVE
Please drive *carefully*.	ADVERB

Good or well

Good is an adjective; its use as an adverb is colloquial and nonstandard.

INCORRECT: He plays *good*.

CORRECT: He looks *good* to be an octogenarian.

The quiche tastes very *good*.

Well may be either an adverb or an adjective. As an adjective, *well* means "in good health."

CORRECT: He plays *well*.	ADVERB
My mother is not *well*.	ADJECTIVE

Bad or badly

Bad is an adjective used after sense verbs such as *look*, *smell*, *taste*, *feel*, or *sound*, or after linking verbs (*is, am, are, was, were*).

INCORRECT: I feel *badly* about the delay.

CORRECT: I feel *bad* about the delay.

Badly is an adverb used after all other verbs.

INCORRECT: It doesn't hurt very *bad*

CORRECT: It doesn't hurt very *badly*.

Real or really

Real is an adjective; its use as an adverb is colloquial and nonstandard. It means "genuine."

INCORRECT: He writes *real* well.

CORRECT: This is *real* leather.

Really is an adverb meaning "very."

INCORRECT: This is *really* diamond.

CORRECT: Have a *really* nice day.

EX: This is *real* amethyst.   ADJECTIVE

This is *really* difficult.   ADVERB

This is a *real* crisis   ADJECTIVE

This is *really* important.   ADVERB

Sort of and kind of

Sort of and *kind of* are often misused in written English by writers who actually mean *rather* or *somewhat*.

INCORRECT: Jan was *kind of* saddened by the results of the test.

CORRECT: Jan was *somewhat* saddened by the results of the test.

Faulty Comparisons

Sentences containing a faulty comparison often sound correct because their problem is not one of grammar but of logic. Read these sentences closely to make sure that like things are being compared, that the comparisons are complete, and that the comparisons are logical.

When comparing two persons or things, use the comparative, not the superlative form, of an adjective or an adverb. Use the superlative form for comparison of more than two persons or things. Use *any, other*, or *else* when comparing one thing or person with a group of which it/he or she is a part.

Most one- and two-syllable words form their comparative and superlative degrees with *-er* and *-est* suffixes. Adjectives and adverbs of more than two syllables form their comparative and superlative degrees with the addition of *more* and *most*.

Positive	Comparative	Superlative
good	better	best
old	older	oldest
friendly	friendlier	friendliest
lonely	lonelier	loneliest
talented	more talented	most talented
beautiful	more beautiful	most beautiful

A double comparison occurs when the degree of the modifier is changed incorrectly by adding both *-er* and *more* or *-est* and *most* to the adjective or adverb.

> INCORRECT: He is the *most nicest* brother.

> CORRECT: He is the *nicest* brother.

> INCORRECT: She is the *more meaner* of the sisters.

> CORRECT: She is the *meaner* sister.

Illogical comparisons occur when there is an implied comparison between two things that are not actually being compared or that cannot be logically compared.

> INCORRECT: The interest at a loan company is higher *than* a bank.

> CORRECT: The interest at a loan company is higher *than* that *at* a bank.

> OR The interest at a loan company is higher *than at* a bank.

Ambiguous comparisons occur when elliptical words (those omitted) create for the reader more than one interpretation of the sentence.

> INCORRECT: I like Mary better than you. (than you *what?*)

> CORRECT: I like Mary better than I like you.

> OR I like Mary better than you do.

Incomplete comparisons occur when the basis of the comparison (the two categories being compared) is not explicitly stated.

> INCORRECT: Skywriting is *more* spectacular.

> CORRECT: Skywriting is *more* spectacular *than* billboard advertising.

Do not omit the words *other, any,* or *else* when comparing one thing or person with a group of which it/he or she is a part.

INCORRECT: Joan writes better *than any* student in her class.

CORRECT: Joan writes better *than any other* student in her class.

Do not omit the second *as* of *as . . . as* when making a point of equal or superior comparison.

INCORRECT: The University of West Florida is *as large* or larger than the University of North Florida.

CORRECT: The University of West Florida is *as large as* or larger than the University of Northern Florida.

Do not omit the first category of the comparison, even if the two categories are the same.

INCORRECT: This is one of the best, if not the best, college in the country.

CORRECT: This is one of the best colleges in the country, if not the best.

The problem with the incorrect sentence is that *one of the best* requires the plural word *colleges,* not *college.*

☞ Drill: Adjectives and Adverbs

DIRECTIONS: Choose the correct option.

1. Although the band performed <u>badly</u>, I feel <u>real bad</u> about missing the concert.

    (A) badly . . . real badly

    (B) bad . . . badly

    (C) badly . . . very bad

    (D) No change is necessary.

2. These reports are <u>relative simple</u> to prepare.

    (A) relatively simple

    (B) relative simply

    (C) relatively simply

    (D) No change is necessary.

3. He did <u>very well</u> on the test although his writing skills are not <u>good</u>.

    (A) real well . . . good

    (B) very good . . . good

    (C) good . . . great

    (D) No change is necessary.

4. Shake the medicine bottle <u>good</u> before you open it.

    (A) very good

    (B) real good

    (C) well

    (D) No change is necessary.

5. Though she speaks <u>fluently</u>, she writes <u>poorly</u> because she doesn't observe <u>closely</u> or think <u>clear</u>.

    (A) fluently, poorly, closely, clearly

    (B) fluent, poor, close, clear

    (C) fluently, poor, closely, clear

    (D) No change is necessary.

DIRECTIONS: Select the sentence that clearly and effectively states the idea and has no structural errors.

6. (A) Los Angeles is larger than any city in California.

    (B) Los Angeles is larger than all the cities in California.

    (C) Los Angeles is larger than any other city in California.

7. (A) Art history is as interesting as, if not more interesting than, music appreciation.

    (B) Art history is as interesting, if not more interesting than, music appreciation.

    (C) Art history is as interesting as, if not more interesting, music appreciation.

8. (A) The baseball team here is as good as any other university.

    (B) The baseball team here is as good as all the other universities.

    (C) The baseball team here is as good as any other university's.

9. (A) I like him better than you.

    (B) I like him better than I like you.

    (C) I like him better.

10. (A) You are the most stingiest person I know.

    (B) You are the most stingier person I know.

    (C) You are the stingiest person I know.

PUNCTUATION

Commas

Commas should be placed according to standard rules of punctuation for purpose, clarity, and effect. The proper use of commas is explained in the following rules and examples:

In a series:

When more than one adjective describes a noun, use a comma to separate and emphasize each adjective. The comma takes the place of the word *and* in the series.

> the long, dark passageway
>
> another confusing, sleepless night
>
> an elaborate, complex, brilliant plan
>
> the old, grey, crumpled hat

Some adjective-noun combinations are thought of as one word. In these cases, the adjective in front of the adjective-noun combination needs no comma. If you inserted *and* between the adjective-noun combination, it would not make sense.

> a stately oak tree
>
> an exceptional wine glass
>
> my worst report card
>
> a china dinner plate

The comma is also used to separate words, phrases, and whole ideas (clauses); it still takes the place of *and* when used this way.

> an apple, a pear, a fig, and a banana
>
> a lovely lady, an elegant dress, and many admirers
>
> She lowered the shade, closed the curtain, turned off the light, and went to bed.

The only question that exists about the use of commas in a series is whether or not one should be used before the final item. It is standard usage to do so, although many newspapers and magazines have stopped using the final comma. Occasionally, the omission of the comma can be confusing.

INCORRECT: He got on his horse, tracked a rabbit and a deer and rode on to Canton.

We planned the trip with Mary and Harold, Susan, Dick and Joan, Gregory and Jean and Charles.

With a long introductory phrase:

Usually if a phrase of more than five or six words or a dependent clause precedes the subject at the beginning of a sentence, a comma is used to set it off.

After last night's fiasco at the disco, she couldn't bear the thought of looking at him again.

Whenever I try to talk about politics, my wife leaves the room.

Provided you have said nothing, they will never guess who you are.

It is not necessary to use a comma with a short sentence.

In January she will go to Switzerland.

After I rest I'll feel better.

During the day no one is home.

If an introductory phrase includes a verb form that is being used as another part of speech (a *verbal*), it must be followed by a comma.

INCORRECT: When eating Mary never looked up from her plate.

CORRECT: When eating, Mary never looked up from her plate.

INCORRECT: Because of her desire to follow her faith in James wavered.

CORRECT: Because of her desire to follow, her faith in James wavered.

INCORRECT: Having decided to leave Mary James wrote her a letter.

CORRECT: Having decided to leave Mary, James wrote her a letter.

To separate sentences with two main ideas:

To understand this use of the comma, you need to be able to recognize compound sentences. When a sentence contains more than two subjects and verbs (clauses), and the two clauses are joined by a conjunction (*and, but, or, nor, for, yet*), use a comma before the conjunction to show that another clause is coming.

I thought I knew the poem by heart, but he showed me three lines I had forgotten.

Are we really interested in helping the children, or are we more concerned with protecting our good names?

He is supposed to leave tomorrow, but he is not ready to go.

Jim knows you are disappointed, and he has known it for a long time.

If the two parts of the sentence are short and closely related, it is not necessary to use a comma.

He threw the ball and the dog ran after it.

Jane played the piano and Michael danced.

Be careful not to confuse a sentence that has a compound verb and a single subject with a compound sentence. If the subject is the same for both verbs, there is no need for a comma.

INCORRECT: Charles sent some flowers, and wrote a long letter explaining why he had not been able to attend.

CORRECT: Charles sent some flowers and wrote a long letter explaining why he had not been able to attend.

INCORRECT: Last Thursday we went to the concert with Julia, and afterwards dined at an old Italian restaurant.

CORRECT: Last Thursday we went to the concert with Julia and afterwards dined at an old Italian restaurant.

INCORRECT: For the third time, the teacher explained that the literacy level for high school students was much lower than it had been in previous years, and, this time, wrote the statistics on the board for everyone to see.

CORRECT: For the third time, the teacher explained that the literacy level for high school students was much lower than it had been in previous years and this time wrote the statistics on the board for everyone to see.

In general, words and phrases that stop the flow of the sentence or are unnecessary for the main idea are set off by commas.

Abbreviations after names:

> Did you invite John Paul, Jr., and his sister?

> Martha Harris, Ph.D., will be the speaker tonight.

Interjections (an exclamation without added grammatical connection):

> Oh, I'm so glad to see you.

> I tried so hard, alas, to do it.

> Hey, let me out of here.

Direct address:

> Roy, won't you open the door for the dog?

> I can't understand, Mother, what you are trying to say.

> May I ask, Mr. President, why you called us together?

> Hey, lady, watch out for that car!

Tag questions:

> I'm really hungry, aren't you?

> Jerry looks like his father, doesn't he?

Geographical names and addresses:

> The concert will be held in Chicago, Illinois, on August 12.

> The letter was addressed to Mrs. Marion Heartwell, 1881 Pine Lane, Palo Alto, California 95824.

(Note: No comma is needed before the zip code, because it is already clearly set off from the state name.)

Transitional words and phrases:

> On the other hand, I hope he gets better.

> In addition, the phone rang constantly this afternoon.

> I'm, nevertheless, going to the beach on Sunday.

> You'll find, therefore, that no one is more loyal than I am.

Parenthetical words and phrases:

> You will become, I believe, a great statesman.

We know, of course, that this is the only thing to do.

In fact, I planted corn last summer.

The Mannes affair was, to put it mildly, a surprise.

Unusual word order:

The dress, new and crisp, hung in the closet.

Intently, she stared out the window.

With nonrestrictive elements:

Parts of a sentence that modify other parts are sometimes essential to the meaning of the sentence and sometimes not. When a modifying word or group of words is not vital to the meaning of the sentence, it is set off by commas. Since it does not restrict the meaning of the words it modifies, it is called "nonrestrictive." Modifiers that are essential to the meaning of the sentence are called "restrictive" and are not set off by commas.

ESSENTIAL: The girl *who wrote the story* is my sister.

NONESSENTIAL: My sister, *the girl who wrote the story*, has always loved to write.

ESSENTIAL: John Milton's famous poem *Paradise Lost* tells a remarkable story.

NONESSENTIAL: Dante's greatest work, *The Divine Comedy*, marked the beginning of the Renaissance.

ESSENTIAL: The cup *that is on the piano* is the one I want.

NONESSENTIAL: The cup, *which my brother gave me last year*, is on the piano.

ESSENTIAL: The people *who arrived late* were not seated.

NONESSENTIAL: George, *who arrived late*, was not seated.

To set off direct quotations:

Most direct quotes or quoted materials are set off from the rest of the sentence by commas.

"Please read your part more loudly," the director insisted.

"I won't know what to do," said Michael, "if you leave me."

> The teacher said sternly, "I will not dismiss this class until I have silence."

> Who was it who said "Do not ask for whom the bell tolls; it tolls for thee"?

Note: Commas always go inside the closing quotation mark, even if the comma is not part of the material being quoted.

Be careful not to set off indirect quotes or quotes that are used as subjects or complements.

> "To be or not to be" is the famous beginning of a soliloquy in Shakespeare's *Hamlet*. (subject)

> She said she would never come back. (indirect quote)

> Back then my favorite poem was "Evangeline." (complement)

To set off contrasting elements:

> Her intelligence, not her beauty, got her the job.

> Your plan will take you a little further from, rather than closer to, your destination.

> It was a reasonable, though not appealing, idea.

> He wanted glory, but found happiness instead.

In dates:

Both forms of the date are acceptable.

> She will arrive on April 6, 1998.

> He left on 5 December 1980.

> In January 1967, he handed in his resignation.

> On October 22, 1992, Frank and Julie were married.

Usually, when a subordinate clause is at the end of a sentence, no comma is necessary preceding the clause. However, when a subordinate clause introduces a sentence, a comma should be used after the clause. Some common subordinating conjunctions are:

after	so that
although	though
as	till
as if	unless

because	until
before	when
even though	whenever
if	while
inasmuch as	since

Semicolons

Questions testing semicolon usage require you to be able to distinguish between the semicolon and the comma, and the semicolon and the colon. This review section covers the basic uses of the semicolon: to separate independent clauses not joined by a coordinating conjunction, to separate independent clauses separated by a conjunctive adverb, and to separate items in a series with internal commas. It is important to be consistent; if you use a semicolon between *any* of the items in the series, you must use semicolons to separate *all* of the items in the series.

Usually, a comma follows the conjunctive adverb. Note also that a period can be used to separate two sentences joined by a conjunctive adverb. Some common conjunctive adverbs are:

accordingly	nevertheless
besides	next
consequently	nonetheless
finally	now
furthermore	on the other hand
however	otherwise
indeed	perhaps
in fact	still
moreover	therefore

Then is also used as a conjunctive adverb, but it is not usually followed by a comma.

Use the semicolon

to separate independent clauses which are not joined by a coordinating conjunction:

I understand how to use commas; the semicolon I have not yet mastered.

to separate two independent clauses connected by a conjunctive adverb:

> He took great care with his work; *therefore*, he was very successful.

to combine two independent clauses connected by a coordinating conjunction if either or both of the clauses contain other internal punctuation:

> Success in college, some maintain, requires intelligence, industry, and perseverance; *but* others, fewer in number, assert that only personality is important.

to separate items in a series when each item has internal punctuation:

> I bought an old, dilapidated chair; an antique table which was in beautiful condition; and a new, ugly, blue and white rug.

> Call our customer service line for assistance: Arizona, 1-800-555-6020; New Mexico, 1-800-555-5050; California, 1-800-555-3140; or Nevada, 1-800-555-3214.

Do not use the semicolon

to separate a dependent and an independent clause:

> INCORRECT: You should not make such statements; even though they are correct.

> CORRECT: You should not make such statements even though they are correct.

to separate an appositive phrase or clause from a sentence:

> INCORRECT: His immediate aim in life is centered around two things; becoming an engineer and learning to fly an airplane.

> CORRECT: His immediate aim in life is centered around two things: becoming an engineer and learning to fly an airplane.

to precede an explanation or summary of the first clause:

Note: Although the sentence below is punctuated correctly, the use of the semicolon provides a miscue, suggesting that the second clause is merely an extension, not an explanation, of the first clause. The colon provides a better clue.

> WEAK: The first week of camping was wonderful; we lived in cabins instead of tents.

> BETTER: The first week of camping was wonderful: we lived in cabins instead of tents.

to substitute for a comma:

> INCORRECT: My roommate also likes sports; particularly football, basketball, and baseball.

> CORRECT: My roommate also likes sports, particularly football, basketball, and baseball.

to set off other types of phrases or clauses from a sentence:

> INCORRECT: Being of a cynical mind; I should ask for a recount of the ballots.

> CORRECT: Being of a cynical mind, I should ask for a recount of the ballots.

> INCORRECT: The next meeting of the club has been postponed two weeks; inasmuch as both the president and vice-president are out of town.

> CORRECT: The next meeting of the club has been postponed two weeks, inasmuch as both the president and vice-president are out of town.

Note: The semicolon is not a terminal mark of punctuation; therefore, it should not be followed by a capital letter unless the first word in the second clause ordinarily requires capitalization.

Colons

While it is true that a colon is used to precede a list, one must also make sure that a complete sentence precedes the colon. The colon signals the reader that a list, explanation, or restatement of the preceding will follow. It is like an arrow, indicating that something is to follow. The difference between the colon and the semicolon and between the colon and the period is that the colon is an introductory mark, not a terminal mark. Look at the following examples:

> The Constitution provides for a separation of powers among the three branches of government.

> **government.** The period signals a new sentence.

> **government;** The semicolon signals an interrelated sentence.

> **government,** The comma signals a coordinating conjunction followed by another independent clause.

> **government:** The colon signals a list.

The Constitution provides for a separation of powers among the three branches of *government*: executive, legislative, and judicial.

Ensuring that a complete sentence precedes a colon means following these rules:

Use the colon to introduce a list (one item may constitute a list):

I hate this one course: English.

Three plays by William Shakespeare will be presented in repertory this summer at the University of Michigan: *Hamlet, Macbeth,* and *Othello.*

To introduce a list preceded by *as follows* or *the following*:

The reasons he cited for his success are as follows: integrity, honesty, industry, and a pleasant disposition.

To separate two independent clauses, when the second clause is a restatement or explanation of the first:

All of my high school teachers said one thing in particular: college is going to be difficult.

To introduce a word or word group which is a restatement, explanation, or summary of the first sentence:

These two things he loved: an honest man and a beautiful woman.

To introduce a formal appositive:

I am positive there is one appeal which you can't overlook: money.

To separate the introductory words from a quotation which follows, if the quotation is formal, long, or paragraphed separately:

The actor then stated: "I would rather be able to adequately play the part of Hamlet than to perform a miraculous operation, deliver a great lecture, or build a magnificent skyscraper."

The colon should only be used after statements that are grammatically complete.

Do *not* use a colon after a verb:

INCORRECT: My favorite holidays are: Christmas, New Year's Eve, and Halloween.

CORRECT: My favorite holidays are Christmas, New Year's Eve, and Halloween.

Do *not* use a colon after a preposition:

> INCORRECT: I enjoy different ethnic foods such as: Greek, Chinese, and Italian.

> CORRECT: I enjoy different ethnic foods such as Greek, Chinese, and Italian.

Do *not* use a colon interchangeably with the dash:

> INCORRECT: Mathematics, German, English: These gave me the greatest difficulty of all my studies.

> CORRECT: Mathematics, German, English—these gave me the greatest difficulty of all my studies.

Information preceding the colon should be a complete sentence regardless of the explanatory information following the clause.

Do *not* use the colon before the words *for example, namely, that is,* or *for instance* even though these words may be introducing a list.

> INCORRECT: We agreed to it: namely, to give him a surprise party.

> CORRECT: There are a number of well-known American women writers: for example, Nikki Giovanni, Phillis Wheatley, Emily Dickinson, and Maya Angelou.

Colon usage questions test your knowledge of the colon preceding a list, restatement, or explanation. These questions also require you to be able to distinguish between the colon and the period, the colon and the comma, and the colon and the semicolon.

Apostrophes

Apostrophe questions require you to know when an apostrophe has been used appropriately to make a noun possessive, not plural. Remember the following rules when considering how to show possession.

Add *'s* to singular nouns and indefinite pronouns:

> Tiffany's flowers
>
> a dog's bark
>
> everybody's computer
>
> at the owner's expense
>
> today's paper

Add *'s* to singular nouns ending in s, unless this distorts the pronunciation:

> Delores's paper
>
> the boss's pen
>
> Dr. Yots' class
>
> for righteousness' sake
>
> Dr. Evans's office OR Dr. Evans' office

Add *an apostrophe* to plural nouns ending in s or *es*:

> two cents' worth
>
> ladies' night
>
> thirteen years' experience
>
> two weeks' pay

Add *'s* to plural nouns not ending in s:

> men's room
>
> children's toys

Add *'s* to the last word in compound words or groups:

> brother-in-law's car
>
> someone else's paper

Add *'s* to the last name when indicating joint ownership:

> Joe and Edna's home
>
> Julie and Kathy's party
>
> women and children's clinic

Add *'s* to both names if you intend to show ownership by each person:

> Joe's and Edna's trucks
>
> Julie's and Kathy's pies
>
> Ted's and Jane's marriage vows

Possessive pronouns change their forms *without* the addition of an apostrophe:

> her, his, hers
>
> your, yours
>
> their, theirs
>
> it, its

Use the possessive form of a noun preceding a gerund:

> His driving annoys me.
>
> My bowling a strike irritated him.
>
> Do you mind our stopping by?
>
> We appreciate your coming.

Add *'s* to words and initials to show that they are plural:

> no if's, and's, or but's
>
> the do's and don't's of dating
>
> three A's
>
> IRA's are available at the bank.

Add *s* to numbers, symbols, and letters to show that they are plural:

> TVs
>
> VCRs
>
> the 1800s
>
> the returning POWs

Quotation Marks and Italics

These kinds of questions test your knowledge of the proper use of quotation marks with other marks of punctuation, with titles, and with dialogue. These kinds of questions also test your knowledge of the correct use of italics and underlining with titles and words used as sample words (for example, *the word is is a common verb*).

The most common use of double quotation marks (") is to set off quoted words, phrases, and sentences.

> "If everybody minded their own business," said the Duchess in a hoarse growl, "the world would go round a great deal faster than it does."
>
> "Then you would say what you mean," the March Hare went on.
>
> "I do," Alice hastily replied: "at least—at least I mean what I say—that's the same thing, you know."
>
> —from Lewis Carroll's *Alice in Wonderland*

Single quotation marks are used to set off quoted material within a quote.

> "Shall I bring 'Rhyme of the Ancient Mariner' along with us?" she asked her brother.

Mrs. Green said, "The doctor told me, 'Go immediately to bed when you get home!'"

"If she said that to me," Katherine insisted, "I would tell her, 'I never intend to speak to you again! Goodbye, Susan!'"

When writing dialogue, begin a new paragraph each time the speaker changes.

"Do you know what time it is?" asked Jane.

"Can't you see I'm busy?" snapped Mary.

"It's easy to see that you're in a bad mood today!" replied Jane.

Use quotation marks to enclose words used as words (sometimes italics are used for this purpose).

"Judgment" has always been a difficult word for me to spell.

Do you know what "abstruse" means?

"Horse and buggy" and "bread and butter" can be used either as adjectives or as nouns.

If slang is used within more formal writing, the slang words or phrases should be set off with quotation marks.

Harrison's decision to leave the conference and to "stick his neck out" by flying to Jamaica was applauded by the rest of the conference attendees.

When words are meant to have an unusual or specific significance to the reader, for instance irony or humor, they are sometimes placed in quotation marks.

For years, women were not allowed to buy real estate in order to "protect" them from unscrupulous dealers.

The "conversation" resulted in one black eye and a broken nose.

To set off titles of TV shows, poems, stories, and book chapters, use quotation marks. (Book, motion picture, newspaper, and magazine titles are underlined when handwritten and italicized when printed.)

The article "Moving South in the Southern Rain," by Jergen Smith in the *Southern News*, attracted the attention of our editor.

The assignment is "Childhood Development," Chapter 18 of *Human Behavior*.

My favorite essay by Montaigne is "On Silence."

"Happy Days" led the TV ratings for years, didn't it?

You will find Keats' "Ode to a Grecian Urn" in Chapter 3, "The Romantic Era," in Lastly's *Selections from Great English Poets.*

Errors to avoid:

Be sure to remember that quotation marks always come in pairs. Do not make the mistake of using only one set.

INCORRECT: "You'll never convince me to move to the city, said Thurman. I consider it an insane asylum."

CORRECT: "You'll never convince me to move to the city," said Thurman. "I consider it an insane asylum."

INCORRECT: "Idleness and pride tax with a heavier hand than kings and parliaments," Benjamin Franklin is supposed to have said. If we can get rid of the former, we may easily bear the latter."

CORRECT: "Idleness and pride tax with a heavier hand than kings and parliaments," Benjamin Franklin is supposed to have said. "If we can get rid of the former, we may easily bear the latter."

When a quote consists of several sentences, do not put the quotation marks at the beginning and end of each sentence; put them at the beginning and end of the entire quotation.

INCORRECT: "It was during his student days in Bonn that Beethoven fastened upon Schiller's poem." "The heady sense of liberation in the verses must have appealed to him." "They appealed to every German." —John Burke

CORRECT: "It was during his student days in Bonn that Beethoven fastened upon Schiller's poem. The heady sense of liberation in the verses must have appealed to him. They appealed to every German." —John Burke

Instead of setting off a long quote with quotation marks, if it is longer than five or six lines you may want to indent and single space it. If you do indent, do not use quotation marks.

In his *First Inaugural Address,* Abraham Lincoln appeals to the war-torn American people:

We are not enemies, but friends. We must not be enemies. Though passion may have strained, it must not break, our bonds of affection. The mystic chords of memory, stretching from every battlefield and patriot grave to every living heart and hearthstone all over this broad land, will yet swell the chorus of the Union when again touched, as surely they will be, by the better angels of our nature.

Be careful not to use quotation marks with indirect quotations.

INCORRECT: Mary wondered "if she would get over it."

CORRECT: Mary wondered if she would get over it.

———————

INCORRECT: The nurse asked "how long it had been since we had visited the doctor's office."

CORRECT: The nurse asked how long it had been since we had visited the doctor's office.

When you quote several paragraphs, it is not sufficient to place quotation marks at the beginning and end of the entire quote. Place quotation marks at the *beginning of each paragraph,* but only at the *end of the last paragraph.* Here is an abbreviated quotation for an example:

"Here begins an odyssey through the world of classical mythology, starting with the creation of the world . . .

"It is true that themes similar to the classical may be found in any corpus of mythology . . . Even technology is not immune to the influence of Greece and Rome . . .

"We need hardly mention the extent to which painters and sculptors . . . have used and adapted classical mythology to illustrate the past, to reveal the human body, to express romantic or antiromantic ideals, or to symbolize any particular point of view."

Remember that commas and periods are *always* placed inside the quotation marks even if they are not actually part of the quote.

INCORRECT: "Life always gets colder near the summit", Nietzsche is purported to have said, "—the cold increases, responsibility grows".

CORRECT: "Life always gets colder near the summit," Nietzsche is purported to have said, "—the cold increases, responsibility grows."

———————

INCORRECT: "Get down here right away", John cried. "You'll miss the sunset if you don't."

CORRECT: "Get down here right away," John cried. "You'll miss the sunset if you don't."

———————

INCORRECT: "If my dog could talk", Mary mused, "I'll bet he would say, 'Take me for a walk right this minute'".

CORRECT: "If my dog could talk," Mary mused, "I'll bet he would say, 'Take me for a walk right this minute'."

Other marks of punctuation, such as question marks, exclamation points, colons, and semicolons, go inside the quotation marks if they are part of the quoted material. If they are not part of the quotation, however, they go outside the quotation marks. Be careful to distinguish between the guidelines for the comma and period, which always go inside the quotation marks, and those for other marks of punctuation.

INCORRECT: "I'll always love you"! he exclaimed happily.

CORRECT: "I'll always love you!" he exclaimed happily.

INCORRECT: Did you hear her say, "He'll be there early?"

CORRECT: Did you hear her say, "He'll be there early"?

INCORRECT: She called down the stairs, "When are you going"?

CORRECT: She called down the stairs, "When are you going?"

INCORRECT: "Let me out"! he cried. "Don't you have any pity"?

CORRECT: "Let me out!" he cried. "Don't you have any pity?"

Remember to use only one mark of punctuation at the end of a sentence ending with a quotation mark.

INCORRECT: She thought out loud, "Will I ever finish this paper in time for that class?".

CORRECT: She thought out loud, "Will I ever finish this paper in time for that class?"

INCORRECT: "Not the same thing a bit!", said the Hatter. "Why, you might just as well say that 'I see what I eat' is the same thing as 'I eat what I see'!".

CORRECT: "Not the same thing a bit!" said the Hatter. "Why, you might just as well say that 'I see what I eat' is the same thing as 'I eat what I see'!"

☞ Drill: Punctuation

__DIRECTIONS:__ Choose the correct option.

1. Indianola, <u>Mississippi, where B.B. King and my father grew up,</u> has a population of less than 50,000 people.

    (A) Mississippi where, B.B. King and my father grew up,

    (B) Mississippi where B.B. King and my father grew up,

    (C) Mississippi; where B.B. King and my father grew up,

    (D) No change is necessary.

2. John Steinbeck's best known novel *The Grapes of Wrath* is the story of the <u>Joads and Oklahoma family</u> who were driven from their dustbowl farm and forced to become migrant workers in California.

    (A) Joads, an Oklahoma family

    (B) Joads, an Oklahoma family,

    (C) Joads; an Oklahoma family

    (D) No change is necessary.

3. All students who are interested in student teaching next <u>semester, must submit an application to the Teacher Education Office.</u>

    (A) semester must submit an application to the Teacher Education Office.

    (B) semester, must submit an application, to the Teacher Education Office.

    (C) semester: must submit an application to the Teacher Education Office.

    (D) No change is necessary.

4. Whenever you travel by <u>car, or plane, you</u> must wear a seatbelt.

    (A) car or plane you   (C) car or plane, you

    (B) car, or plane you   (D) No change is necessary.

5. Wearing a seatbelt is not just a good <u>idea, it's</u> the law.

   (A) idea; it's   (C) idea. It's

   (B) idea it's   (D) No change is necessary.

6. Senators and representatives can be reelected <u>indefinitely; a</u> president can only serve two terms.

   (A) indefinitely but a   (C) indefinitely a

   (B) indefinitely, a   (D) No change is necessary.

7. Students must pay a penalty for overdue library <u>books, however, there</u> is a grace period.

   (A) books; however, there   (C) books: however, there

   (B) books however, there   (D) No change is necessary.

8. Among the states that seceded from the Union to join the Confederacy in 1860-1861 <u>were</u>: Mississippi, Florida, and Alabama.

   (A) were   (C) were.

   (B) were;   (D) No change is necessary.

9. The art exhibit displayed works by many famous <u>artists such as:</u> Dali, Picasso, and Michelangelo.

   (A) artists such as;   (C) artists. Such as

   (B) artists such as   (D) No change is necessary.

10. The National Shakespeare Company will perform <u>the following plays:</u> *Othello, Macbeth, Hamlet,* and *As You Like It.*

   (A) the following plays,   (C) the following plays

   (B) the following plays;   (D) No change is necessary.

CAPITALIZATION

When a word is capitalized, it calls attention to itself. This attention should be for a good reason. There are standard uses for capital letters. In general, capitalize (1) all proper nouns, (2) the first word of a sentence, and (3) the first word of a direct quotation.

You should also capitalize

Names of ships, aircraft, spacecraft, and trains:

Apollo 13	Mariner IV
DC-10	S.S. United States
Sputnik 11	Boeing 707

Names of deities:

God	Jupiter
Allah	Holy Ghost
Buddha	Venus
Jehovah	Shiva

Geological periods:

Neolithic age	Cenozoic era
late Pleistocene times	Ice Age

Names of astronomical bodies:

Mercury	Big Dipper
the Milky Way	Halley's comet
Ursa Major	North Star

Personifications:

Reliable Nature brought her promised Spring.

Bring on Melancholy in his sad might.

She believed that Love was the answer to all her problems.

Historical periods:

the Middle Ages	World War I
Reign of Terror	Great Depression
Christian Era	Roaring Twenties
Age of Louis XIV	Renaissance

Organizations, associations, and institutions:

Girl Scouts	North Atlantic Treaty Organization
Kiwanis Club	League of Women Voters
New York Yankees	Unitarian Church

Smithsonian Institution	Common Market
Library of Congress	Franklin Glen High School
New York Philharmonic	Harvard University

Government and judicial groups:

United States Court of Appeals	Senate
Committee on Foreign Affairs	Parliament
New Jersey City Council	Peace Corps
Arkansas Supreme Court	Census Bureau
House of Representatives	Department of State

A general term that accompanies a specific name is capitalized only if it follows the specific name. If it stands alone or comes before the specific name, it is put in lowercase:

Washington State	the state of Washington
Senator Dixon	the senator from Illinois
Central Park	the park
Golden Gate Bridge	the bridge
President Clinton	the president of the United States
Pope John XXIII	the pope
Queen Elizabeth I	the queen of England
Tropic of Capricorn	the tropics
Monroe Doctrine	the doctrine of expansion
the Mississippi River	the river
Easter Day	the day
Treaty of Versailles	the treaty
Webster's Dictionary	the dictionary
Equatorial Current	the equator

Use a capital to start a sentence:

Our car would not start.

When will you leave? I need to know right away.

Never!

Let me in! Please!

When a sentence appears within a sentence, start it with a capital letter:

> We had only one concern: When would we eat?
>
> My sister said, "I'll find the Monopoly game."
>
> He answered, "We can only stay a few minutes."

The most important words of titles are capitalized. Those words not capitalized are conjunctions (*and, or, but*) and short prepositions (*of, on, by, for*). The first and last word of a title must always be capitalized:

A Man for All Seasons	*Crime and Punishment*
Of Mice and Men	*Rise of the West*
Strange Life of Ivan Osokin	"Sonata in G Minor"
"Let Me In"	"Ode to Billy Joe"
"Rubaiyat of Omar Khayyam"	
"All in the Family"	

Capitalize newspaper and magazine titles:

> *U.S. News & World Report*
>
> *National Geographic*
>
> the *New York Times*
>
> the *Washington Post*

Capitalize radio and TV station call letters:

ABC	NBC
WNEW	WBOP
CNN	HBO

Do not capitalize compass directions or seasons:

west	north
east	south
spring	winter
autumn	summer

Capitalize regions:

the South	the Northeast
the West	Eastern Europe

> BUT: the south of France
>
>   the east part of town

Capitalize specific military units:

> the U.S. Army
>
> the 7th Fleet
>
> the German Navy
>
> the 1st Infantry Division

Capitalize political groups and philosophies:

Democrat	Communist
Marxist	Nazism
Whig	Federalist
Existentialism	Transcendentalism

BUT do not capitalize systems of government or individual adherents to a philosophy:

democracy	communism
fascist	agnostic

☞ Drill: Capitalization

DIRECTIONS: Choose the correct option.

1.   Mexico is the southernmost country in <u>North America</u>. It borders the United States on the north; it is bordered on the <u>south</u> by Belize and Guatemala.

    (A)   north America . . . South

    (B)   North America . . . South

    (C)   North america . . . south

    (D)   No change is necessary.

2.   (A)   Until 1989, Tom Landry was the only Coach the Dallas cowboys ever had.

    (B)   Until 1989, Tom Landry was the only coach the Dallas Cowboys ever had.

(C) Until 1989, Tom Landry was the only Coach the Dallas Cowboys ever had.

3. The <u>Northern Hemisphere</u> is the half of the <u>earth</u> that lies north of the
<u>Equator.</u>

(A) Northern hemisphere . . . earth . . . equator

(B) Northern hemisphere . . . Earth . . . Equator

(C) Northern Hemisphere . . . earth . . . equator

(D) No change is necessary.

4. (A) My favorite works by Ernest Hemingway are "The Snows of
Kilamanjaro," *The Sun Also Rises,* and *For Whom the Bell
Tolls.*

(B) My favorite works by Ernest Hemingway are "The Snows Of
Kilamanjaro," *The Sun Also Rises,* and *For Whom The Bell
Tolls.*

(C) My favorite works by Ernest Hemingway are "The Snows of
Kilamanjaro," *The Sun also Rises,* and *For whom the Bell
Tolls.*

5. Aphrodite (<u>Venus in Roman Mythology</u>) was the <u>Greek</u> goddess of
love.

(A) Venus in Roman mythology . . . greek

(B) venus in roman mythology . . . Greek

(C) Venus in Roman mythology . . . Greek

(D) No change is necessary.

6. The <u>Koran</u> is considered by <u>Muslims</u> to be the holy word.

(A) koran . . . muslims   (C) Koran . . . muslims

(B) koran . . . Muslims   (D) No change is necessary.

7. (A) The freshman curriculum at the community college includes
english, a foreign language, Algebra I, and history.

(B) The freshman curriculum at the community college includes
English, a foreign language, Algebra I, and history.

(C) The Freshman curriculum at the Community College includes English, a foreign language, Algebra I, and History.

8. At the <u>spring</u> graduation ceremonies, the university awarded over 2,000 <u>bachelor's</u> degrees.

(A) Spring . . . Bachelor's   (C) Spring . . . bachelor's

(B) spring . . . Bachelor's   (D) No change is necessary.

9. The fall of the <u>Berlin wall</u> was an important symbol of the collapse of <u>Communism</u>.

(A) berlin Wall . . . communism

(B) Berlin Wall . . . communism

(C) berlin wall . . . Communism

(D) No change is necessary.

10. A photograph of <u>mars</u> was printed in <u>the *New York Times*</u>.

(A) Mars . . . *The New York Times*

(B) mars . . . *The New York times*

(C) mars . . . *The New York Time*s

(D) No change is necessary.

SPELLING

Spelling questions test your ability to recognize misspelled words. This section reviews spelling tips and rules to help you spot incorrect spellings. Problems such as the distinction between *to* and *too* and *lead* and *led* are covered under the Word Choice Skills section of this review.

• Remember, *i* before *e* except after *c*, or when sounded as "a" as in *neighbor* and *weigh*.

• There are only three words in the English language that end in -*ceed*:

proceed, succeed, exceed

• There are several words that end in -*cede*:

secede, recede, concede, precede

- There is only one word in the English language that ends in *-sede*:

  supersede

Many people learn to read English phonetically; that is, by sounding out the letters of the words. However, many English words are not pronounced the way they are spelled, and those who try to spell English words phonetically often make spelling *errors*. It is better to memorize the correct spelling of English words rather than relying on phonetics to spell correctly.

Frequently Misspelled Words

The following list of words are frequently misspelled words. Study the spelling of each word by having a friend or teacher drill you on the words. Then mark down the words that you misspelled and study those select ones again. (The words appear in their most popular spellings.)

a lot	adequate	amateur
ability	advantage	American
absence	advantageous	among
absent	advertise	amount
abundance	advertisement	analysis
accept	advice	analyze
acceptable	advisable	angel
accident	advise	angle
accommodate	advisor	annual
accompanied	aerial	another
accomplish	affect	answer
accumulation	affectionate	antiseptic
accuse	again	anxious
accustomed	against	apologize
ache	aggravate	apparatus
achieve	aggressive	apparent
achievement	agree	appear
acknowledge	aisle	appearance
acquaintance	all right	appetite
acquainted	almost	application
acquire	already	apply
across	although	appreciate
address	altogether	appreciation
addressed	always	approach

appropriate	benefit	charity
approval	benefited	chief
approve	between	choose
approximate	bicycle	chose
argue	board	cigarette
arguing	bored	circumstance
argument	borrow	citizen
arouse	bottle	clothes
arrange	bottom	clothing
arrangement	boundary	coarse
article	brake	coffee
artificial	breadth	collect
ascend	breath	college
assistance	breathe	column
assistant	brilliant	comedy
associate	building	comfortable
association	bulletin	commitment
attempt	bureau	committed
attendance	burial	committee
attention	buried	communicate
audience	bury	company
August	bushes	comparative
author	business	compel
automobile	cafeteria	competent
autumn	calculator	competition
auxiliary	calendar	compliment
available	campaign	conceal
avenue	capital	conceit
awful	capitol	conceivable
awkward	captain	conceive
bachelor	career	concentration
balance	careful	conception
balloon	careless	condition
bargain	carriage	conference
basic	carrying	confident
beautiful	category	congratulate
because	ceiling	conquer
become	cemetery	conscience
before	cereal	conscientious
beginning	certain	conscious
being	changeable	consequence
believe	characteristic	consequently

considerable

consistency

consistent

continual

continuous

controlled

controversy

convenience

convenient

conversation

corporal

corroborate

council

counsel

counselor

courage

courageous

course

courteous

courtesy

criticism

criticize

crystal

curiosity

cylinder

daily

daughter

daybreak

death

deceive

December

deception

decide

decision

decisive

deed

definite

delicious

dependent

deposit

derelict

descend

descent

describe

description

desert

desirable

despair

desperate

dessert

destruction

determine

develop

development

device

dictator

died

difference

different

dilemma

dinner

direction

disappear

disappoint

disappointment

disapproval

disapprove

disastrous

discipline

discover

discriminate

disease

dissatisfied

dissection

dissipate

distance

distinction

division

doctor

dollar

doubt

dozen

earnest

easy

ecstasy

ecstatic

education

effect

efficiency

efficient

eight

either

eligibility

eligible

eliminate

embarrass

embarrassment

emergency

emphasis

emphasize

enclosure

encouraging

endeavor

engineer

English

enormous

enough

entrance

envelope

environment

equipment

equipped

especially

essential

evening

evident

exaggerate

exaggeration

examine

exceed

excellent

except

exceptional

exercise

exhausted

exhaustion

exhilaration	grievous	insistent
existence	grocery	instead
exorbitant	guarantee	instinct
expense	guess	integrity
experience	guidance	intellectual
experiment	half	intelligence
explanation	hammer	intercede
extreme	handkerchief	interest
facility	happiness	interfere
factory	healthy	interference
familiar	heard	interpreted
fascinate	heavy	interrupt
fascinating	height	invitation
fatigue	heroes	irrelevant
February	heroine	irresistible
financial	hideous	irritable
financier	himself	island
flourish	hoarse	its
forcibly	holiday	it's
forehead	hopeless	itself
foreign	hospital	January
formal	humorous	jealous
former	hurried	journal
fortunate	hurrying	judgment
fourteen	ignorance	kindergarten
fourth	imaginary	kitchen
frequent	imbecile	knew
friend	imitation	knock
frightening	immediately	know
fundamental	immigrant	knowledge
further	incidental	labor
gallon	increase	laboratory
garden	independence	laid
gardener	independent	language
general	indispensable	later
genius	inevitable	latter
government	influence	laugh
governor	influential	leisure
grammar	initiate	length
grateful	innocence	lesson
great	inoculate	library
grievance	inquiry	license

light	muscle	panicky
lightning	mysterious	parallel
likelihood	mystery	parallelism
likely	narrative	particular
literal	natural	partner
literature	necessary	pastime
livelihood	needle	patience
loaf	negligence	peace
loneliness	neighbor	peaceable
loose	neither	pear
lose	newspaper	peculiar
losing	newsstand	pencil
loyal	niece	people
loyalty	noticeable	perceive
magazine	o'clock	perception
maintenance	obedient	perfect
maneuver	obstacle	perform
marriage	occasion	performance
married	occasional	perhaps
marry	occur	period
match	occurred	permanence
material	occurrence	permanent
mathematics	ocean	perpendicular
measure	offer	perseverance
medicine	often	persevere
million	omission	persistent
miniature	omit	personal
minimum	once	personality
miracle	operate	personnel
miscellaneous	opinion	persuade
mischief	opportune	persuasion
mischievous	opportunity	pertain
misspelled	optimist	picture
mistake	optimistic	piece
momentous	origin	plain
monkey	original	playwright
monotonous	oscillate	pleasant
moral	ought	please
morale	ounce	pleasure
mortgage	overcoat	pocket
mountain	paid	poison
mournful	pamphlet	policeman

political
population
portrayal
positive
possess
possession
possessive
possible
post office
potatoes
practical
prairie
precede
preceding
precise
predictable
prefer
preference
preferential
preferred
prejudice
preparation
prepare
prescription
presence
president
prevalent
primitive
principal
principle
privilege
probably
procedure
proceed
produce
professional
professor
profitable
prominent
promise
pronounce
pronunciation

propeller
prophet
prospect
psychology
pursue
pursuit
quality
quantity
quarreling
quart
quarter
quiet
quite
raise
realistic
realize
reason
rebellion
recede
receipt
receive
recipe
recognize
recommend
recuperate
referred
rehearsal
reign
relevant
relieve
remedy
renovate
repeat
repetition
representative
requirements
resemblance
resistance
resource
respectability
responsibility
restaurant

rhythm
rhythmical
ridiculous
right
role
roll
roommate
sandwich
Saturday
scarcely
scene
schedule
science
scientific
scissors
season
secretary
seize
seminar
sense
separate
service
several
severely
shepherd
sheriff
shining
shoulder
shriek
siege
sight
signal
significance
significant
similar
similarity
sincerely
site
soldier
solemn
sophomore
soul

source	technical	vacuum
souvenir	telegram	valley
special	telephone	valuable
specified	temperament	variety
specimen	temperature	vegetable
speech	tenant	vein
stationary	tendency	vengeance
stationery	tenement	versatile
statue	therefore	vicinity
stockings	thorough	vicious
stomach	through	view
straight	title	village
strength	together	villain
strenuous	tomorrow	visitor
stretch	tongue	voice
striking	toward	volume
studying	tragedy	waist
substantial	transferred	weak
succeed	treasury	wear
successful	tremendous	weather
sudden	tries	Wednesday
superintendent	truly	week
suppress	twelfth	weigh
surely	twelve	weird
surprise	tyranny	whether
suspense	undoubtedly	which
sweat	United States	while
sweet	university	whole
syllable	unnecessary	wholly
symmetrical	unusual	whose
sympathy	useful	wretched
synonym	usual	

☞ Drill: Spelling

DIRECTIONS: Identify the misspelled word in each set.

1.   (A) probly

    (B) accommodate

    (C) acquaintance

2. (A) auxiliary

   (B) atheletic

   (C) beginning

3. (A) environment

   (B) existence

   (C) Febuary

4. (A) ocassion

   (B) occurrence

   (C) omitted

5. (A) perspiration

   (B) referring

   (C) priviledge

DIRECTIONS: Choose the correct option.

6. <u>Preceding</u> the <u>business</u> session, lunch will be served in a <u>separate</u> room.

   (A) preceeding . . . business . . . seperate

   (B) proceeding . . . bussiness . . . seperate

   (C) proceeding . . . business . . . seperite

   (D) No change is necessary.

7. Monte <u>inadvertently</u> left <u>several</u> of his <u>libary</u> books in the cafeteria.

   (A) inadverdently . . . serveral . . . libery

   (B) inadvertently . . . several . . . library

   (C) inadvertentely . . . several . . . librery

   (D) No change is necessary.

8. Sam wished he had more <u>liesure</u> time so he could <u>persue</u> his favorite hobbies.

   (A) leisure . . . pursue   (B) Liesure . . . pursue

(C)   leisure . . . persue   (D)   No change is necessary.

9.   One of my <u>favrite charecters</u> in <u>litrature</u> is Bilbo from *The Hobbit*.

   (A)   favrite . . . characters . . . literature

   (B)   favorite . . . characters . . . literature

   (C)   favourite . . . characters . . . literature

   (D)   No change is necessary.

10.   Even <u>tho</u> Joe was badly hurt in the <u>accidant</u>, the company said they were not <u>lible</u> for damages.

   (A)   though . . . accidant . . . libel

   (B)   though . . . accident . . . liable

   (C)   though . . . acident . . . liable

   (D)   No change is necessary.

ENGLISH LANGUAGE SKILLS

ANSWER KEY

Drill: Word Choice Skills

1. (D)	4. (C)	7. (A)	10. (B)
2. (D)	5. (A)	8. (B)	
3. (A)	6. (C)	9. (C)	

Drill: Sentence Structure Skills

1. (C)	4. (B)	7. (B)	10. (B)
2. (B)	5. (A)	8. (C)	
3. (B)	6. (A)	9. (B)	

Drill: Verbs

1. (C)	4. (A)	7. (A)	10. (D)
2. (D)	5. (A)	8. (C)	
3. (D)	6. (B)	9. (A)	

Drill: Pronouns

1. (A)	4. (A)	7. (B)	10. (C)
2. (C)	5. (D)	8. (B)	
3. (A)	6. (A)	9. (A)	

Drill: Adjectives and Adverbs

1. (C)	4. (C)	7. (A)	10. (C)
2. (A)	5. (A)	8. (C)	
3. (D)	6. (C)	9. (B)	

Drill: Punctuation

1.	(D)	4.	(C)	7.	(A)	10.	(D)
2.	(A)	5.	(A)	8.	(A)		
3.	(A)	6.	(D)	9.	(B)		

Drill: Capitalization

1.	(D)	4.	(A)	7.	(B)	10.	(A)
2.	(B)	5.	(C)	8.	(D)		
3.	(C)	6.	(D)	9.	(B)		

Drill: Spelling

1.	(A)	4.	(A)	7.	(B)	10.	(B)
2.	(B)	5.	(C)	8.	(A)		
3.	(C)	6.	(D)	9.	(B)		

DETAILED EXPLANATIONS
OF ANSWERS

Drill: Word Choice Skills

1.   **(D)**   Choice (D) is correct. No change is necessary. *Principal* as a noun means "head of a school." *Principle* is a noun meaning "axiom" or "rule of conduct."

2.   **(D)**   Choice (D) is correct. No change is necessary. *Affect* is a verb meaning "to influence" or "to change." *Effect* as a noun meaning "result."

3.   **(A)**   Choice (A) is correct. Use *amount* with noncountable, mass nouns (*amount* of food, help, money); use *number* with countable, plural nouns (*number* of children, classes, bills).

4.   **(C)**   Choice (C) is correct. *Supposed to* and *used to* should be spelled with a final *d*. *Achieving* follows the standard spelling rule—*i* before *e*.

5.   **(A)**   Choice (A) is correct. Use *that*, not *because*, to introduce clauses after the word *reason*. Choice (A) is also the only choice that contains the correct spelling of "succeeded."

6.   **(C)**   Choice (C) is correct. *Converge together* is redundant, and *single* is not needed to convey the meaning of *a highway*.

7.   **(A)**   Choice (A) is correct. It is economical and concise. The other choices contain unnecessary repetition.

8.   **(B)**   Choice (B) is correct. Choices (A) and (C) pad the sentences with loose synonyms that are redundant. Choice (D), although a short sentence, does not convey the meaning as clearly as choice (B).

9.   **(C)**   Choice (C) is correct. The other choices all contain unnecessary repetition.

10.   **(B)**   Choice (B) is correct. Choices (A) and (C) contain circumlocution; they fail to get to the point. Choice (D) does not express the meaning of the sentence as concisely as choice (B).

Drill: Sentence Structure Skills

1.   **(C)**   Choice (C) is correct. Each response contains items in a series. In choices (A) and (B), the word group after the conjunction is not an adjective like the first words in the series. Choice (C) contains three adjectives.

2.   **(B)**   Choice (B) is correct. Choices (A), (C), and (D) combine conjunctions incorrectly.

3.   **(B)**   Choice (B) is correct. Choices (A) and (C) appear to be parallel because the conjunction *and* connects two word groups that both begin with *because*, but the structure on both sides of the conjunction are very different. *Because he kept his campaign promises* is a clause; *because of his refusal to accept political favors* is a prepositional phrase. Choice (B) connects two dependent clauses.

4.   **(B)**   Choice (B) is correct. Choices (A) and (C) contain the elliptical clause *While . . . taking a shower*. It appears that the missing subject in the elliptical clause is the same as that in the independent clause—the *doorbell* in choice (A) and *someone* in choice (C), neither of which is a logical subject for the verbal *taking a shower*. Choice (B) removes the elliptical clause and provides the logical subject.

5.   **(A)**   Choice (A) is correct. Who swung the bat? Choices (B) and (C) both imply that it is the runner who swung the bat. Only choice (A) makes it clear that as *he* swung the bat, someone else (the *runner*) stole second base.

6.   **(A)**   Choice (A) is correct. The punctuation in the original sentence and in choice (B) creates a fragment. *Cotton being the state's principal crop* is not an independent thought because it lacks a complete verb—*being* is not a complete verb.

7.   **(B)**   Choice (B) is correct. The punctuation in the original sentence and in choice (A) creates a fragment. Both the semicolon and the period should be used to separate two independent clauses. The word group *one that I have never seen before* does not express a complete thought and therefore is not an independent clause.

8.   **(C)**   Choice (C) is correct. The dependent clause *because repairs were being made* in choices (B) and (C) is punctuated as if it were a sentence. The result is a fragment.

9.   **(B)**   Choice (B) is correct. Choices (A) and (C) do not separate the complete thoughts in the independent clauses with the correct punctuation.

10.   **(B)**   Choice (B) is correct. Choices (A) and (C) do not separate the independent clauses with the correct punctuation.

Drill: Verbs

1.   **(C)**   Choice (C) is correct. The past participle form of each verb is required because of the auxiliaries (helping verbs) *had been* (concerned) and *would have* (gone).

2.   **(D)**   Choice (D) is correct. The forms of the irregular verb meaning *to rest* are *lie (rest), lies (rests), lay (rested),* and *has lain (has rested).* The forms of the verb meaning *to put* are *lay (put), lays (puts), laying (putting), laid (put),* and *have laid (have put).*

3.   **(D)**   Choice (D) is correct. The present tense is used for universal truths and the past tense is used for historical truths.

4.   **(A)**   Choice (A) is correct. The present tense is used for customary happenings. Choice (B), *had begun,* is not a standard verb form. Choice (C), *was beginning,* indicates that 10:30 a.m. is not the regular class time.

5.   **(A)**   Choice (A) is correct. The past tense is used for historical statements, and the present tense is used for statements about works of art.

6.   **(B)**   Choice (B) is correct. The subject of the sentence is the plural noun *sales,* not the singular noun *Christmas,* which is the object of the prepositional phrase.

7.   **(A)**   Choice (A) is correct. The subject *specialty* is singular.

8.   **(C)**   Choice (C) is correct. Subjects preceded by *every* are considered singular and therefore require a singular verb form.

9.   **(A)**   Choice (A) is correct. The subject of the sentence is the gerund *hiding,* not the object of the gerund phrase *mistakes. Hiding* is singular; therefore, the singular verb form *does* should be used.

10. **(D)** Choice (D) is correct. Though the form of the subject *Board of Regents* is plural, it is singular in meaning.

Drill: Pronouns

1. **(A)** Choice (A) is correct. Do not use the reflexive pronoun *myself* as a substitute for I.

2. **(C)** Choice (C) is correct. In the clause *whoever consumes them*, *whoever* is the subject. *Whomever* is the objective case pronoun and should be used only as the object of a sentence, never as the subject.

3. **(A)** Choice (A) is correct. Use the nominative case pronoun *who* as the subject complement after the verb *is*.

4. **(A)** Choice (A) is correct. In this sentence use the nominative case/subject pronouns *she who* as the subject complement after the *be* verb *was*.

5. **(D)** Choice (D) is correct. *Student* is an indefinite, genderless noun that requires a singular personal pronoun. While *his* is a singular personal pronoun, a genderless noun includes both the masculine and feminine forms and requires *his or her* as the singular personal pronoun.

6. **(A)** Choice (A) is correct. The antecedent *company* is singular, requiring the singular pronoun *it*, not the plural *they*.

7. **(B)** Choice (B) is correct. Choice (A) contains a person shift: *Your* is a second person pronoun, and *his* and *her* are third person pronouns. The original sentence uses the third person plural pronoun *their* to refer to the singular antecedent *every car owner*. Choice (B) correctly provides the masculine and feminine forms *his or her* required by the indefinite, genderless *every car owner*.

8. **(B)** Choice (B) is correct. The implied antecedent is *teaching*. Choices (A) and (C) each contain a pronoun with no antecedent. Neither *it* nor *this* are suitable substitutions for *teacher*.

9. **(A)** Choice (A) is correct. The pronoun *they* in the original sentence has no conspicuous antecedent. Since the doer of the action is obviously unknown (and therefore genderless), choice (B), *he*, is not the correct choice.

10. **(C)**   Choice (C) is correct. The original sentence is ambiguous: the pronoun *she* has two possible antecedents; we don't know whether it is Margaret or her sister who is away at college.

Drill: Adjectives and Adverbs

1. **(C)**   Choice (C) is correct. *Bad* is an adjective; *badly* is an adverb. *Real* is an adjective meaning *genuine* (*a real problem, real leather*). To qualify an adverb of degree to express how bad, how excited, how boring, etc., choose *very*.

2. **(A)**   Choice (A) is correct. Use an adverb as a qualifier for an adjective. *How simple? Relatively simple.*

3. **(D)**   Choice (D) is correct. *Good* is an adjective; *well* is both an adjective and an adverb. As an adjective, *well* refers to health; it means "not ill."

4. **(C)**   Choice (C) is correct. All the other choices use *good* incorrectly as an adverb. *Shake* is an action verb that requires an adverb, not an adjective.

5. **(A)**   Choice (A) is correct. The action verbs *speaks, writes, observe,* and *think* each require adverbs as modifiers.

6. **(C)**   Choice (C) is correct. The comparisons in choices (A) and (B) are illogical: these sentences suggest that Los Angeles is not in California because it *is larger than any city in California.*

7. **(A)**   Choice (A) is correct. Do not omit the second *as* of the correlative pair *as . . . as* when making a point of equal or superior comparison, as in choice (B). Choice (C) omits *than* from "if not more interesting [than]".

8. **(C)**   Choice (C) is correct. Choice (A) illogically compares *baseball team* to a *university*, and choice (B) illogically compares *baseball team* to *all the other universities*. Choice (C) logically compares the baseball team here to the one at any other university, as implied by the possessive ending on university—*university's.*

9. **(B)**   Choice (B) is correct. Choices (A) and (C) are ambiguous;

because these sentences are too elliptical, the reader does not know where to place the missing information.

10.　**(C)**　Choice (C) is correct. Choice (A) is redundant; there is no need to use *most* with *stingiest*. Choice (B) incorrectly combines the comparative word *more* with the superlative form *stingiest*.

Drill: Punctuation

1.　**(D)**　Choice (D) is correct. Nonrestrictive clauses, like other nonrestrictive elements, should be set off from the rest of the sentence with commas.

2.　**(A)**　Choice (A) is correct. Use a comma to separate a nonrestrictive appositive from the word it modifies. "An Oklahoma family" is a nonrestrictive appositive.

3.　**(A)**　Choice (A) is correct. Do not use unnecessary commas to separate a subject and verb from their complement. Both choices (B) and (C) use superfluous punctuation.

4.　**(C)**　Choice (C) is correct. Do not separate two items in a compound with commas. The original sentence incorrectly separates "car or plane." Choice (A) omits the comma after the introductory clause.

5.　**(A)**　Choice (A) is correct. Use a semicolon to separate two independent clauses/sentences that are not joined by a coordinating conjunction, especially when the ideas in the sentences are interrelated.

6.　**(D)**　Choice (D) is correct. Use a semicolon to separate two sentences not joined by a coordinating conjunction.

7.　**(A)**　Choice (A) is correct. Use a semicolon to separate two sentences joined by a conjunctive adverb.

8.　**(A)**　Choice (A) is correct. Do not use a colon after a verb or a preposition. Remember that a complete sentence must precede a colon.

9.　**(B)**　Choice (B) is correct. Do not use a colon after a preposition, and do not use a colon to separate a preposition from its objects.

10.　**(D)**　Choice (D) is correct. Use a colon preceding a list that is introduced by words such as *the following* and *as follows*.

Drill: Capitalization

1. **(D)** Choice (D) is correct. *North America,* like other proper names, is capitalized. *North, south, east,* and *west* are only capitalized when they refer to geographic regions (*the Southwest, Eastern Europe);* as compass directions, they are not capitalized.

2. **(B)** Choice (B) is correct. Although persons' names are capitalized, a person's title is not (*coach,* not *Coach*). Capitalize the complete name of a team, school, river, etc. (Dallas Cowboys).

3. **(C)** Choice (C) is correct. Capitalize all geographic units, and capitalize *earth* only when it is mentioned with other planets. *Equator* is not capitalized.

4. **(A)** Choice (A) is correct. Capitalize the first word in a title and all other words in a title except articles, prepositions with fewer than five letters, and conjunctions.

5. **(C)** Choice (C) is correct. Capitalize proper adjectives (proper nouns used as adjectives): *Greek* goddess, *Roman* mythology.

6. **(D)** Choice (D) is correct. Capitalize all religious groups, books, and names referring to religious deities.

7. **(B)** Choice (B) is correct. Do not capitalize courses unless they are languages (English) or course titles followed by a number (Algebra I).

8. **(D)** Choice (D) is correct. Do not capitalize seasons unless they accompany the name of an event such as *Spring Break.* Do not capitalize types of degrees (*bachelor's degrees*); capitalize only the name of the degree (*Bachelor of Arts degree*).

9. **(B)** Choice (B) is correct. As a landmark, *Berlin Wall* is capitalized; however, do not capitalize systems of government or individual adherents to a philosophy, such as *communism.*

10. **(A)** Choice (A) is correct. The names of planets, as well as the complete names of newspapers and other periodicals, are capitalized.

Drill: Spelling

1.   **(A)**   The correct spelling of choice (A) is "probably."

2.   **(B)**   The correct spelling is "athletic."

3.   **(C)**   Choice (C) should be spelled "February."

4.   **(A)**   The correct spelling of this word is "occasion."

5.   **(C)**   Choice (C) should be spelled "privilege."

6.   **(D)**   Choice (D) is the best response. *Business* has only three -*s's*. Separate has an -*e* at the beginning and the end, not in the middle.

7.   **(B)**   Choice (B) is the best response. *Library* has two *r's*.

8.   **(A)**   Choice (A) is the best response. *Leisure* is one of the few English words that does not follow the *i* before *e* except after *c* rule. *Pursue* has two *u's* and only one *e*.

9.   **(B)**   Choice (B) is the best response. "Favorite," "characters," and "literature" are commonly mispronounced, and when someone who mispronounces them tries to spell them phonetically, he or she often misspells them.

10.   **(B)**   Choice (B) is the best response. Advertisements often misspell words to catch the consumer's eye (*lite* for light, *tho* for though, etc.), and these misspellings are becoming more common in student writing. "Accident" and "liable" are examples of words that are not pronounced the way they are spelled.

SAT II: Writing

Chapter 4
Essay Writing
Review

Chapter 4

ESSAY WRITING REVIEW

The SAT II: Writing Subject Test contains one writing exercise. You will have 20 minutes to plan and write an essay on a given topic. You must write on only that topic. Since you will have only 20 minutes to complete the essay, efficient use of your time is essential.

Writing under pressure can be frustrating, but if you study this review, practice and polish your essay skills, and have a realistic sense of what to expect, you can turn problems into possibilities. The following review will show you how to plan and write a logical, coherent, and interesting essay.

PRE-WRITING/PLANNING

Before you begin to actually write, there are certain preliminary steps you need to take. A few minutes spent planning pays off—your final essay will be more focused, well-developed, and clearer. For a 20-minute essay, you should spend about five minutes on the pre-writing process.

Understand the Question

Read the essay question very carefully and ask yourself the following questions:

- What is the meaning of the topic statement?

- Is the question asking me to persuade the reader of the validity of a certain opinion?

- Do I agree or disagree with the statement? What will be my thesis (main idea)?

- What kinds of examples can I use to support my thesis? Explore personal experiences, historical evidence, current events, and literary subjects.

Consider Your Audience

Essays would be pointless without an audience. Why write an essay if no one wants or needs to read it? Why add evidence, organize your ideas, or correct bad grammar? The reason to do any of these things is because someone out there needs to understand what you mean or say.

What does the audience need to know to believe you or to come over to your position? Imagine someone you know listening to you declare your position or opinion and then saying, "Oh, yeah? Prove it!" This is your audience—write to them. Ask yourself the following questions so that you will not be confronted with a person who says, "Prove it!"

- What evidence do I need to prove my idea to this skeptic?

- What would s/he disagree with me about?

- What does he or she share with me as common knowledge? What do I need to tell the reader?

WRITING YOUR ESSAY

Once you have considered your position on the topic and thought of several examples to support it, you are ready to begin writing.

Organizing Your Essay

Decide how many paragraphs you will write. In a 20-minute exercise, you will probably have time for no more than four or five paragraphs. In such a format, the first paragraph will be the introduction, the next two or three will develop your thesis with specific examples, and the final paragraph should be a strong conclusion.

The Introduction

The focus of your introduction should be the thesis statement. This statement allows your reader to understand the point and direction of your essay. The statement identifies the central idea of your essay and should clearly state your attitude about the subject. It will also dictate the basic content and organization of your essay. If you do not state your thesis clearly, your essay will suffer.

The thesis is the heart of the essay. Without it, readers won't know what your major message or central idea is in the essay.

The thesis must be something that can be argued or needs to be proven, not just an accepted fact. For example, "Animals are used every day in cosmetic and medical testing," is a fact—it needs no proof. But if the writer says, "Using animals for cosmetic and medical testing is cruel and should be stopped," we have a point that must be supported and defended by the writer.

The thesis can be placed in any paragraph of the essay, but in a short essay, especially one written for evaluative exam purposes, the thesis is most effective when placed in the last sentence of the opening paragraph.

Consider the following sample question:

ESSAY TOPIC:

"That government is best which governs least."

ASIGNMENT: Do you agree or disagree with this statement? Choose a specific example from current events, personal experience, or your reading to support your position.

After reading the topic statement, decide if you agree or disagree. If you agree with this statement, your thesis statement could be the following:

> "Government has the right to protect individuals from interference but no right to extend its powers and activities beyond this function."

This statement clearly states the writer's opinion in a direct manner. It also serves as a blueprint for the essay. The remainder of the introduction should give two or three brief examples that support your thesis.

Supporting Paragraphs

The next two or three paragraphs of your essay will elaborate on the supporting examples you gave in your introduction. Each paragraph should discuss only one idea. Like the introduction, each paragraph should be coherently organized, with a topic sentence and supporting details.

The topic sentence is to each paragraph what the thesis statement is to the essay as a whole. It tells the reader what you plan to discuss in that paragraph. It has a specific subject and is neither too broad nor too narrow. It also establishes the author's attitude and gives the reader a sense of the direction in which the writer is going. An effective topic sentence also arouses the reader's interest.

Although it may occur in the middle or at the end of the paragraph, the topic sentence usually appears at the beginning of the paragraph. Placing it at the beginning is advantageous because it helps you stay focused on the main idea.

The remainder of each paragraph should support the topic sentence with examples and illustrations. Each sentence should progress logically from the previous one and be centrally connected to your topic sentence. Do not include any extraneous material that does not serve to develop your thesis.

Conclusion

Your conclusion should briefly restate your thesis and explain how you have shown it to be true. Since you want to end your essay on a strong note, your conclusion should be concise and effective.

Do not introduce any new topics that you cannot support. If you were watching a movie that suddenly shifted plot and characters at the end, you would be disappointed or even angry. Similarly, conclusions must not drift away from the major focus and message of the essay. Make sure your conclusion is clearly on the topic and represents your perspective without any confusion about what you really mean and believe. The reader will respect you for staying true to your intentions.

The conclusion is your last chance to grab and impress the reader. You can even use humor, if appropriate, but a dramatic close will remind the reader you are serious, even passionate, about what you believe.

EFFECTIVE USE OF LANGUAGE

Clear organization, while vitally important, is not the only factor the graders of your essay consider. You must also demonstrate that you can express your ideas clearly, using correct grammar, diction, usage, spelling, and punctuation. For rules on grammar, usage, and mechanics, consult the English Language Skills Review in this book.

Point-of-View

Depending on the audience, essays may be written from one of three points of view:

1. *Subjective/Personal* Point of View:

    "I think . . ."

    "I believe cars are more trouble than they are worth."

    "I feel . . ."

2.   *Second Person* Point of View (We . . . You; I . . . You):

> "If *you* own a car, *you* will soon find out that it is more trouble than it is worth."

3.   *Third Person* Point of View (focuses on the idea, not what "I" think of it):

> "*Cars* are more trouble than *they* are worth."

It is very important to maintain a consistent point of view throughout your essay. If you begin writing in the first-person ("I"), do not shift to the second- or third-person in the middle of the essay. Such inconsistency is confusing to your reader and will be penalized by the graders of your essay.

Tone

A writer's tone results from his or her attitude towards the subject and the reader. If the essay question requires you to take a strong stand, the tone of your essay should reflect this.

Your tone should also be appropriate for the subject matter. A serious topic demands a serious tone. For a more light-hearted topic, you may wish to inject some humor into your essay.

Whatever tone you choose, be consistent. Do not make any abrupt shifts in tone in the middle of your essay.

Verb Tense

Make sure to remain in the same verb tense in which you began your essay. If you start in the past, make sure all verbs are past tense. Staying in the same verb tense improves the continuity and flow of ideas. Avoid phrases such as "now was," a confusing blend of present and past. Consistency of time is essential to the reader's understanding.

Transitions

Transitions are like the links of a bracelet, holding the beads or major points of your essay together. They help the reader follow the smooth flow of your ideas and show a connection between major and minor ideas. Transitions are used either at the beginning of a paragraph, or to show the connections among ideas within a single paragraph. Without transitions, you will jar the reader and distract him from your true ideas.

Here are some typical transitional words and phrases:

Linking similar ideas

again	for example	likewise
also	for instance	moreover
and	further	nor
another	furthermore	of course
besides	in addition	similarly
equally important	in like manner	too

Linking dissimilar/contradictory ideas

although	however	otherwise
and yet	in spite of	provided that
as if	instead	still
but	nevertheless	yet
conversely	on the contrary	on the other hand

Indicating cause, purpose, or result

as	for	so
as a result	for this reason	then
because	hence	therefore
consequently	since	thus

Indicating time or position

above	before	meanwhile
across	beyond	next
afterwards	eventually	presently
around	finally	second
at once	first	thereafter
at the present time	here	thereupon

Indicating an example or summary

as a result	in any event	in short
as I have said	in brief	on the whole
for example	in conclusion	to sum up
for instance	in fact	in other words

Common Writing Errors

The four writing errors most often made by beginning writers are run-ons (also known as fused sentences), fragments, lack of subject-verb agreement, and incorrect use of object:

1. **Run-ons**: "She swept the floor it was dirty" is a run-on, because the pronoun "it" stands as a noun subject and starts a new sentence. A period or semicolon is needed after "floor."

2. **Fragments**: "Before Jimmy learned how to play baseball" is a fragment, even though it has a subject and verb (Jimmy learned). The word "before" fragmentizes the clause, and the reader needs to know what happened before Jimmy learned how to play baseball.

3. **Problems with subject-verb agreement**: "Either Maria or Robert are going to the game" is incorrect because either Maria is going or Robert is going, but not both. The sentence should say, "Either Maria or Robert is going to the game."

4. **Incorrect object**: Probably the most common offender in this area is saying "between you and I," which sounds correct, but isn't. "Between" is a preposition that takes the objective case "me." The correct usage is "between you and me."

SAT II: Writing test graders also cite lack of thought and development, misspellings, incorrect pronouns or antecedents, and lack of development as frequently occurring problems. Finally, keep in mind that clear, coherent handwriting always works to your advantage. Readers will appreciate an essay they can read with ease.

Five Words Weak Writers Overuse

Weak and beginning writers overuse the vague pronouns "you, we, they, this, and it" often without telling exactly who or what is represented by the pronoun.

1. Beginning writers often shift to second person **"you,"** when the writer means, "a person." This shift confuses readers and weakens the flow of the essay. Although "you" is commonly accepted in creative writing, journalism, and other arenas, in a short, formal essay, it is best to avoid "you" altogether.

2. **"We"** is another pronoun that should be avoided. If by "we" the writer means "Americans," "society," or some other group, then he or she should say so.

3. **"They"** is often misused in essay writing, because it is overused in conversation: "I went to the doctor, and they told me to take some medicine." Tell the reader who "they" are.

4. **"This"** is usually used incorrectly without a referent: "She told me she received a present. This sounded good to me." This what? This idea? This news? This present? Be clear—don't make your readers guess what you mean. The word "this" should be followed by a noun or referent.

5. **"It"** is a common problem among weak writers. To what does "it" refer? Your readers don't appreciate vagueness, so take the time to be clear and complete in your expression of ideas.

Use Your Own Vocabulary

Is it a good idea to use big words that sound good in the dictionary or thesaurus, but that you don't really use or understand? No. So whose vocabulary should you use? Your own. You will be most comfortable with your own level of vocabulary.

This "comfort zone" doesn't give you license to be informal in a formal setting or to violate the rules of standard written English, but if you try to write in a style that is not yours, your writing will be awkward and lack a true voice.

You should certainly improve and build your vocabulary at every opportunity, but remember: you should not attempt to change your vocabulary level at this point.

Avoid the Passive Voice

In writing, the active voice is preferable because it is emphatic and direct. A weak passive verb leaves the doer unknown or seemingly unimportant. However, the passive voice is essential when the action of the verb is more important than the doer, when the doer is unknown, or when the writer wishes to place the emphasis on the receiver of the action rather than on the doer.

PROOFREADING

Make sure to leave yourself enough time at the end to read over your essay for errors such as misspellings, omitted words, or incorrect punctuation. You will not have enough time to make large-scale revisions, but take this chance to make any small changes that will make your essay stronger. Consider the following when proofreading your work:

- Are all your sentences really sentences? Have you written any fragments or run-on sentences?

- Are you using vocabulary correctly?

- Did you leave out any punctuation? Did you capitalize correctly?

- Are there any misspellings, especially of difficult words?

If you have time, read your essay backwards from end to beginning. By doing so, you may catch errors that you missed reading forward only.

☞ Drill: Essay Writing

DIRECTIONS: You have 20 minutes to plan and write an essay on the topic below. You may write only on the assigned topic.

Make sure to give specific examples to support your thesis. Proofread your essay carefully and take care to express your ideas clearly and effectively. Write your essay on the lined pages.

Write your essay on the lined pages at the back of the book.

ESSAY TOPIC:

In the last 20 years, the deterioration of the environment has become a growing concern among both scientists and ordinary citizens.

ASSIGNMENT: Choose one pressing environmental problem, explain its negative impact, and discuss possible solutions.

DETAILED EXPLANATIONS OF ANSWERS

Drill: Essay Writing

This Answer Key provides three sample essays which represent possible responses to the essay topic. Compare your own response to those given on the next few pages. Allow the strengths and weaknesses of the sample essays help you to critique your own essay and improve your writing skills.

ESSAY I (Score: 5–6)

There are many pressing environmental problems facing both this country and the world today. Pollution, the misuse and squandering of resources, and the cavalier attitude many people express all contribute to the problem. But one of the most pressing problems this country faces is the apathetic attitude many Americans have towards recycling.

Why is recycling so imperative? There are two major reasons. First, recycling previously used materials conserves precious national resources. Many people never stop to think that reserves of metal ores are not unlimited. There is only so much gold, silver, tin, and other metals in the ground. Once it has all been mined, there will never be any more unless we recycle what has already been used.

Second, the United States daily generates more solid waste than any other country on earth. Our disposable consumer culture consumes fast food meals in paper or styrofoam containers, uses disposable diapers with plastic liners that do not biodegrade, receives pounds, if not tons, of unsolicited junk mail every year, and relies more and more on prepackaged rather than fresh food.

No matter how it is accomplished, increased recycling is essential. We have to stop covering our land with garbage, and the best ways to do this are to reduce our dependence on prepackaged goods and to minimize the amount of solid waste disposed of in landfills. The best way to reduce solid waste is to recycle it. Americans need to band together to recycle, to preserve our irreplaceable natural resources, reduce pollution, and preserve our precious environment.

Analysis

This essay presents a clearly defined thesis, and the writer elaborates on this thesis in a thoughtful and sophisticated manner. Various aspects of the problem under consideration are presented and explored, along with possible solutions. The support provided for the writer's argument is convincing and logical. There are few usage or mechanical errors to interfere with the writer's ability to communicate effectively. This writer demonstrates a comprehensive understanding of the rules of written English.

ESSAY II (Score: 3–4)

A pressing environmental problem today is the way we are cutting down too many trees and not planting any replacements for them. Trees are beneficial in many ways, and without them, many environmental problems would be much worse.

One of the ways trees are beneficial is that, like all plants, they take in carbon dioxide and produce oxygen. They can actually help clean the air this way. When too many trees are cut down in a small area, the air in that area is not as good and can be unhealthy to breath.

Another way trees are beneficial is that they provide homes for many types of birds, insects, and animals. When all the trees in an area are cut down, these animals lose their homes and sometimes they can die out and become extinct that way. Like the spotted owls in Oregon, that the loggers wanted to cut down the trees they lived in. If the loggers did cut down all the old timber stands that the spotted owls lived in, the owls would have become extinct.

But the loggers say that if they can't cut the trees down then they will be out of work, and that peoples' jobs are more important than birds. The loggers can do two things—they can either get training so they can do other jobs, or they can do what they should have done all along, and start replanting trees. For every mature tree they cut down, they should have to plant at least one tree seedling.

Cutting down the trees that we need for life, and that lots of other species depend on, is a big environmental problem that has a lot of long term consaquences. Trees are too important for all of us to cut them down without thinking about the future.

Analysis

This essay has a clear thesis, which the author does support with good examples. But the writer shifts between the chosen topic, which is that indiscriminate tree-cutting is a pressing environmental problem, and a list of the ways in which trees are beneficial and a discussion about the logging profession. Also, while there are few mistakes in usage and mechanics, the writer does have some problems with sentence structure. The writing is pedestrian and the writer does not elaborate on the topic as much as he or she could have. The writer failed to provide the kind of critical analysis that the topic required.

ESSAY III (Score: 1–2)

The most pressing environmental problem today is that lots of people and companies don't care about the environment, and they do lots of things that hurt the environment.

People throw littur out car windows and don't use trash cans, even if their all over a park, soda cans and fast food wrappers are all over the place. Cigarette butts are the worst cause the filters never rot. Newspapers and junk mail get left to blow all over the neighborhood, and beer bottles too.

Companies pollute the air and the water. Sometimes the ground around a company has lots of tocsins in it. Now companies can buy credits from other companies that let them pollute the air even more. They dump all kinds of chemacals into lakes and rivers that kills off the fish and causes acid rain and kills off more fish and some trees and small animuls and insects and then noone can go swimming or fishing in the lake.

People need to respect the environment because we only have one planet, and if we keep polluting it pretty soon nothing will grow and then even the people will die.

Analysis

The writer of this essay does not define his or her thesis for this essay. Because of this lack of a clear thesis, the reader is left to infer the topic from the body of the essay. It is possible to perceive the writer's intended thesis; however, the support for this thesis is very superficial. The writer presents a list of common complaints about polluters, without any critical discussion of the problems and possible solutions. Many sentences are run-ons and the writer has made several spelling errors. While the author manages to communicate his or her position on the issue, he or she does so on such a superficial level and with so many errors in usage and mechanics that the writer fails to demonstrate an ability to effectively communicate.

SAT II: Writing

Practice Test 1

SAT II: WRITING TEST 1

Part A: Essay

TIME: 20 Minutes

DIRECTIONS: You have 20 minutes to plan and write an essay on the topic below. You may write only on the assigned topic.

Make sure to give specific examples to support your thesis. Proofread your essay carefully and take care to express your ideas clearly and effectively.

Write your essay on the lined pages at the back of the book.

ESSAY TOPIC:

In the twentieth century, the concept of heroism is dead.

ASSIGNMENT: Do you agree or disagree with the statement? Support your opinion with specific examples from history, current events, literature, or personal experience.

Part B: Multiple-Choice

(Answer sheets appear in the back of this book.)

TIME: 40 Minutes
60 Questions

DIRECTIONS: Each of the following sentences may contain an error in diction, usage, idiom, or grammar. Some sentences are correct. Some sentences contain one error. No sentence contains more than one error.

If there is an error, it will appear in one of the underlined portions labeled A, B, C, or D. If there is no error, choose the portion labeled E. If there is an error, select the letter of the portion that must be changed in order to correct the sentence.

EXAMPLE:

He drove <u>slowly</u> and <u>cautiously</u> in order to <u>hopefully</u> avoid having an
          A   **B**   **C**

<u>accident</u>. <u>No error</u>.
  D   **E**   Ⓐ Ⓑ ● Ⓓ Ⓔ

---

1. In 1877 Chief Joseph of the Nez Perces, <u>together with</u> 250 warriors
                                                A

    and 500 women and children, <u>were praised</u> by newspaper reporters
                                  B

    for <u>bravery</u> during the 115-day fight <u>for</u> freedom. <u>No error</u>.
        C   **D**   **E**

2. The ideals <u>upon which</u> American society <u>is based</u> <u>are</u> primarily those
                  A   **B**   **C**

    of Europe and not ones <u>derived from</u> the native Indian culture.
                             D

    <u>No error</u>.
      E

3. <u>An astute and powerful</u> woman, Frances Nadel <u>was</u> a beauty contest
        A   **B**

119

winner before she <u>became</u> president of the company <u>upon the death</u>
               C   **D**

of her husband. <u>No error</u>.
                  E

4.   Representative Wilson <u>pointed out</u>, however, that the legislature
                                 A

    <u>had not finalized</u> the state budget and salary increases <u>had depended</u>
         B   **C**

    on decisions <u>to be made</u> in a special session. <u>No error</u>.
                  D   **E**

5.   Now the <u>city</u> librarian, doing more than checking out books, must
                A

    help <u>to plan</u> puppet shows and movies for children, garage sales for
          B

    <u>used</u> books, and <u>arranging for</u> guest lecturers and exhibits for adults.
    C   **D**

    <u>No error</u>.
    E

6.   In order <u>to completely understand</u> the psychological <u>effects</u> of the
                     A   **B**

    Bubonic plague, <u>one must</u> realize that one-fourth to one-third of the
                   C

    population in an <u>affected</u> area died. <u>No error</u>.
                 D   **E**

7.   Rural roads, <u>known</u> in the United States as farm to market roads,
               A

    have always been a vital <u>link in</u> the economy of <u>more advanced</u>
                         B   **C**

    nations because transportation of goods to markets <u>is</u> essential.
                                              D

    <u>No error</u>.
    E

8.   <u>Many a</u> graduate <u>wishes</u> to return to college and <u>abide in</u> the pro-
    A   **B**   **C**

tected environment of a university, particularly if <u>someone else</u> pays

                                                        D

the bills. <u>No error</u>.

          E

9. <u>Confronted with</u> a choice of either <u>cleaning up</u> his room or <u>cleaning</u>

    A   **B**   **C**

<u>out</u> the garage, the teenager became very <u>aggravated</u> with his parents.

                                              D

<u>No error</u>.

E

10. My brother and <u>I</u> dressed as <u>quickly</u> as we could, but we missed the

                A   **B**

school bus, <u>which</u> made <u>us</u> late for class today. <u>No error</u>.

          C   **D**   **E**

11. <u>Among</u> the activities <u>offered at</u> the local high school <u>through</u> the

    A   **B**   **C**

community education program <u>are</u> singing in the couples' chorus,

                                    D

ballroom dancing, and Chinese cooking. <u>No error</u>.

                                           E

12. If you are <u>disappointed by</u> an <u>inexpensive</u> bicycle, then an option you

                   A   **B**

might consider is to work this summer and <u>save</u> your money for a

                                            C

<u>more expensive</u> model. <u>No error</u>.

       D   **E**

13. Also being presented to the city council this morning <u>is</u> the mayor's

                                                 A

city budget for next year and plans <u>to renovate</u> the <u>existing</u> music

                                      B   **C**

theater, so the session <u>will focus</u> on financial matters. <u>No error</u>.

                      D   **E**

14. Even a movement <u>so delicate</u> as a <u>fly's walking</u> triggers the Venus

                     A   **B**

flytrap <u>to grow</u> extra cells on the outside of <u>its</u> hinge, immediately
       C   D

closing the petals of the trap. <u>No error</u>.
                               E

15. Although <u>outwardly</u> Thomas Hardy seemed quite <u>the picture</u> of
               A   B

<u>respectability</u> and contentment, his works, especially the prose,
 C

<u>deals with</u> the theme of man's inevitable suffering. <u>No error</u>.
 D   E

16. Though <u>unequal in</u> social standing, the everyday lives of ancient
           A

Egyptian kings and commoners <u>alike</u> is visible in the pictures of <u>them</u>
                               B   C

found <u>inside of</u> tombs and temples. <u>No error</u>.
        D   E

17. Sometimes considered <u>unsafe for</u> crops, land around river <u>deltas</u>
                         A   B

<u>can be</u> excellent land for farming because periodic flooding deposits
 C

silt rich <u>in</u> nutrients. <u>No error</u>.
         D   E

18. For years <u>people</u> concerned with the environment <u>have compiled</u> in-
           A   B

formation which <u>show</u> many species are extinct and others <u>are either</u>
               C   D

endangered or bordering on becoming endangered. <u>No error</u>.
                                               E

19. Little is known about Shakespeare's boyhood or his early career as an

actor and playwright, but he <u>appears to have been</u> a financial success
                                        A

<u>because he bought</u> many properties, including <u>one of the finest</u> homes
     B   C

in Stratford, the town he <u>was born in</u>. <u>No error</u>.
                          D   E

20. *Scared Straight,* a program designed <u>to inhibit</u> criminal <u>behavior in</u>
A B
juvenile offenders <u>who</u> seemed bound for prison as adults, had a
C
significant <u>affect</u> on the youngsters. <u>No error</u>.
D E

21. The <u>average</u> American tourist feels <u>quite</u> at home in a Japanese sta-
A B
dium filled <u>at capacity</u> with sports fans watching Japan's <u>most</u> popu-
C D
lar sport, baseball. <u>No error</u>.
E

22. My brother is <u>engaged</u> to a woman <u>who</u> my parents <u>have</u> not met
A B C
because she has not yet <u>emigrated from</u> her native country of Ecua-
D
dor. <u>No error</u>.
E

23. Colonel Jones <u>denies that</u> he <u>illegally</u> delivered funds to a foreign
A B
government agent or that <u>he</u> was involved in <u>any other</u> covert activ-
C D
ity. <u>No error</u>.
E

24. In the United States, <u>testing for</u> toxicity, determining the <u>proper</u>
A B
dose and timing between doses, and evaluating the vaccine for
<u>effectiveness</u> <u>is</u> the method used in researching new drugs. <u>No error</u>.
C D E

25. George wants <u>to know if</u> <u>it is her</u> driving that expensive red sports car
A B
<u>at a rate of speed</u> <u>obviously exceeding</u> the posted speed limit.
C D
<u>No error</u>.
E

26. Unless an athlete is physically fit, there is no sense in <u>him</u> sacrificing
                                                              A
    <u>himself</u> for victory in <u>any one game</u> <u>and, therefore, facing</u> a lifetime
     B   **C**   **D**
    injury. <u>No error</u>.
            E

27. <u>Insensible of</u> the pain from his burn, Father was <u>more concerned</u> with
    A   **B**
    cooling off the overheated car and <u>assessing any</u> <u>damage to</u> the en-
                                        C   **D**
    gine. <u>No error</u>.
          E

28. <u>Parasitic</u> plants, attaching <u>themselves</u> to other plants and <u>drawing</u>
    A   **B**   **C**
    <u>nourishment</u> from them, thereby <u>sapping</u> the strength of the host
    D (sapping)
    plant, usually killing it. <u>No error</u>.
                               E

29. The Alaskan pipeline <u>stretches from</u> Prudhoe Bay <u>through</u> three
                         A   **B**
    mountain ranges and <u>over</u> eight hundred rivers to Valdes, the north-
                        C
    ernmost ice-free <u>port in</u> the United States. <u>No error</u>.
                     D   **E**

30. Current statistics show that <u>environmental</u> factors, once the most im-
                                 A
    portant element <u>in determining</u> susceptibility to cancer, may not be <u>so</u>
                    B   **C**
    significant <u>as diet and lifestyle</u> in maintaining a person's good health.
                D
    <u>No error</u>.
    E

DIRECTIONS: In each of the following sentences, some portion of the sentence is underlined. Under each sentence are five choices. The first choice has the same wording as the original. The other four choices are reworded. Sometimes the first choice containing the original wording is the best; sometimes one of the other choices is the best. Choose the letter of the best choice. Your choice should produce a sentence which is not ambiguous or awkward and which is correct, clear, and precise.

This is a test of correct and effective English expression. Keep in mind the standards of English usage, punctuation, grammar, word choice, and construction.

EXAMPLE:

When you listen to opera, <u>a person may not appreciate it.</u>

(A)   a person may not appreciate it.

(B)   it may not be appreciated by a person.

(C)   which may not be appreciated by one.

(D)   you may not appreciate it.

(E)   appreciating it may be a problem for you.

31. <u>Being that you bring home more money than I do</u>, it is only fitting you should pay proportionately more rent.

    (A) Being that you bring home more money than I do

    (B) Bringing home the more money of the two of us

    (C) When more money is made by you than by me

    (D) Because you bring home more money than I do

    (E) If your bringing home more money than me

32. So tenacious is their grip on life, that sponge cells will regroup and form a new sponge even <u>when they are squeezed</u> through silk.

    (A) when they are squeezed

    (B) since they have been

    (C) as they will be

(D) after they have been

(E) because they should be

33. <u>Seeing as how the plane is late</u>, wouldn't you prefer to wait for a while on the observation deck?

   (A) Seeing as how the plane is late

   (B) When the plane comes in

   (C) Since the plane is late

   (D) Being as the plane is late

   (E) While the plane is landing

34. Only with careful environmental planning can we protect the <u>world we live in</u>.

   (A) world we live in

   (B) world in which we live in

   (C) living in this world

   (D) world's living

   (E) world in which we live

35. In the last three years we have added more varieties of vegetables to our garden <u>than those you suggested in the beginning</u>.

   (A) than those you suggested in the beginning

   (B) than the ones we began with

   (C) beginning with your suggestion

   (D) than what you suggested to us

   (E) which you suggested in the beginning

36. As you know, I am not easily fooled by flattery, and while <u>nice words please you</u>, they don't get the job done.

   (A) nice words please you

   (B) nice words are pleasing

   (C) nice words please a person

(D) flattering words please people

(E) flattering words are pleasing to some

37. Some pieces of the puzzle, in spite of Jane's search, <u>are still missing and probably will never be found</u>.

(A) are still missing and probably will never be found

(B) is missing still but never found probably

(C) probably will be missing and never found

(D) are still probably missing and to never be found

(E) probably are missing and will not be found

38. *Gone With The Wind* <u>is the kind of a movie</u> producers would like to release because it would bring them fame.

(A) is the kind of a movie

(B) is the sort of movie

(C) is the kind of movie

(D) is the type of a movie

(E) is the category of movie

39. Eighteenth century architecture, with its columns and balanced lines, <u>was characteristic of those of previous times in Greece and Rome</u>.

(A) was characteristic of those of previous times in Greece and Rome

(B) is similar to characteristics of Greece and Rome

(C) is similar to Greek and Roman building styles

(D) is characteristic with earlier Greek and Roman architecture

(E) was similar to architecture of Greece and Rome

40. Plato, one of the famous Greek philosophers, won many wrestling prizes when he was a young man, thus <u>exemplifying the Greek ideal of balance between the necessity for physical activity and using one's mind</u>.

(A) exemplifying the Greek ideal of balance between the necessity for physical activity and using one's mind

(B) serving as an example of the Greek ideal of balance between physical and mental activities

(C) an example of balancing Greek mental and athletic games

(D) this as an example of the Greek's balance between mental physical pursuits

(E) shown to be exemplifying the balancing of two aspects of Greek life, the physical and the mental

41. Allied control of the Philippine Islands during World War II proved to be <u>another obstacle as the Japanese scattered resistance</u> until the end of the war.

(A) another obstacle as the Japanese scattered resistance

(B) difficult because of the Japanese giving resistance

(C) continuing scattered Japanese resistance as obstacles

(D) as another scattered obstacle due to Japanese resistance

(E) difficult because the Japanese gave scattered resistance

42. Flooding abated and the river waters receded as the <u>rainfall finally let up</u>.

(A) rainfall finally let up

(B) rain having let up

(C) letting up of the rainfall

(D) rainfall, when it finally let up

(E) raining finally letting up

43. Unless China slows its population growth to zero, that country <u>would still have</u> a problem feeding its people.

(A) would still have

(B) will have still had

(C) might have had still

(D) will still have

(E) would have still

44. In *The Music Man* Robert Preston portrays a fast-talking salesman who comes to a small town in Iowa <u>inadvertently falling in love with</u> the librarian.

(A) inadvertently falling in love with

(B) and inadvertently falls in love with

(C) afterwards he inadvertently falls in love with

(D) after falling inadvertently in love with

(E) when he inadvertently falls in love with

45. Many naturalists have a reverence for the woods and wildlife <u>which exhibits itself through their</u> writings or paintings.

(A) which exhibits itself through their

(B) this exhibits itself through their

(C) showing up in

(D) and exhibiting itself in

(E) when they produce

46. The art <u>of any region</u> is influenced by the cultural and physical environment of that region.

(A) of any region

(B) of any other region

(C) of the region

(D) from that region

(E) for regions

47. <u>Ringing loudly, Doug's girlfriend called him on the telephone to insist</u> he come over right away.

(A) Ringing loudly, Doug's girlfriend called him on the telephone to insist

(B) Doug's loud girlfriend rang him on the telephone to insist

(C) Loudly ringing, the telephone was the insisting girlfriend of Doug

(D) When the telephone rang loudly, Doug's girlfriend insisting

(E) The telephone rang loudly, and Doug's girlfriend was calling to insist

48. Women live longer and have fewer illnesses than men, <u>which proves that women are the strongest sex</u>.

(A) which proves that women are the strongest sex.

(B) which proves that women are the stronger sex.

(C) facts which prove that women are the stronger sex.

(D) proving that women are the strongest sex.

(E) a proof that women are the stronger sex.

Questions 49–54 are based on the following passage.

(1) In 1840 Dickens came up with the idea of using a raven as a character in his new novel, *Barnaby Rudge*. (2) Soon, the word got out among his friends and neighbors that the famous author was interested in ravens and wanted to know more about them. (3) When someone gave a raven as a pet, he was delighted. (4) The raven was named Grip by Dickens' children and became a successful member of the family. (5) Grip began to get his way around the household, and if he wanted something, he took it, and Grip would bite the children's ankles when he felt displeased. (6) The

raven in *Barnaby Rudge* is depicted as a trickster who slept "on horse-back" in the stable and "has been known, by the mere superiority of his genius, to walk off unmolested with the dog's dinner." (7) So we get an idea of what life with Grip was like.

(8) Poe, however, was dissatisfied. (9) This was a comical presentation of the raven. (10) Poe felt that the large black bird should have a more prophetic use. (10) So, about a year after *Barnaby Rudge* was published, Poe began work on his poem, "The Raven." (11) Any schoolchild can quote the famous line, "Quoth the Raven, 'Nevermore,'" but almost no one knows about Grip. (12) What happened to Grip? (13) Well, when he died, the Dickens family had become so attached to him that they had him stuffed and displayed him in the parlor.

49. Which of the following is the best revision of the underlined portion of sentence 3 below?

    When <u>someone gave a raven as a pet, he was delighted</u>.

    (A) giving someone a raven as a pet, he was delighted.

    (B) someone gave Dickens a raven for a pet, the author was de-lighted.

    (C) someone delightedly gave a raven for a pet to Dickens.

    (D) someone gave Dickens a raven as a pet, the result was that the author was delighted with the gift.

    (E) receiving a raven as a pet, Dickens was delighted.

50. Which of the following is the best revision of the underlined portion of sentence 5 below?

    Grip began to get his way around the household, and <u>if he wanted something, he took it, and Grip would bite the children's ankles when he felt displeased</u>.

    (A) if he wanted something, he took it; if he felt displeased, he bit the children's ankles.

    (B) if wanting something, he would take, and if unhappy, he would bite.

    (C) when he wanted something, he would take it; being displeased, he would bite the children's ankles.

    (D) when taking something that he wanted, he would bite the children's ankles.

(E) if displeased and if wanting something, Grip would bite the children's ankles and he would take it.

51. In the context of the sentences preceding and following sentence 7, which of the following is the best revision of sentence 7?

(A) So, you can get an idea of what life with Grip was like.

(B) Therefore, the challenges of living with Grip must have been numerous and varied.

(C) So, an idea of the life with Grip can be gotten.

(D) So, life with Grip must have been entertaining.

(E) These are some examples I have given of what life with Grip was like.

52. Which of the following is the best way to combine sentences 8, 9, and 10?

(A) Having dissatisfaction with the comical presentation of the big black bird, Poe felt it should be more prophetic.

(B) As a result of dissatisfaction, Poe felt the big black bird should be presented more prophetically than comically.

(C) However, Poe felt the comical presentation was not as good as the prophetic one.

(D) Poe, however, dissatisfied with the comical presentation of the big black bird, felt a more prophetic use would be better.

(E) Poe, however, was dissatisfied with this comical presentation and felt that the large black bird should have a more prophetic use.

53. In relation to the passage as a whole, which of the following best describes the writer's intention in the first paragraph?

(A) To provide background information

(B) To provide a concrete example of a humorous episode

(C) To arouse sympathy in the reader

(D) To evaluate the effectiveness of the treatment of the subject

(E) To contrast with treatment of the subject in the second paragraph

54. Which of the following is the best revision of the underlined portion of sentence 4 below?

    The raven was named Grip <u>by Dickens' children and became a successful member of the family</u>.

    (A) by the children and it became a successful member of his family.

    (B) by Dickens' children and was becoming a successful member of his family.

    (C) by Dickens' children and became a successful member of the family.

    (D) , Dickens' children named him that, and he became a successful member of the family.

    (E) by Dickens' children and the raven also became a successful member of his family.

Questions 55–60 are based on the following passage.

(1) Medieval literature and art, throughout the predominance of religious themes, was greatly varied. (2) In literature, for example, the chivalric tradition embodied in such works as the Arthurian legends, as well as the Anglo-Saxon epic *Beowulf* and the French epic *Song of Roland,* showed the richness of themes. (3) Originating in France during the mid-1100s, the Gothic style spread to other parts of Europe. (4) However, it was in Gothic architecture that the Medieval religious fervor best exhibited itself. (5) Gothic cathedrals were the creation of a community, many artisans and craftsman working over many generations. (6) Most of the populace could not read or write, so donating funds or working on the building and its furnishings become a form of religious devotion as well as a means of impressing neighboring areas and attracting tourism. (7) The first Gothic structures were parts of an abbey and a cathedral. (8) Later during the twelfth and thirteenth centuries Gothic architecture reached its peak in the great cathedrals of Notre Dame in Paris, Westminster Abbey in England, and Cologne Cathedral in Germany.

(9) Gothic architecture strives to emphasize height and light. (10) Characteristic internal structures are the ribbed vault and pointed arches. (11) Thick stone walls give way to stained glass windows depicting religious scenes, and the masonry is embellished with delicate tracery. (12) Outside, slender beams called "flying buttresses" provide support for the height of the building. (13) Great spires complete the illusion of rising to the sky.

55. Which of the following would most appropriately replace "through-out" in sentence 1?

(A) beyond

(D) unless

(B) until

(E) under

(C) despite

56. Which of the following should be plural rather than singular?

(A) "art" in sentence 1

(B) "architecture" in sentence 4

(C) "craftsman" in sentence 5

(D) "tracery" in sentence 11

(E) "populace" in sentence 6

57. Which of the following would improve and clarify the structure of the first paragraph?

(A) Eliminate sentence 5.

(B) Place sentence 3 after sentence 7.

(C) Reverse the order of sentences 2 and 4.

(D) Place the first sentence at the end.

(E) No change is necessary.

58. Which of the following words is used incorrectly in Sentence 6?

(A) populace

(D) devotion

(B) donating

(E) tourism

(C) become

59. How would the following underlined portion of sentence 8 be better clarified by punctuation?

Later during the twelfth and thirteenth centuries Gothic architecture reached its peak in the great cathedrals of Notre Dame in Paris, Westminster Abbey in England, and Cologne Cathedral in Germany.

(A) Later during the twelfth and thirteenth centuries, Gothic architecture reached its peak, in the great cathedrals

(B) Later, during the twelfth and thirteenth centuries: Gothic archi-tecture reached its peak in the great cathedrals

(C) Later, during the twelfth, and thirteenth centuries, Gothic archi-tecture reached its peak, in the great cathedrals

(D) Later, during the twelfth and thirteenth centuries, Gothic archi-tecture reached its peak in the great cathedrals

(E) None of these.

60. Which of the following would best fit between sentences 10 and 11?

(A) Often, you can find gargoyles, grotesque demonic-looking crea-tures carved on the outside of the building.

(B) Particularly impressive to me are the carvings of realistic ani-mals and plants on the pulpits.

(C) Tall, thin columns reach to the ceiling and help to support the roof.

(D) These buildings were designed to impress everyone who saw them with the glory of God.

(E) In the twelfth century, the Gothic style had reached its peak.

SAT II: WRITING
TEST 1

ANSWER KEY

1. (B)	16. (D)	31. (D)	46. (A)
2. (E)	17. (E)	32. (D)	47. (E)
3. (B)	18. (C)	33. (C)	48. (C)
4. (C)	19. (D)	34. (E)	49. (B)
5. (D)	20. (D)	35. (A)	50. (A)
6. (A)	21. (C)	36. (B)	51. (D)
7. (C)	22. (B)	37. (A)	52. (E)
8. (E)	23. (C)	38. (C)	53. (A)
9. (D)	24. (E)	39. (E)	54. (C)
10. (C)	25. (B)	40. (B)	55. (C)
11. (E)	26. (A)	41. (E)	56. (C)
12. (A)	27. (A)	42. (A)	57. (B)
13. (A)	28. (D)	43. (D)	58. (C)
14. (A)	29. (E)	44. (B)	59. (D)
15. (D)	30. (C)	45. (A)	60. (C)

DETAILED EXPLANATIONS OF ANSWERS

Part A: Essay

Sample Essays with Commentary

ESSAY I (Score: 5–6)

A poll was recently conducted to determine American heroes. Sadly, most of the heroes listed in the top ten are cartoon characters or actors who portray heroic roles. What does this say about American ideals? Perhaps we do not know enough, or perhaps we know too much in order to have heroes. Having access to instant information about a variety of military, political and religious figures, citizens of modern society have outgrown the innocence of previous centuries.

The ancient hero possessed many idealized virtues, such as physical strength, honesty, courage, and intelligence. Oedipus saved his people from pestilence by solving the riddle of the Sphinx. As leader, he was sworn to find the murderer of the previous king; Oedipus' brave pursuit of justice was conducted with honesty and integrity. Beowolf, another famous ancient hero, existed at a time when life was wild, dangerous, unpredictable.

Modern society is missing several of the ingredients necessary to produce a hero of this calibre. For one thing, there are no mythical monsters such as the Sphinx or Grendel. War is left as the stuff of heroic confrontation, but modern wars only add to our confusion. Men have been decorated for killing their brothers and friends in the Civil War; America fought the Germans in World War I and the Germans and Japanese in World War II, but our former enemies are our current allies. As for honesty, modern role models too often let us down. The media exposes politicians who are involved in scandal, sports figures who do drugs, and religious leaders who make multi-million dollar incomes.

No wonder Americans name Superman and actors John Wayne and Clint Eastwood to the list of modern heroes. These heroes are larger than life on the theatre screen, and their vices are at least predictable and reasonably innocuous. Wisely, we have chosen those who will not surprise us with ugly or mundane reality.

ANALYSIS

Essay I has a score range of 5–6. It is the strongest of the four essays. Although it is not perfect, it shows a good command of the English language and depth of thought. The writer employs a traditional essay structure: the first paragraph is the introduction and ends with the thesis statement; the second and third paragraphs discuss traditional and contemporary heroes, as stated in the last sentence of the thesis paragraph; the fourth paragraph concludes. Each of the two body paragraphs has a clear topic sentence. The writer gives several distinct examples to support his ideas. Vocabulary is effective, and sentence structure is varied.

ESSAY II (Score: 4–5)

Heroes are people who perform the extraordinary and who are highly regarded by society. These outstanding people have characteristics that are desirable to everyone, but the ways in which heroes use their talents glorify them even more. A true hero will do anything in his power to help others.

Two heroes from modern literature exhibit the quality of self-sacrifice. In Remarque's novel *All Quiet on the Western Front,* Paul Baumer is a German ground soldier who endures many disappointments and difficulties while fighting for his country. Paul does not shirk his duties as a soldier of the German people. Moreover, Paul goes out of his way to train the raw recruits and to care for a soldier suffering from shell shock. Another hero, Willy Loman in *Death of a Salesman* makes all the everyday sacrifices a father makes for children and a husband makes for his wife. Willy drives long distances in order to make a living. When Willy feels he is hindering his family, he makes the ultimate sacrifice of suicide to get out of the way.

The true heroes of today are the common people, not unlike Willy and Paul. Stories regularly appear in the newspapers of everyday heroes. The woman with knowledge of CPR saves a drowning child from certain death. A neighbor saves two children from an apartment fire. Teachers take the extra time to listen to a student's personal problem. Parents stand tough against their child's unreasonable demands. Adults who stop to help a stranded motorist are all heroic in their own way.

Every day they stand behind their ideals, living up to their moral standards, in order to help others. It is the day-to-day dedication that makes these twentieth-century heroes extraordinary.

ANALYSIS

Essay II has a score range of 4–5. It still has the traditional essay organization, but the thesis paragraph and conclusion are a bit less focused and less interesting than in Essay I. The paper is supported by examples, but the sentence structure is not varied enough. The last sentence of the third paragraph is weak.

ESSAY III (Score: 3-4)

I would say that there are some heroes still left in modern society. Although we don't have heroes like we used to, our heroes are different now.

When I was a child, I thought that Superman was a real person. He was my hero. He was strong and always won the fights he got into. Villains didn't stand a chance with him. My parents thought I should watch *Sesame Street,* but I wanted to go to the moves to see Luke Skywalker. Even though I later knew it was not real, I still enjoy going to the movies. I want to see a good conflict between the forces of good and the forces of evil, especially when justice rules.

Now I am more realistic. My heroes are good people or successful people. My uncle, for example. He owns his own business and lets me work there part time to earn money. That's what I want to be, someone who is successful and independent but will still help out a young person. When a person is brave, that's heroism too. My friend's brother has a medal for being a hero in Viet Nam. You have different ways to be brave now. The innocent days of childhood are gone, but there are still people to be admired.

ANALYSIS

Essay III has a score range of 3–4. There is a thesis in the opening paragraph, and the remaining two paragraphs are organized so as to support that thesis. However, this paper is not as strong as the previous two. The conclusion is not well defined. Also, the writer uses mixed voice, slang and contractions. His use of the first person pronoun becomes intrusive, and all examples are drawn from his personal experience. The sentence structure could be better, and there is even a fragment.

ESSAY IV (Score: 1–2)

It is not true that there are no heroes nowadays. Everywhere you look, a person see heroes to believe in.

When you go to the movie theatre, many movies are about good guys versus bad buys. Not just Westerns. Sometimes the good cop gets killed. But he usually kills a few criminals for himself before he dies. In many movies, justice wins when the villain is defeated. No matter who wins, people in the audience know what is right and what is wrong because the heroes kill because he needs to defend themselves or because the guy needed to be killed. Rambo would not kill anyone except the enemy. This teaches good values about heroes and their motives since people like to go to the movies, they see alot of heroes.

ANALYSIS

Essay IV has a score range of 1–2. It is the weakest of the four essays. The ideas are inexact, and the sentences are ill-formed. This essay uses mixed voice and slang. There is an agreement error and a fragment. The most serious faults of this essay are the lack of specific examples and the use of sweeping generalizations. The concluding two sentences are exceptionally poor in clarity of thought and wording.

Part B: Multiple-Choice

1. **(B)** "Were praised" is a plural verb; since the subject is Chief Joseph, a singular proper noun, the verb should be "was praised." The intervening phrase of choice (A), "*together with* 250 warriors and 500 women and children," does not change the singular subject. Choice (C), "bravery," is the correct noun form, and choice (D), "for," is idiomatically correct in that phrase.

2. **(E)** Choice (A), "upon which," is a correct prepositional phrase. Choice (B), "is based," agrees with its subject, "society." In choice (C) "are" agrees with its subject, "ideals." "Derived from" in choice (D) is correct idiomatic usage.

3. **(B)** Two past actions are mentioned. The earlier of two past actions should be indicated by past perfect tense, so the answer is "had been." Choice (C) is correct. Choice (A) contains two adjectives as part of an appositive phrase modifying the subject, and choice (D), "upon the death," is idiomatically correct.

4. **(C)** Choice (C) should be "depend," not "had depended" because that use of past perfect would indicate prior past action. There is a series of events in this sentence: first, the legislature "had not finalized" the budget (B); then, Representative Wilson "pointed out" this failure (A). Choice (C), needs to be present tense as this situation still exists, and (D) is future action.

5. **(D)** In order to complete the parallelism, choice (D) should be "arrangements." Choice (A) is a noun used as an adjective. "To plan" (B) is an infinitive phrase followed by noun objects: "puppet shows and movies" and "garage sales." Choice (C), "used," is a participate modifying books.

6. **(A)** An infinitive, "to understand," should never be split by any adverbial modifier, "completely." Choice (B), "effects," is the noun form, and choice (D), "affected," is the adjective form. "One must," choice (C), is used in standard English.

7. **(C)** "More" is used to compare two things. Since the number of nations is not specified, "more" cannot be used in this sentence. Choice

(A), "known," modifies "roads"; choice (B) is idiomatically correct; choice (D), "is," agrees in number with its subject, "transportation."

8. **(E)** Choice (A), "many a," should always be followed by the singular verb, "wishes," of choice (B). Choice (C) is idiomatically correct. In "someone else," (D), "else" is needed to indicate a person other than the student would pay the bills.

9. **(D)** Choice (D) should read, "became very irritated." "To aggravate" means "to make worse"; "to irritate" means "to excite to impatience or anger." A situation is "aggravated" and becomes worse, but one does not become "aggravated" with people. Choices (A), (B), and (C) are correctly-used idioms.

10. **(C)** The reference in choice (C) is vague because it sounds as if the bus made the two students late. Choice (A) is a correct subject pronoun; choice (B) is the correct adverb form to modify "dressed"; choice (D) is a correct object pronoun.

11. **(E)** Choice (A), "among," indicates choice involving more than two things. The prepositions in (B) and (C) are correct. "Are," (D), is a plural verb, agreeing in number with the compound subject "singing...dancing...cooking."

12. **(A)** One is "disappointed by" a person or action but "disappointed in" what is not satisfactory. "Inexpensive," (B), is the adjective form. Parallel with "to work," choice (C), "save," had the word "to" omitted. Choice (D) compares the two models, one "inexpensive" and one "more expensive."

13. **(A)** The verb should be plural, "are," in order to agree with the compound subject, "budget...plans." Choice (B) begins an infinitive phrase which includes a participle, "existing," (C). Choice (D) is idiomatically correct.

14. **(A)** The expression should be phrased, "as delicate as." Choice (B) uses a possessive before a gerund; choice (C) is correctly used; and choice (D) is a possessive pronoun of neuter gender which is appropriate to use in referring to a plant.

15. **(D)** The verb "deal" must agree with the subject, "works," and not

a word in the intervening phrase. "Outwardly," choice (A), is an adverb modifying "seemed." Choices (B) and (C), "the picture of respectability," describe the subject; (D) is idiomatically correct.

16. **(D)** The word "of" in "inside of" is redundant and should not be used. Choice (A) is idiomatically correct and signals two classes of people once considered unequal in merit, and choice (B), "alike," is appropriate when comparing the two. Choice (C), "them," is correct pronoun usage.

17. **(E)** Choice (A), "unsafe for," is idiomatically correct; choice (B), "deltas," is a plural noun. Choice (C), "can be excellent," is grammatically correct. The preposition "in," choice (D), is correct.

18. **(C)** The verb in this subordinate clause is incorrect; the clause begins with, "which," and this word refers to "information." Therefore, the clause, in order to agree with antecedent, must read, "which shows." The verb "shows" should not be made to agree with "species" and "others." Choices (A), "people," and (B), "have compiled," agree in number. "Either" in choice (D) is correctly placed after the verb to show a choice of "endangered" or "becoming endangered."

19. **(D)** Do not end a sentence with a preposition; the phrase should read, "in which he was born." The verbs show proper time sequence in (A) and (B); choice (C) is correct pronoun usage and correct superlative degree of adjective.

20. **(D)** The noun form, "effect," is the correct one to use. Choice (A), "to inhibit," is an infinitive; choice (B) is correctly worded; in choice (C), the nominative case "who" is the correct subject of "seemed."

21. **(C)** The idiom should be "filled to capacity." The adjective in choice (A), "average," is correct, as is the adverb in choice (B). Choice (D), "most," is appropriate for the superlative degree.

22. **(B)** The subordinate clause, "who my parents have not met," has as its subject "parents," which agrees with choice (C), "have ... met." Therefore, the pronoun is a direct object of the verb and should be in the objective case, "whom." Both choice (A) and choice (D) are idiomatically correct.

23. **(C)** The pronoun reference is unclear. The meaning of the sentence

indicated that Colonel Jones denies involvement in any other covert activity. The agent from a foreign country may or may not have been involved in other covert activities, but that is not the issue here. The verb tense of choice (A) is correct. Choice (B) is the correct adverb form, and "other" in choice (D) is necessary to the meaning of the sentence.

24. **(E)**   Choice (A), "testing," is parallel to "determining" and "evaluating." "Proper" in choice (B) and "effectiveness" in choice (C) are correct. In choice (D) "is" must be singular because all three steps mentioned comprise the one process.

25. **(B)**   Choice (A) is correct. Choice (B) should read, "it is she"; nominative case pronoun is required following a linking verb. Choice (C) is proper English, and correct form of the modifiers appears in choice (D).

26. **(A)**   "Sacrificing" is a gerund, and a possessive form is always used before a gerund. The phrase should read, "no sense in his sacrificing." Choice (B) is the reflexive form of the pronoun, and the pronoun in choice (C) is correct also. The punctuation in choice (D) is correct as "therefore" is an interrupter.

27. **(A)**   The correct idiom is "insensible to" pain. Choice (B), "more concerned," is the correct comparative degree; choices (C) and (D) are correct.

28. **(D)**   This is a fragment which can be corrected by changing "sapping" to "sap." Choice (A), "parasitic," is an adjective form; the pronoun "themselves," choice (B), refers to "plants." Choice (C), "drawing nourishment," is parallel to "attaching."

29. **(E)**   Every preposition in this sentence is used correctly.

30. **(C)**   The phrase should read, "as significant as," in order to complete the correctly-written choice (D). Choice (A), "environmental," is an adjective form, and choice (B) is idomatically correct.

31. **(D)**   "Because" is the correct word to use in the cause and effect relationship in this sentence. Choice (A), "being that"; choice (E), "than me"; and choice (D), "the more" are not grammatically correct. Choice (C), "is made by you," is in the passive voice and not as direct as (D).

32. **(D)** "After they have been" completes the proper time sequence. Choice (A), "when"; choice (B), "have been"; and choice (C), "will be," are the wrong time sequences. Choice (E), "should be," is an idea not contained in the original sentence.

33. **(C)** "Since the plane is late" shows correct time sequence and good reasoning. Choice (A), "seeing as how," and choice (D), "being as," are poor wording. Choices (B), "when," and (E), "while," are the wrong time, logically, to be on the observation deck.

34. **(E)** Since a sentence should not end with a preposition, choices (A) and (B) are eliminated. Choices (C), "living in this world," and (D), "world's living," introduce new concepts.

35. **(A)** The construction, "than those," clarifies the fact that more vegetables have been added. Choice (C), "your suggestion"; choice (D), "than what"; and choice (E), "which," do not contain the idea of adding more varieties of vegetables. Choice (B) ends with a preposition.

36. **(B)** The voice must be consistent with "I", so (B) is the only possible correct answer. All other choices have a noun or pronoun that is not consistent with "I"; choice (A), "you"; choice (C), "a person"; choice (D), "people"; and choice (E), "some."

37. **(A)** The correct answer has two concepts—pieces are missing and pieces will probably never be found. Choice (B) has a singular verb, "is." Choice (C) indicates the pieces "probably will be" missing, which is not the problem. Choice (D) and choice (E) both indicate the pieces are "probably" missing, which is illogical because the pieces either are or are not missing.

38. **(C)** Choice (A), "the kind of a," and choice (D), "the type of a," are incorrect grammatical structures. Choice (E) introduces the new concept of "category." Choice (B), "sort of," is poor wording.

39. **(E)** Choice (E) is clear and concise and shows the correct comparison of architecture. The antecedent of "those" in choice (A) is not clear. Choice (B) is comparing "characteristics," not just architecture. Choice (C) is awkward, and choice (D) incorrectly uses an idiom, "characteristic with."

40. **(B)**   Choice (B) is clear and direct. Choices (A) and (E) are too wordy. Choice (C) has the wrong concept, "balancing games." Choice (D) "this as an example" is poorly worded.

41. **(E)**   An opposing force "gives" scattered resistance; therefore, choice (A) is incorrect. Choices (B), (C), and (D) are poorly worded and do not have the correct meaning.

42. **(A)**   Choice (A) produces a complete sentence: "rainfall" is the subject and "let up" is the verb. None of the other choices produces a complete sentence.

43. **(D)**   This choice uses the correct tense, "will have," showing action in the future. All the other verbs listed do not show correct future verb construction.

44. **(B)**   The correct choice has a compound verb: "comes" and "falls in love." The salesman comes to town first, then he meets and falls in love with the librarian. Choice (A), with its misplaced participial phrase, sounds as if either the town or Iowa is in love with the librarian. Choice (C) would produce a run-on sentence. Choices (D) and (E) have unclear tense.

45. **(A)**   Choice (A) has clear reference. Choice (B) will produce a run-on sentence. Choices (C) and (D) do not indicate whose writings or paintings. Choice (E) sounds as if the only time naturalists feel reverence is when they write or paint.

46. **(A)**   This choice is correct when used in conjunction with "of that region." Choices (B), (C), and (D) imply the mention of a specific region; in addition, (D) would be repetitious. Choice (E) does not agree in number, "regions."

47. **(E)**   This choice indicates that the telephone has a loud ring and that it is Doug's girlfriend who is calling. Choice (A) is a misplaced participial phrase. Choice (B) has an error, "Doug's loud girlfriend"; choice (C) has an error, "the telephone was the insisting girlfriend" and choice (D) is missing a verb to make it a complete sentence.

48. **(C)**   General reference should be avoided. The pronoun "which" does not have a clear reference in choices (A) or (B). In (C) "which" clearly refers to "facts." The reference "proving" in choice (D) is too

general. In choice (E) "a proof" is an incorrect number to refer to the two strengths of women.

49. **(B)**   Choice (B) clears up the pronoun usage problem, eliminating the ambiguous reference of "he"; it is clear that Dickens is delighted. Choice (A) does not clearly identify the antecedent of "he." Choice (C) incorrectly identified the "delighted" person as the giver, not Dickens. Choices (D) and (E) both create fragments.

50. **(A)**   Choice (A) combines all the elements correctly and uses parallel structure, creating a balanced sentence. Choice (B) is not exactly parallel, and the many commas create confusion. Choice (C) does not have parallel verbs: "wanted" and "being." Choices (D) and (E) incorrectly combine the two ideas, making it seem as if the children are blocking Grip's action.

51. **(D)**   Choice (D) keeps the formal tone of the essay and avoids passive voice. Choice (A) and choice (E) both break the formal tone and use another voice: "you" and "I." Choice (B) is perhaps too formal and not straightforward. Choice (C) uses the passive voice.

52. **(E)**   Choice (E) smoothly combines both major ideas as a cause-and-effect sequence. Choice (A) is the next best choice, but it is not as smoothly worded in the first half; also, this choice eliminates the idea of "use" in the second half. Choice (B) does not clarify the source of Poe's dissatisfaction. Choice (C) does not clearly present the idea that the prophetic use was Poe's, not Dickens'. Choice (D) has too many interruptions.

53. **(A)**   Choice (A) is incorrect; the paragraph gives information on the origin of the bird. Although the paragraph gives one or two humorous incidents, choice (B) cannot be the main intention. Choice (C) is unlikely; the bird's biting is presented as more humorous than tragic. Choice (D) would be a more effective label for paragraph two. Choice (E) is partly correct, but the second paragraph returns to the Dickens' household.

54. **(C)**   Choice (C) clears up the confusion caused by the possessive pronoun "his," which in this sentence would incorrectly refer to "Dickens' children." "Their" would also be fine, but "the" is probably best, as it is clear from the context which family we are referring to. Choice (A) adds "it," which is unnecessary and redundant. Choice (B) replaces the past

with the past progressive tense, which does not agree with the verb tense throughout the passage. Choice (D) replaces a neat prepositional phrase with an awkward clause. Choice (E) is repetitive; it is clear that "the raven" is still the subject of the sentence.

55. **(C)** "Despite" best fits the relation between the religious and secular themes. Choice (A), "beyond" would be the next best choice, though it sounds a bit overzealous. Choice (B), "until" would be inappropriate since the rest of the passage does not suggest that the secular themes preceded the religious, but rather that they coexisted. "Unless" (D) and "under" (E) are nonsensical in this context.

56. **(C)** "Craftsman" should be plural to agree with the other noun "artisans." We assume that there was not only one "craftsman" "working over many generations," so the singular would be nonsensical.

57. **(B)** Sentence 3, as it stands, introduces a wholly new subject without transition. Sentence 4 best carries this transition, and should follow Sentence 2. Sentence 3 introduces the spread of Gothic style throughout Europe, and this point is directly supported in Sentence 8.

58. **(C)** "Become" should be in the past tense ("became") to accord with the rest of the passage.

59. **(D)** Choice (D) sets the clause off with commas, and best clarifies the sentence. Choice (A) uses commas to disrupt the main idea of the sentence. Choice (B) sets the clause off well, but the colon is inappropriate and should be a comma. Choice (C) employs too many commas; the second and fourth should be eliminated, as they disrupt the flow of the sentence.

60. **(C)** Choice (C) continues to describe the internal physical characteristics of Gothic cathedrals, and best fits between Sentences 10 and 11. Choice (A) switches to the external aspect of the building. Choice (B) introduces the author's opinion, which is not necessary at this part of the passage. Choice (D) is a relevant thought, but would best be placed elsewhere: it describes the purpose of the architecture, where Sentences 10 and 11 are describing the physical qualities of the interior of the buildings. Choice (E) is an unrelated, and possibly factually incorrect, statement.

SAT II: Writing

Practice Test 2

SAT II: WRITING
TEST 2

Part A: Essay

TIME: 20 Minutes

DIRECTIONS: You have 20 minutes to plan and write an essay on the topic below. You may write only on the assigned topic.

Make sure to give specific examples to support your thesis. Proofread your essay carefully and take care to express your ideas clearly and effectively.

Write your essay on the lined pages at the back of the book.

ESSAY TOPIC:

Many leaders have suggested over the last few years that instead of a military draft we should require all young people to serve the public in some way for a period of time. The service could be military or any other reasonable form of public service.

ASSIGNMENT: Do you agree or disagree with the statement? Support your opinion with specific examples from history, current events, literature, or personal experience.

Part B: Multiple-Choice

(Answer sheets appear in the back of this book.)

TIME: 40 Minutes
60 Questions

DIRECTIONS: Each of the following sentences may contain an error in diction, usage, idiom, or grammar. Some sentences are correct. Some sentences contain one error. No sentence contains more than one error.

If there is an error, it will appear in one of the underlined portions labeled A, B, C, or D. If there is no error, choose the portion labeled E. If there is an error, select the letter of the portion that must be changed in order to correct the sentence.

EXAMPLE:

He drove <u>slowly</u> and <u>cautiously</u> in order to <u>hopefully</u> avoid having an
      A   **B**   **C**

<u>accident</u>. <u>No error</u>.
  D &nb;   **E**
                       Ⓐ Ⓑ ⬤ Ⓓ Ⓔ

---

1. *Huckleberry Finn*, by <u>general consensus agreement</u> Mark Twain's
                             A

    <u>greatest</u> work, is <u>supremely</u> the American <u>Classic</u>; it is also one of the
      B   **C**   **D**

    great books of the world. <u>No error</u>.
                      E

2. The U.S. <u>Constitution</u> <u>supposes</u> what the history of all governments
           A   **B**

    <u>demonstrate</u>, that the executive is the branch <u>most</u> interested in war
       C   **D**

    and most prone to it. <u>No error</u>.
                 E

3. Mama, the <u>narrator</u> of Alice Walker's short story "Everyday Use,"
         A

speaks fondly of her daughter upon her return home after a long
   B

absence like Mama is proud of her. No error.
      C   D   E

4.   Nearly one hundred years after the impoverished Vincent Van Gogh
      A   B

died, his paintings had sold for more than a million dollars. No error.
              C   D   E

5.   Many athletes recruited for football by college coaches expect that
              A   B

they will, in fact, receive an education when they accept a scholar-
          C   D

ship. No error.
      E

6.   Hopefully, by the end of the Twentieth Century, computer scientists
      A   B

will invent machines with enough intelligence to work without break-
                    C

ing down continually. No error.
          D   E

7.   Studies showing that the earth includes a vast series of sedimentary
         A   B

rocks, some with embedded fossils that prove the existence of ancient
              C   D

organisms. No error.
      E

8.   When Martin Luther King, Jr., wrote his famous letter from the Bir-
                        A

mingham jail, he advocated neither evading or defying the law; but
                              B   C

he accepted the idea that a penalty results from breaking a law, even
                                    D

an unjust one. No error.
          E

9. The Eighteenth Century philosopher Adam Smith asserted that a na-
    <u>A</u>   <u>B</u>
    tion achieves the best economic results when individuals work both
         <u>C</u>
    for their own interests and to gain more goods. No error.
                               <u>D</u>   <u>E</u>
                                D   E

10. According to Niccolo Machiavelli, wise rulers cannot and should not
                                                 <u>A</u>   <u>B</u>
    keep their word when such integrity would be to their disadvantage
                                                   <u>C</u>
    and when the reasons for the promise no longer exist. No error.
                                                   <u>D</u>   <u>E</u>
                                                    D   E

11. The Milky Way galaxy, which comprises millions of stars, has both
                                 <u>A</u>
    thin and congested spots, but shines their brightest in the constella-
    <u>B</u>   <u>C</u>   <u>D</u>
    tion Sagittarius. No error.
                      <u>E</u>

12. To learn an ancient language like Latin or Greek is one way to dis-
    <u>A</u>   <u>B</u>
    cover the roots of Western Culture; studying Judaeo-Christian reli-
    gious beliefs is another. No error.
          <u>C</u> <u>D</u>   <u>E</u>

13. Many political conservatives contribute the problems of modern
                                 <u>A</u>
    American society to the twin evils of the New Deal and secular
                                                         <u>B</u>
    humanism, both of which are presumed to stem from Marxism. No
              <u>C</u>   <u>D</u>
    error.
    <u>E</u>

14. Having minimal exposure to poetry when they attended school, most
    <u>A</u>   <u>B</u>
    Americans chose to watch television or to read popular magazines for
              <u>C</u>   <u>D</u>

entertainment. <u>No error</u>.
              E

15. What makes <u>we</u> humans <u>different from</u> other animals <u>can be defined</u>
          A   B   C

    at least <u>partly</u> by our powerful and efficient intelligence. <u>No error</u>.
               D   E

16. When one contrasts the ideas of the Romantic William Wordsworth

    <u>with</u> <u>those</u> of Neoclassicist John Dryden, <u>one finds</u> that neither of the
     A   B   C

    poets <u>differ</u> as much as one would expect. <u>No error</u>.
            D   E

17. Carl Jung's hypothesis of the collective unconscious <u>suggests</u> that we
                                                 A

    inherit <u>cultural-experimental</u> memory in the form of mythological
                B

    archetype, <u>which arise</u> from repeated <u>patterns</u> of human behavior.
              C   D

    <u>No error</u>.
     E

18. Bertrand Russell believed that a free <u>person's</u> liberation is <u>effected</u> by
                                   A   B

    a contemplation of <u>Fate</u>; one achieves emancipation through passion-
                    C

    ate pursuit of eternal things, <u>not through</u> the pursuit of private happi-
                              D

    ness. <u>No error</u>.
         E

19. <u>Latin American</u> literature <u>includes</u> the works of Gabriel Garcia
     A   B

    Marquez, Pablo Neruda, and Jorge Luis Borges; each of these

    <u>acclaimed</u> artists has won <u>their</u> share of prizes. <u>No error</u>.
      C   D   E

20. The reason <u>a large percentage</u> of American college students <u>located</u>
                  A   **B**
    Moscow in California is <u>because</u> they <u>were not required</u> to learn the
                            C   **D**
    facts of geography. <u>No error</u>.
                       E

21. Astronomers and physicists <u>tell</u> us that the universe is <u>constant</u> ex-
                            A   **B**
    panding <u>and that</u> it <u>comprises</u> numerous galaxies like ours. <u>No error</u>.
           C   **D**   **E**

22. <u>Less</u> students chose liberal arts and <u>sciences</u> majors in the 1980s
    A   **B**
    than in the 1960s <u>because of</u> the contemporary view that a college
                        C
    education <u>is</u> a ticket to enter the job market. <u>No error</u>.
             D   **E**

23. Span of control is the term <u>that</u> refers to the <u>limits</u> of a leader's <u>ability</u>
                              A   **B**   **C**
    <u>for managing</u> those employees <u>under</u> his/her supervision. <u>No error</u>.
             D   **E**

24. <u>Because some</u> people believe <u>strongly</u> that channelling, the <u>process</u>
      A   **B**   **C**
    <u>by which</u> an individual goes into a trance-like state and communi-
    cates the thoughts of an ancient warrior or guru to an audience, helps
    them cope with modern problems, but others condemn the whole
    ideas <u>as</u> mere superstition. <u>No error</u>.
          D   **E**

25. The reed on a woodwind instrument is <u>essential</u> <u>being that</u> it <u>controls</u>
                                         A   **B**   **C**
    <u>the quality</u> of <u>tone and sound</u>. <u>No error</u>.
          D   **E**

26. <u>As far as</u> taking on SAT preparation course, educators <u>discourage it</u>
    A   **B**

    <u>because</u> at best the course may <u>alleviate</u> test anxiety. <u>No error</u>.
    C   **D**   **E**

27. In the <u>South,</u> <u>they</u> like to eat <u>cured</u> or smoked <u>pork products</u> such as
            A   **B**   **C**   **D**

    ham, bacon, and barbecue. <u>No error</u>.
                         E

28. Both <u>Japan and the United States</u> <u>want</u> to remain a <u>net exporter</u> of
            A   **B**   **C**

    goods to avoid <u>unfavorable trade imbalances</u>. <u>No error</u>.
                     D   **E**

29. As an <u>avid cyclist</u>, Jon <u>rode</u> more <u>miles a day</u> <u>than his friend's</u>
          A   **B**   **C**   **D**

    bicycle. <u>No error</u>.
          E

30. After the end of the <u>Mesozoic Era</u>, dinosaurs, <u>once the dominant</u>
                 A   **B**

    <u>species are</u> <u>extinct</u>. <u>No error</u>.
      C   **D**   **E**

DIRECTIONS: In each of the following sentences, some portion of the sentence is underlined. Under each sentence are five choices. The first choice has the same wording as the original. The other four choices are reworded. Sometimes the first choice containing the original wording is the best; sometimes one of the other choices is the best. Choose the letter of the best choice. Your choice should produce a sentence which is not ambiguous or awkward and which is correct, clear, and precise.

This is a test of correct and effective English expression. Keep in mind the standards of English usage, punctuation, grammar, word choice, and construction.

EXAMPLE:

When you listen to opera, <u>a person may not appreciate it.</u>

(A)   a person may not appreciate it.

(B)   it may not be appreciated by a person.

(C)   which may not be appreciated by one.

(D)   you may not appreciate it.

(E)   appreciating it may be a problem for you.

31. Two-thirds of American 17-year-olds do not know that the Civil War <u>takes place</u> between 1850–1900.

    (A) takes place   (D) have taken place

    (B) took place   (E) is taking place

    (C) had taken place

32. Both professional and amateur ornithologists, <u>people that study birds,</u> recognize the Latin or scientific names of bird species.

    (A) people that study birds

    (B) people which study birds

    (C) the study of birds

    (D) people who study birds

    (E) in which people study birds

33. Many of the oil-producing states spent their huge surplus tax revenues during the oil boom of the 1970s and early 1980s <u>in spite of the fact that</u> oil production from new wells began to flood the world market as early as 1985.

    (A) in spite of the fact that

    (B) even in view of the fact that

    (C) however clearly it was known that

    (D) even though

    (E) when it was clear that

34. The president of the community college reported <u>as to the expectability of the tuition increase as well as the actual amount</u>.

    (A) as to the expectability of the tuition increase as well as the actual amount

    (B) that the tuition will likely increase by a specific amount

    (C) as to the expectability that tuition will increase by a specific amount

    (D) about the expected tuition increase of five percent.

    (E) regarding the expectation of a tuition increase expected to be five percent

35. Although Carmen developed an interest in classical music, <u>she did not read notes and had never played an instrument</u>.

    (A) she did not read notes and had never played an instrument

    (B) she does not read notes and has never played an instrument

    (C) it is without being able to read notes or having played an instrument

    (D) she did not read notes nor had she ever played them

    (E) it is without reading notes nor having played an instrument

36. Political candidates must campaign on issues and ideas that strike a chord within their constituency but <u>with their goal to sway</u> undecided voters to support their candidacy.

    (A) with their goal to sway

(B) need also to sway

(C) aiming at the same time to sway

(D) also trying to sway

(E) its goal should also be in swaying

37. The major reason students give for failing courses in college <u>is that</u> <u>they have demanding professors and work at</u> full- or part-time jobs.

(A) is that they have demanding professors and work at

(B) are demanding professors and they work at

(C) is having demanding professors and having

(D) are demanding professors, in addition to working at

(E) are that they have demanding professors and that they have

38. <u>Having command of color, symbolism, as well as technique</u>, Georgia O'Keeffe is considered to be a great American painter.

(A) Having command of color, symbolism, as well as technique

(B) Having command of color, symbolism, and her technical ability

(C) Because of her command of color, symbolism, and technique

(D) With her command of color and symbolism and being technical

(E) By being in command of both color and symbolism and also technique

39. <u>Whether the ancient ancestors of American Indians actually migrated</u> <u>or did not</u> across a land bridge now covered by the Bering Strait remains uncertain, but that they could have has not been refuted by other theories.

(A) Whether the ancient ancestors of American Indians actually migrated or did not

(B) That the ancient ancestors of American Indians actually did migrate

(C) The actuality of whether the ancient ancestors of American Indians migrated

(D) Whether in actuality the ancient ancestors of American Indians migrated or not

(E) That the ancient ancestors of American Indians may actually have migrated

40. Caution in scientific experimentation can <u>sometimes be related more to integrity than to lack of knowledge</u>.

(A) sometimes be related more to integrity than to lack of knowledge

(B) sometimes be related more to integrity as well as lack of knowledge

(C) often be related to integrity as to lack of knowledge

(D) be related more to integrity rather than lack of knowledge

(E) be related often to integrity, not only to lack of knowledge

41. Separated by their successful rebellion against England from any existing form of government, the citizens of the United States <u>have developed a unique constitutional political system</u>.

(A) have developed a unique constitutional political system

(B) had developed a very unique constitutional political system

(C) had developed their constitutional political system uniquely

(D) have developed their political system into a very unique constitutional one

(E) have a unique political system, based on a constitution

42. <u>Returning to the ancestral home after 12 years, the house itself seemed much smaller to Joe</u> than it had been when he visited it as a child.

(A) Returning to the ancestral home after 12 years, the house itself seemed much smaller to Joe

(B) When Joe returned to the ancestral home after 12 years, he thought the house itself much smaller

(C) Joe returned to the ancestral home after 12 years, and then he thought the house itself much smaller

(D) After Joe returned to the ancestral home in 12 years, the house itself seemed much smaller

(E) Having returned to the ancestral home after 12 years, it seemed a much smaller house to Joe

43. Historians say that the New River of North Carolina, Virginia, and West Virginia, which is 2,700 feet above sea level and 2,000 feet above the surrounding foothills, is the oldest river in the United States.

(A) which is 2,700 feet above sea level and 2,000 feet above

(B) with a height of 2,700 feet above sea level as well as 2,000 feet above that of

(C) 2,700 feet higher than sea level and ascending 2,000 feet above

(D) being 2,700 feet above sea level and 2,000 feet high measure from that of

(E) located 2,700 feet high above sea level while measuring 2,000 feet above

44. The age of 36 having been reached, the Ukrainian-born Polish sailor Teodor Josef Konrad Korzeniowski changed his name to Joseph Conrad and began a new and successful career as a British novelist and short story writer.

(A) The age of 36 having been reached

(B) When having reached the age of 36

(C) When he reached the age of 36

(D) The age of 36 being reached

(E) At 36, when he reached that age

45. During the strike, Black South African miners threw a cordon around the gold mine, and they thereby blocked it to all White workers.

(A) gold mine, and they thereby blocked it to all White workers

(B) gold mine, by which all White workers were therefore blocked

(C) gold mine, and therefore this had all White workers blocked

(D) gold mine and therefore blocking it to all White workers

(E) gold mine, thereby blocking it to all White workers

46. Because of the long half-life of low-level nuclear <u>wastes, this means</u> <u>that waste depositories could emit dangerous doses of radiation thou-</u> <u>sands of years into the future</u>.

   (A) wastes, this means that waste depositories could emit dangerous doses of radiation thousands of years into the future

   (B) wastes is the reason why waste depositories could emit danger- ous doses of radiation thousands of years into the future

   (C) wastes, this is the reason why waste depositories could emit dangerous doses of radiation thousands of years into the future

   (D) wastes, depositories for these wastes could still emit dangerous doses of radiation thousands of years into the future

   (E) wastes, the future means that waste depositories could emit dan- gerous doses of radiation for thousands of years

47. <u>The more you listen to and understand classical music</u>, the more our ears will prefer music for the mind to music for the body.

   (A) The more you listen to and understand classical music

   (B) The more we listen to and understand classical music

   (C) The more classical music is listened to and understood

   (D) As understanding and listening to classical music increases

   (E) As people listen to and understand classical music

48. As modern archaeologists discover new fossils, biologists are amend- ing Darwin's theory of evolution <u>that once served as the standard</u>.

   (A) that once served as the standard

   (B) by which all others were measured

   (C) having served as the standard for over a hundred years

   (D) thereby changing the standard

   (E) and creating a new standard

DIRECTIONS: The following passages are considered early draft efforts of a student. Some sentences need to be rewritten to make the ideas clearer and more precise.

Read each passage carefully and answer the questions that follow. Some of the questions are about particular sentences or parts of sentences and ask you to make decisions about sentence structure, diction, and usage. Some of the questions refer to the entire essay or parts of the essay and ask you to make decisions about organization, development, appropriateness of language, audience, and logic. Choose the answer that most effectively makes the intended meaning clear and follows the requirements of standard written English. After you have chosen your answer, fill in the corresponding oval on your answer sheet.

EXAMPLE:

(1) On the one hand, I think television is bad, But it also does some good things for all of us. (2) For instance, my little sister thought she wanted to be a policemen until she saw police shows on television.

Which of the following is the best revision of the underlined portion of Sentence 1 below?

On the one hand, I think television is bad. But it also does some good things for all of us.

(A)   is bad; But it also

(B)   is bad. but is also

(C)   is bad, and it also

(D)   is bad, but it also

(E)   is bad because it also

Questions 49-54 are based on the following passage.

(1) The melt-water stream draining out along the floor of a glacier cave gives evidence of its origin. (2) It goes without saying that the origin of another kind of cave can be gotten from the pounding of sea waves at the mouth of a sea cave. (3) Solution caves, however, have always been a source of wonder to man. (4) How do these extensive, complex, and in some places beautifully decorated passageways develop? (5) Solution caves are formed in limestone and similar rocks by the action of the water. (6) Think of them as part of a huge subterranean

plumbing system. (7) After a rain water seeps into cracks and pores of soil and rock and percolates beneath the land surface. (8) Eventually, some of the water reaches a zone of soil and rock where all the cracks are already filled with water. (9) The term <u>water table</u> refers to the upper surface of this saturated zone. (10) Calcite (calcium carbonate), the main mineral of limestone, is barely soluble in pure water. (11) Rainwater, however, absorbs some carbon dioxide as it passes through soil and decaying vegetation. (12) The water, combining chemically with the carbon dioxide, forms a weak carbonic acid solution which slowly dissolves calcite. (13) This acid slowly dissolves calcite, forms solution cavities, and excavates passageways. (14) This results in a solution cave.

(15) A second stage in cave development is when there is lowering of the water table. (16) During this stage, the solution cavities are stranded in the unsaturated zone where air can enter. (17) This leads to the deposition of calcite, which forms <u>dripstone</u> features, beautiful formations in strange shapes on the inside of caves.

49. Which of the following is the best revision of sentence 2 below?

   It goes without saying that the origin of another kind of cave can be gotten from the pounding of sea waves at the mouth of a sea cave.

   (A) It goes without saying that a sea cave can be formed by the pounding of waves at its mouth.

   (B) The pounding waves at the mouth of a sea cave offer evidence of the origin of this cave.

   (C) Evidence is offered of the origin of sea caves by the pounding of the waves.

   (D) In saying that another kind of cave can be formed by the pounding of waves at the entrance of sea caves.

   (E) It goes without saying that the pounding waves at the mouth of a sea cave offers evidence as to the origin of this kind of cave.

50. In the context of the sentences preceding and following sentence 6, which of the following is the best revision of sentence 6?

   (A) These caves can be considered part of a huge subterranean plumbing system.

   (B) You can think of these caves as part of a huge subterranean plumbing system.

(C) The formation of these caves can be thought of in terms of a huge subterranean plumbing system.

(D) If you think of it, these caves are similar to a huge subterranean plumbing system.

(E) When one visualizes the formation of these caves, one could compare them to part of a huge subterranean plumbing system.

51. Which of the following is the best way to combine sentences 13 and 14?

(A) This acid dissolving results in solution cavities, passageways, and caves.

(B) Solution caves are formed when this acid dissolves solution cavities and passageways.

(C) Slowly, this acid dissolves calcite, and the resulting effects are that cavities and passageways become caves.

(D) Excavating cavities, passageways, and caves, the acid slowly dissolves calcite.

(E) This acid slowly dissolves calcite, excavating cavities and passageways which eventually become solution caves.

52. In relation to the passage as a whole, which of the following best describes the writer's intention in paragraph 2?

(A) To provide an example

(B) To propose a solution to a problem

(C) To describe a location

(D) To examine opposing evidence

(E) To explain a process

53. Which of the following is the best revision of the underlined portion of sentence 15 below?

A second stage in cave development is when there is lowering of the water table.

(A) is because there is lowering of the water table

(B) is due to the water table going lower

(C) occurs after a lowering of the water table

(D) happens to be when the water table is lowered

(E) being when there is a lowering of the water table

54. Which of the following is the best punctuation of the underlined portion of sentence 7?

After a rain water seeps into cracks and pores of soil and rock and percolates beneath the land surface.

(A) After a rain, water seeps into

(B) After, a rain water seeps into

(C) After a rain: water seeps into

(D) After a rain-water seeps into

(E) Best as it is

Questions 55-60 are based on the following passage.

(1) Dripstone features are called speleotherms, and they can take several beautiful forms. (2) When these structures are highlighted by lanterns or electric lights, they transform a cave into a natural wonderland. (3) Some people feel that electric lights have no place in a cave. (4) The most familiar decorative dripstone features are stalactites and stalagmites. (5) Stalactites hang downward from the ceiling and are formed as drop after drop of water slowly trickles through cracks in the cave roof. (6) Each drop of water hangs from the ceiling. (7) The drop of water loses carbon dioxide. (8) It then deposits a film of calcite. (9) Stalagmites grow upward from the floor of the cave generally as a result of water dripping from overhead stalactites. (10) An impressive column forms when a stalactite and stalagmite grow until they join. (11) A curtain or drapery begins to form in an inclined ceiling when the drops of water trickle along a slope. (12) Gradually, a thin sheet of calcite grows downward from the ceiling and hangs in graceful decorative folds like a drape.

(13) These impressive and beautiful features appear in caves in almost every state, making for easy access for tourists looking for a thrill. (14) In addition, the size and depth of many caves in the United States also impress even the most experienced tourist accustomed to many very unique sights. (15) Seven caves have more than 15 passage miles, the longest being the Flint-Mammoth Cave system in Kentucky with more than 169 miles. (16) The deepest cave in the United States is Neff Canyon in Utah.

(17) Although many people seem to think that the deepest cave is Carlsbad Caverns, located in New Mexico. (18) However, Carlsbad Caverns boasts the largest room, the Big Room which covers 14 acres. (19) These are sights not to be missed by those who appreciate the handiwork of Mother Nature.

55. Which of the following sentences breaks the unity of paragraph 1 and should be omitted?

   (A) Sentence 1   (D) Sentence 10

   (B) Sentence 3   (E) Sentence 12

   (C) Sentence 4

56. Which of the following is the best way to combine sentences 6, 7, and 8?

   (A) Each drop of water deposits a film of calcite as it is hanging from the ceiling and losing carbon dioxide.

   (B) When hanging, water drops lose carbon dioxide and create a film of calcite.

   (C) In the process of losing carbon dioxide, the drops of water hang from the ceiling and deposit calcite.

   (D) Hanging from the ceiling, losing carbon dioxide, and depositing calcite are the drops of water.

   (E) Hanging from the ceiling, each drop of water loses carbon dioxide and deposits a film of calcite.

57. In relation to the passage as a whole, which of the following best describes the writer's intention in paragraph 2?

   (A) To describe some examples

   (B) To provide a summary

   (C) To convince the reader to change an opinion

   (D) To persuade the reader to follow a course of action

   (E) To detail a chain of events

58. Which of the following is the best revision of the underlined portion of sentence 14 below?

    In addition, the size and depth of many caves in the United States also impress even the most experienced tourist accustomed to many very unique sights.

    (A) impressed the most experienced tourist also accustomed to very unique sights

    (B) impress even the most experienced tourist also accustomed to very unique sights

    (C) impress even the most experienced tourist accustomed to many unique sights

    (D) also impress very experienced tourists accustomed to very unique sights

    (E) also impress even the most experienced tourist accustomed to many unique sights

59. In the context of the sentences preceding and following sentence 17, which of the following is the best revision of sentence 17?

    (A) Although many people are thinking that the deepest cave is Carlsbad Caverns in New Mexico.

    (B) Although, many people think the deepest cave is existing is Carlsbad Caverns in New Mexico.

    (C) As a matter of fact, many people think the deepest cave exists in New Mexico in Carlsbad Caverns.

    (D) However, many people think the deepest cave is Carlsbad Caverns in New Mexico.

    (E) In addition, many people think the deepest cave is located in New Mexico in Carlsbad Caverns.

60. Which of the following corrects the grammatical error in sentence 12?

    (A) Gradually, a thin sheet of calcite grow downward from the ceiling and hang in graceful decorative folds like a drape.

    (B) Gradually, a thin sheet of calcite grows downward from the ceiling and hangs in graceful decorative folds like a drape.

(C) Gradually, a thin sheet of calcite grows downward from the ceiling and gracefully hang in decorative folds like a drape.

(D) Gradually, a thin sheet of calcite grows downward from the ceilings and hang in graceful decorative folds like a drape.

(E) Gradually, a thin sheet of calcite grows downward from the ceiling and hang from the ceiling like a drape.

SAT II: WRITING
TEST 2

ANSWER KEY

1. (A)	16. (D)	31. (B)	46. (D)
2. (C)	17. (E)	32. (D)	47. (B)
3. (C)	18. (E)	33. (D)	48. (A)
4. (C)	19. (D)	34. (B)	49. (B)
5. (B)	20. (C)	35. (A)	50. (A)
6. (A)	21. (B)	36. (B)	51. (E)
7. (A)	22. (A)	37. (E)	52. (E)
8. (B)	23. (C)	38. (C)	53. (C)
9. (D)	24. (A)	39. (B)	54. (A)
10. (E)	25. (B)	40. (A)	55. (B)
11. (C)	26. (A)	41. (A)	56. (E)
12. (A)	27. (B)	42. (B)	57. (D)
13. (A)	28. (C)	43. (A)	58. (C)
14. (C)	29. (D)	44. (C)	59. (D)
15. (A)	30. (C)	45. (E)	60. (B)

DETAILED EXPLANATIONS
OF ANSWERS

Part A: Essay

Sample Essays with Commentary

ESSAY I (Score: 5–6)

The cynic in me wants to react to the idea of universal public service for the young with a reminder about previous complaints aimed at the military draft. These complaints suggest that wars might never be fought if the first people drafted were the adult leaders and lawmakers. Still the idea of universal public service sounds good to this concerned citizen who sees everywhere—not just in youth—the effects of a selfish and self indulgent culture.

One reads and hears constantly about young people who do not care about the problems of our society. These youngsters seem interested in money and the luxuries money can buy. They do not want to work from the minimum wage up, but want instead to land a high paying job without "paying their dues." An informal television news survey of high school students a few years ago suggested that students had the well entrenched fantasy that with no skills or higher education they would not accept a job paying less than $20 an hour. Perhaps universal service helping out in an urban soup kitchen for six months would instill a sense of selflessness rather than selfishness.

The shiny gleam of a new expensive sports sedan bought on credit by a recent accounting student reflects self indulgence that might be toned down by universal service. That self indulgence may reflect merely a lack of discipline, but it also may reflect a lack of purpose in life. Philosophers, theologians and leaders of all types suggest throughout the ages that money and objects do not ultimately satisfy. Helping others—service to our fellow human beings—often does. Universal public service for that accounting student might require a year helping low income or senior citizens prepare income tax forms. This type of service would dim that self indulgence, give the person some experience in the real world, and also give satisfaction that one's life is not lived only to acquire things.

Universal service might also help young people restore faith in their nation and what it means to them. Yes, this is the land of opportunity, but it is also a land of forgotten people, and it is a land that faces outside threats. Part of the requisite public service should remind young people of their past and of their responsibility to the future.

ANALYSIS

Essay I has a score range of 5-6. It uses a traditional structure: the first paragraph states the topic, the second and third present development with specific examples from personal observation. The fourth ends the essay, but it is not as strong a conclusion as it could be. The writer probably ran out of time. The essay as a whole is unified and uses pertinent examples to support the opinion stated. The sentence structure varies, and the vocabulary is effective. Generally, it is well done within the 20-minute time limit.

ESSAY II (Score: 4–5)

In the U.S. today, when a boy turns 18 he is obligated, by law, to register for the military draft. This is done so that in case of a war or something catastrophic these boys and men can be called on for active duty in the military. It is good to know that we will have the manpower in case of a war but my opinion on the military draft is negative. I don't like the idea of forcing someone to sign up at a certain age for something that they don't want to happen. Of course, I know that we need some sort of military manpower on hand just in case, but it would be so much better if it was left to the individual to decide what area to serve in and what time.

When a boy turns 18, he's a rebel of sorts. He doesn't want someone telling him what to do and when to do it; he's just beginning to live. In Switzerland, when a boy turns 18, he goes into some branch of the military for a time of training. He is given his gun, uniform and badge number. Then, once a year for about two weeks he suits up for retraining. He does this until he is about 65 years old. Now in a way this is like a draft but the men love it and feel that it is honorable. I think that they like it because it does not discriminate and their jobs pay them for the time away. Switzerland seems to give the 18 year old somewhat of a choice what division to go in and whether or not to join. They're not as strict on joining as we are so it's more of an honorable thing to do.

Of course, I'd love to see it as strictly up to the individual but it can't be that way. We have too many enemies that we might go to war with and we would need a strong military. Switzerland has nothing to worry about as long as they have their banks.

ANALYSIS

Essay II has a score range of 4-5. It displays competence in overall thought. It does not state its topic quite as well as Essay I. The extended example of Swiss military conscription is the main strength of the essay. The writer hedges a bit but manages to convey an opinion. Sentences have some variety, and the vocabulary is competent. Some spelling and grammatical errors interfere with the communication.

ESSAY III (Score: 3–4)

I agree with the many leaders who suggest we require young people to serve the public in some way, rather than the military draft.

There are several reasons this could benefit our country. The first being giving the young people, perhaps just out of high school, with no job experience, an opportunity to give something to his community. In return for this, he gains self-respect and pride.

Whether it be taking flowers to shut-ins or just stopping for a chat in a rest home, a young person would have gained something and certainly given, perhaps hope, to that elder person. I can tell from my own experience, not quite old enough for the military draft, how enriched I feel when visiting the elderly. They find joy in the simplest things, which in turn, teaches me I should do the same.

Another thing gained by doing voluntary type work, is a sense of caring about doing the job right—quality! If you can't do it for your country, what else matters?

ANALYSIS

Essay III has a score range of 3-4. It has major faults, not the least of them the lack of a clear sense of overall organization. The thoughts do have some coherence, but they don't seem to have a plan, except to express agreement with the statement. Examples from personal observation do help, but the paragraphs are not well developed. Several severe grammatical problems interfere with the communication.

ESSAY IV (Score: 1–2)

Feeling strongly against the draft, as I do. I could not agree with the idea of requiring young people to serve in the military. I feel this would say something about the world situation. I believe the leaders and people would have to give up the idea of peace totally. Which would eventually lead to our own destruction.

Although I do believe young people should serve their country in a peaceful more useful way. They should be more politically aware of what the government is trying to do. They should work in a peaceful way to try and make changes that work for the good of all people of the world.

There has never in the history of the world been a military state that survived.

ANALYSIS

Essay IV has a score range of 1-2. It has many problems. Not only does it fail to present a coherent argument, it also shows a fundamental lack of understanding of sentence structure. The concluding statement seems to come out of nowhere. The writer also confuses the topic with that of required military service, which would be only part of universal service.

Part B: Multiple-Choice

1.   **(A)**   Choice (A) is obviously wordy, "consensus" meaning the same as "general agreement," so it is the best choice. None of the others has a usage error. Choice (B) is acceptable in that it implies a well-known fact that Twain wrote many other works. Choice (C) underscores the claim made in the whole sentence be establishing the book as the "best" American work. Finally, choice (D) is acceptable because of commas in other parts of the sentence. Choice (E) clearly does not apply.

2.   **(C)**   This question has several potential errors. Choice (A) requires that you know to capitalize important historical documents, so it is correct. Choice (B) calls to question the attribution of human rationality to an inanimate object, but since the Constitution actually does have logical premises, we can correctly say that the document can posit the premise stated. Choice (D) is acceptable because the superlative is referenced within the sentence; one should know that the U.S. government has three branches. That leaves choices (C) and (E). Choice (C) is the verb in the clause beginning with the word "what"; it is plural, and therefore, incorrect because it does not agree with its subject "history," a singular noun. Do not be fooled by the intervening plural word "governments." Since choice (C) is the error, choice (E) would no longer be considered.

3.   **(C)**   Even though people use "like" as a conjunction in conversation and public speaking, it is a preposition, and formal written English requires "as," "as if," or "as though" when what follows is a clause. No other choice is even suspect.

4.   **(C)**   One could question the use of "nearly" (A), but it is correct. One might argue also that "million dollars" (D) should be written "$1 million," but choice (C) is so clearly an incorrect use of the past perfect tense that the other possibilities, remote at best, pale by comparison. The simple past tense ("sold"), the present progressive tense ("are selling"), or the present perfect progressive tense ("have been selling") could each be used correctly depending on the meaning intended.

5.   **(B)**   This choice is not as obvious, but authorities agree that the use of "expect" to mean "suppose" or "believe" (the usage here) is either informal or colloquial, but again not formal written English. The next most likely choice, (E), would suggest that informal or colloquial usage is

appropriate. The third most likely choice, (D), brings to mind the distinction between "accept" and "except," a word pair often confused. However, "accept" is correct here.

6.   **(A)**   Regardless of its popular usage "hopefully" is an adverb trying to be a clause ("it is hoped" or "I hope"). However, instances still exist that require a distinction between the two uses. To be clear, use "hopefully" when you mean "in a hopeful manner." ["He wished hopefully that she would accept his proposal of marriage."] Capitalizing "Twentieth Century" (B) is appropriate as it is here used as the specific historical period (like the "Middle Ages"). We would not capitalize the phrase if it were used simply to count, as in "The twentieth century from now will surely find enormous changes in the world." Choice (C), "enough," is correct as used. Choice (D) appears suspicious. "Continually" means recurrence at intervals over a period of time, so it is correctly used to imply that machines do break down often. It is incorrect to hyphenate a number-noun phrase like this one when it stands alone as a noun phrase.

7.   **(A)**   The two most suspicious choices are (A) and (D) because the item is a sentence fragment. No reasonable substitute for (D) would solve both the logic problem (incomplete thought) and the punctuation problem (comma splice if you omit "that"). Changing "showing" to "show" would, however, make the clause into a complete sentence with correct punctuation. Neither (B) or (C) provoke suspicion.

8.   **(B)**   Again, the two most questionable choices, (B) and (C), compete for our attention. The use of "but" makes sense because it shows contrast to the previous idea. ("Don't evade or defy the law, *but* if caught breaking a law, accept the penalty.") The use of "or," however, is clearly not parallel to the immediately preceding use of "neither." The proper phrase is "neither . . . nor" for negative alternate choices. Neither choice (A) nor choice (D) demands a second look.

9.   **(D)**   This choice involves parallel construction, or the lack of it. The word "both" introduces a pair of phrases, one a prepositional phrase ("for their own interests"), the other an infinitive phrase ("to gain more goods"). Aside from being inelegant, "to gain more goods" is also not the same structure and should be changed to "their own gain" to make the two phrases perfectly parallel. Choices (B) and (C) are not problematic. Choice (A) is another candidate because of the capitalization and the lack of a hyphen between "Eighteenth" and "Century." The capitalization is correct

and no hyphen is needed when the phrase becomes an adjective that has meaning as a single phrase, which the capitalization suggests, or if the first word forms a familiar pair with the following word and if there is no danger of confusion. [The sentence clearly does not mean that Smith is the eighteenth (small "e") philosopher, but *the* Eighteenth Century philosopher.]

10. **(E)**   The other choices all fail to exhibit inappropriate usage. Choice (A), "cannot," is spelled as one word; choice (B), "should not," is parallel to "cannot" and adds meaning necessary to the thought. Choice (C) is a correct plural possessive pronoun, the antecedent of which is "rulers." Finally, choice (D) is a third-person plural verb agreeing with its subject, "reasons."

11. **(C)**   "Milky Way galaxy" is the singular antecedent, for which the pronoun referent should be "its" (inanimate object). Do not be confused by the intervening words ("stars" and "spots"); it is the galaxy which shines in this sentence, not the stars or the spots. Choice (A) is the correct usage of "comprises." Choice (B) is an appropriate pair of adjectives with no apparent problem. Choice (D) is appropriate because the sentence has an internally supplied superlative sense; it does not need a "brightest of" phrase.

12. **(A)**   Again, non-parallel structure is the key of this and many other test items. Because of the overwhelming importance of understanding balance in sentence structure, tests like this one emphasize parallel sentence structures. "To learn" clashes with "studying" in the parallel clause. You cannot choose "studying." "Learning" substituted for "To learn" would make the clauses parallel. Choice (B) is a correct use of "like" as a preposition (objects: "Latin," "Greek"). Choice (D) is correctly singular as the verb of the noun phrase "studying . . . beliefs." Nothing is incorrect about choice (C).

13. **(A)**   This is a colloquial, nonstandard substitution for the correct word, "attribute." Choice (B) is correctly lowercase, not capitalized. Choice (C) is a correct, if a bit stiff, phrase. Choice (D) is a correct plural verb the subject of which is "both," also plural.

14. **(C)**   This is an incorrect simple past verb tense. You have to spot the context clue "most Americans" "attended" school (B) in the past, which suggests they no longer do so now. They must then "choose" their

entertainment. Choice (A) is questionable, but the present participial phrase suggests coincidence with the time "most Americans" "attended school." It is, therefore, correct. Choice (D) is correctly an infinitive that is parallel to "to watch."

15. **(A)** The two most questionable choices are (A) and (B). Choice (A) is incorrectly a subjective case pronoun when it should be objective (object of verb "makes," subject "What"). If you know the difference between "different from" (correctly used in this sentence) and "difference than" (correctly used only to introduce a clause), then choice (B) is no longer viable. Besides being a passive construction, choice (C) has no objectionable qualities; it is grammatically correct. So is choice (D) correctly an adverb that has meaning in context.

16. **(D)** This is a case of subject-verb disagreement related to the definition of the word "neither" (subject) as singular. Its verb must also be singular, and "differ" is plural. Choice (A) correctly uses English idiom ("compare to"—"contrast with"). Choice (B) refers clearly to "ideas," its antecedent, and agrees with it (both plural). Choice (C) is a singular verb agreeing with its subject, "one."

17. **(E)** Everything in the sentence is acceptable or correct usage, even though some of it may be a bit stuffy and pedantic, i.e., choice (B). You might question choice (A) in that instead of suggesting, perhaps asserting or stating would be more appropriate. Even though these terms clearly differ, there is nothing wrong with using "suggests" (correct subject-verb agreement with "hypothesis") because a hypothesis can suggest as well as theorize, assert, etc. Choice (C) correctly agrees with its subject "which" (plural, antecedent "archetypes"). Choice (D) might be considered redundant ("repeated" and "patterns"), but that is not apparent from the context.

18. **(E)** You are likely to have chosen either (B) or (C) here. The affect/effect word pair often confuses students, and this instance is one in which "effected" is correctly used as a verb meaning "brought about" or "caused to happen." The question in choice (C) is whether or not to capitalize the word "Fate." When it refers to the collective term for the Greek concept of destiny (actually gods, the Fates), as it does here, it is appropriately capitalized. Choices (A) and (D) do not seem questionable.

19. **(D)** Again, the problem here is pronoun-antecedent agreement. "Their" does not refer to the three writers collectively; its antecedent is

"each," which is always singular, not plural ("each one"). There is nothing wrong with choices (A), (B), and (C).

20. **(C)**   The error here is known as faulty predication ("reason . . . is because"). The usage rule is that "because" is redundant for "reason." Choice (A) is appropriate, if a bit general (not 30 or 70 percent, for example). The verb in choice (B) is correct and in the past tense, as is the verb phrase in choice (D).

21. **(B)**   Choice (A) is a verb correctly in agreement with its compound subject. Choice (C) is an appropriate parallel structure requiring no punctuation. Choice (D) correctly uses the word "comprises" and makes it agree with its subject. Only (B) seems incorrect. The structure requires the adverb form "constantly," since it describes an adjective, "expanding."

22. **(A)**   This is the classic confusion of "less" for the correct "fewer." "Few(er)" refers to countable things or persons; "little (less)" refers to things that can be measured or estimated but not itemized. The only other choice to examine is (D), but it is the appropriate tense referring to the "contemporary" (now) view.

23. **(C)**   Choice (A) is a correct use of the relative pronoun. Nothing is unusual about (B). (C) is the culprit here: it should be the infinitive form to adhere to the idiom, "ability to (verb)." (D) is an appropriate reference to hierarchy and responsibility.

24. **(A)**   The sentence as it stands is illogical. Removing "Because" will make it sensible. (B) is an appropriate adverb modifying "believe"; (C) is a clear and effective subordination of an explanation of a term. (D) uses "as" properly as a preposition.

25. **(B)**   "Being that" is colloquial for "because," which is better for at least the reason that it is shorter, but also that it is more formal. No other choices seem out of bounds.

26. **(A)**   "As far as" is an incomplete comparison that should always include "is" (or variant form of "to be") "concerned." "As for" can be substituted for "as far as . . . is (are concerned)." The others are acceptable.

27. **(B)**   This is the classic vague pronoun reference. Out of context,

there is no antecedent for "they." Every pronoun must have an identifiable antecedent. (A) is acceptable, by the way; geographical region is capitalized. No problems show up in the other choices.

28. **(C)**   This is a problem often called agreement of nominative forms. The compound subject ("Japan and the United States") is plural, and the form to match is "net exporters" in this case. Choice (B) is a verb correctly agreeing with its plural subject. "Imbalances" is correct in (D) because all nations, particularly the two mentioned, want an imbalance of trade in their favor.

29. **(D)**   This problem demonstrates a faulty comparison: "Jon" and "his friend's bicycle" are not equivalents and should not be compared. "His friend" would have been correct. (B) is acceptable because it indicates the rides are in the past, which does not conflict with any other part of the sentence.

30. **(C)**   The problem here is appropriate verb tense. Both "After" and "once the dominant species" signal requirement of the past tense. Changing "are" to "became" would solve the problem. (A) is correctly capitalized as a geologic period. Nothing is amiss with either (B) or (D).

31. **(B)**   This question of appropriate verb tense requires the simple past tense verb "took" because the Civil War happened in a finite time period in the past. The other choices all fail that test. The original and choice (E) are present tense, and do not logically fit the facts. Choice (D) is the present perfect tense, which suggests a continuous action from the past to the present. Choice (C) is the past perfect tense, which suggests a continuing action from one time in the past to another in the more recent past.

32. **(D)**   We can eliminate fairly quickly choices (C) and (E) as either inappropriate or awkward appositives to "ornithology," instead of "ornithologists." Neither is (A) the best choice even though some may consider it acceptable. Likewise, choice (B) tends to be limited to nonrestrictive clauses, unlike this one. Choice (D) then correctly uses a "personal" relative pronoun.

33. **(D)**   Choices (A), (D), and (E) are the best candidates because they are more concise than the other two choices. Each does express the same idea, but (E) does not as strongly indicate the contrast between the two

clauses in the sentence as do choices (A) and (D). Choice (D) clearly makes its point in fewer words and is the better choice.

34. **(B)** The phrase "as to" often is overblown and unclear, so it is best to eliminate it when there are other choices. Likewise, "expectability" does not exactly roll of your tongue. That leaves choices (B) and (D). Choice (D) adds a definite figure, unwarranted by the original sentence. It also is duller than (B), which does change the wording for the better and also indicates that the "actual amount" is to be announced, rather than that it is already known.

35. **(A)** Choices (C) and (E) introduce unnecessary absolute phrases beginning with "it," which makes the sentences wordy. They can be eliminated immediately. Choice (D) has an illogical comparison suggesting notes = instrument, so it, too, is not the best choice. Between (A) and (B) the difference boils down to the present tense vs. the past tense. Choice (A) uses past tenses, which seem better in sequence to follow the past tense verb "developed."

36. **(B)** Choices (A), (C), and (D) can be disqualified quickly because they are not parallel to the structure of the main clause. Choice (E) is ungainly and introduces a vague pronoun "its" (unclear antecedent). Choice (B) reads well and has the virtue of brevity.

37. **(E)** The choices are easy to discern in this sentence. The original verb does not agree with its subject, nor is the structure parallel. The former reason also eliminates choice (C). Choice (B) does not have parallel structure (phrase and clause). Choice (D) does not logically agree with the subject ("reasons") since it names one ("demanding professors") but relegates the other reason to an afterthought. Choice (D) has both parallel structure and subject-verb agreement; it also names two reasons.

38. **(C)** The original suffers from inadequate causal relationship and non-parallel structure. Choices (D) and (E) are both unnecessarily wordy; (D) is still not parallel, and (E) is internally illogical ("both" with three things). Choice (B) switches its structure at the end. Although it is technically parallel, it is still awkward because of the addition of the possessive pronoun "her." Choice (C) solves both problems by clearly showing cause and by being parallel (three nouns in series).

39. **(B)** This sentence presents an incomplete comparison and a redun-

dancy ("Whether"/"or did not"/"remains uncertain"). Choice (B) eliminates both problems clearly. Choice (C) tries to undo the damage, but it remains inelegant in syntax and leaves partial redundancy ("whether"/ "remains uncertain"). Choice (D) is worse in both respects. Choice (E) clears up the syntax but leaves some redundancy ("may actually have"/ "remains uncertain"). Choice (B) eliminates both problems clearly.

40. **(A)**   The sentence as is reads well; it is perfectly balanced. Choice (B) introduces an incomplete comparison ("more" but no "than"). Choice (C) awkwardly uses "as to." Choices (D) and (E) make a scrambled mess by introducing illogical structures.

41. **(A)**   "Unique" means just that; it should not have qualifiers like "very" or "nearly." That eliminates choices (B) and (D). Choice (C) changes the meaning by making the development unique, instead of the system. Choice (E) uses an inappropriate verb tense because the first of the sentence suggests the Revolutionary War period, definitely in the past.

42. **(B)**   The original sentence (A) has a dangling modifier (participial phrase); it remains that way in choice (E). The house cannot return to itself, nor can "it" (pronoun for house). Choice (D) seems to leave something out: "returned to . . . home in 12 years." Choice (C) solves the original problem but is unnecessarily wordy. Choice (B) properly solves the dangling modifier problem by subordinating the return in an adverbial clause.

43. **(A)**   Choice (A) is the only response that makes sense. Each of the others introduces illogical comparisons or structures (non-parallel); (B), (D), and (E) are also verbose. Choice (C) is concise but not parallel.

44. **(C)**   This sentence suggests causal relationships between the parts of the sentence that do not belong there. Choices (B) and (D) echo the original (A) in that regard. Choice (E) has garbled syntax. (C) shows clearly that the cause-effect relationship is, rather, a time relationship.

45. **(E)**   This is essentially a problem of wordiness. (E) is the shortest and most clear of all the choices. The punctuation is weak in (C), and the syntax of (B) complicates the idea unnecessarily. (D) does not use the appropriate conjunctive adverb; "thereby" is more precise than "therefore" when referring to an event.

46. **(D)**   All the other responses repeat the cause-effect relationship stated in the phrase "Because of." (D) is the only choice which does not do so.

47. **(B)**   Choice (B) would solve the problem of needless pronoun voice shift from second person to first person ("you" to "our"). It correctly substitutes first person "we" for "you." (C) uses the passive voice awkwardly. (D) introduces non-parallel structure (and incomplete comparison). (E) is a similar voice shift from third to first person.

48. **(A)**   This is the best response from the choices. The sentence implies a change of the standard. For that reason, (B) is an incorrect choice. (C) is unnecessarily awkward and wordy. (D) is redundant and (E) states more than the sentence implies.

49. **(B)**   Choice (B) is the most concise, least repetitive form of this sentence. Choices (A) and (E) contain the unnecessary phrase, "It goes without saying." Choice (C) leaves out the fact that waves are pounding at the mouth of a sea cave. Choice (D) is a fragment.

50. **(A)**   Choice (A) is the best revision because it is precise and uses a voice consistent with the rest of the passage. Choice (B) and (C) both slip into the less formal "you." Choice (E) is too formal, using "one." Choice (C) is somewhat acceptable but uses the passive voice construction, "can be thought of."

51. **(E)**   Choice (E) clearly shows the pattern of events, a sequence of cause-and-effect. Choice (A) contains the incorrect construction, "This acid dissolving"; it should be, "This acid's dissolving." Choice (B) neglects to extend clearly the process of cave formation to show that the passageways become caves. Choice (C) is somewhat acceptable, but it contains the awkward phrasing, "effects are that." Choice (D) reverses the cause with the effect, and so confuses the issues.

52. **(E)**   The second paragraph explains the process (E) by which drip-stone features are formed in a cave. This process takes place in a location—caves—but description, choice (C), is not the main intent of the paragraph. Choices (A), (B), and (D) would be more suitable to persuasion.

53. **(C)**   Choice (C) is the most precise wording and uses an action

verb, "occurs." Choices (A), (D), and (E) use two forms of the verb "to be" in the same sentence, thus producing a weaker construction. Choice (B) uses, "is due to," and so is a bit more awkward than choice (C).

54. **(A)** Choice (A) sets the prepositional phrase apart from the main subject and verb ("water sweeps"). Choice (B) makes it seem as though we are talking about "a rain water." In (C) and (D) both a colon and a hyphen are inappropriate. In (E), the sentence as it stands is ambiguous, especially because we use the phrase "rain water" in other contexts, and unless the prepositional phrase is set-off by a comma, the sense is unclear.

55. **(B)** Choice (B) breaks the unity of the paragraph by digressing slightly into an opinion about the presence of electric lights in a natural setting. As the main thrust of the passage is to discuss the beauty of caves in the United States, this idea is out of place. This sentence also mentions the opinions of "some people," a vague reference. The other choices contain no digressions.

56. **(E)** Choice (E) concisely combines ideas while effectively showing the sequence of events. Choice (A) puts the cause, "losing carbon dioxide," after the effect, "deposits a film of carbon dioxide." Choice (B) could be better worded by revising, "When hanging, water drops." Choice (C) erroneously presents hanging from the ceiling as part of the process of losing carbon dioxide. Choice (D) completely loses the cause-and-effect and lists events as an unrelated list.

57. **(D)** The intent of the second paragraph builds to the last sentence, in which the persuasive (D) intent becomes evident. Although the paragraph provides some examples, choice (A), those examples bolster the persuasive intent. Choice (C) could be plausible if the writer had indicated an acknowledgment of the reader's aversion to caves. Choices (B) and (E) are more appropriate for the first paragraph.

58. **(C)** Choice (C) is the most concise and accurate. Choices (A) and (B) use the incorrect grammatical structure, "very unique." A sight is unique, meaning "one of a kind"; therefore, "very unique" is incorrect. The sentence begins with the phrase, "in addition," so choices (D) and (E) are repetitive because they use the word "also."

59. **(D)** Choice (D) makes a complete sentence that is correctly punctuated. Choice (A) is a fragment and contains the awkward "people are

thinking." Choice (B) contains the poor phrase "is existing." Choices (C) and (E) could be moderately acceptable, but they have two prepositional phrases in a row beginning with "in" at the end of the sentence.

60. **(B)**   Choice (B) is correct because both verbs must agree with the singular noun "sheet." Choice (A) brings "grow" into accord with "hang," but the plural verbs do not agree with the singular subject. Choice (C) uses "gracefully" as an adverb correctly, but does not correct the verb agreement problem. Choice (D) may appear correct: "hang" would be correct if it modified the plural "ceilings" but it modifies "sheet" which is singular. Similarly, (E) does not correct the subject-verb disagreement.

SAT II: Writing

Practice Test 3

SAT II: WRITING
TEST 3

Part A: Essay

TIME: 20 Minutes

DIRECTIONS: You have 20 minutes to plan and write an essay on the topic below. You may write only on the assigned topic.

Make sure to give specific examples to support your thesis. Proofread your essay carefully and take care to express your ideas clearly and effectively.

Write your essay on the lined pages at the back of the book.

ESSAY TOPIC:

"There is a wonderful, mystical law of nature that the three things we crave most in life—happiness, freedom, and peace of mind—are always attained by giving them to someone else."

ASSIGNMENT: Do you agree or disagree with this statement? Support your opinion with specific examples from history, current events, literature, or personal experience.

Part B: Multiple-Choice

(Answer sheets appear in the back of this book.)

TIME: 40 Minutes
60 Questions

DIRECTIONS: Each of the following sentences may contain an error in diction, usage, idiom, or grammar. Some sentences are correct. Some sentences contain one error. No sentence contains more than one error.

If there is an error, it will appear in one of the underlined portions labeled A, B, C, or D. If there is no error, choose the portion labeled E. If there is an error, select the letter of the portion that must be changed in order to correct the sentence.

EXAMPLE:

He drove <u>slowly</u> and <u>cautiously</u> in order to <u>hopefully</u> avoid having an
      A   **B**   **C**

<u>accident</u>. <u>No error</u>.
  D   **E**   Ⓐ Ⓑ ● Ⓓ Ⓔ

---

1. <u>Which</u> suspension bridge <u>is</u> the <u>longest</u>, the Verrazano-Narrows
     A   **B**   **C**
Bridge in New York City <u>or</u> the Golden Gate Bridge in San Fran-
                      D
cisco? <u>No error</u>.
      E

2. A main function <u>of proteins</u>, whether <u>they come</u> from <u>plant or animal</u>
             A   **B**   **C**
<u>sources, is</u> the building of body tissue. <u>No error</u>.
   D   **E**

3. <u>Recognizing</u> that we <u>had worked</u> very hard to complete our project,
     A   **B**
the teacher told Janice and <u>I</u> that we could give it to her <u>tomorrow</u>.
                   C   **D**
<u>No error</u>.
 E

4. <u>According to</u> the United States Constitution, the legislative branch of
     A

    the government <u>has</u> powers <u>different than</u> <u>those</u> of the executive
              B   **C**   **D**

    branch. <u>No error.</u>
         E

5. After <u>being studied</u> for the <u>preceding ten years</u> by the National Heart,
       A   **B**

    Lung, and Blood Institute, the relationship of high levels of

    cholesterol in the blood to the possibility of <u>having</u> heart attacks
                                               C

    <u>was reported</u> in 1984. <u>No error.</u>
      D   **E**

6. The book *Cheaper By the Dozen* <u>demonstrates</u> that each of the chil-
                                A

    dren of Frank and Lillian Gilbreth <u>was expected</u> <u>to use</u> <u>his or her</u> time
                             B   **C**   **D**

    efficiently. <u>No error.</u>
            E

7. His aversion <u>with</u> snakes made camping an unpleasant activity
             A

    <u>for him</u> and <u>one</u> <u>that</u> he tried diligently to avoid. <u>No error.</u>
     B   **C** **D**   **E**

8. The story of the American pioneers, <u>those</u> who willingly left the
                                 A

    safety of <u>their</u> homes to move into unsettled territory, <u>show</u> <u>us</u> great
           B   **C** **D**

    courage in the face of danger. <u>No error.</u>
                       E

9. <u>Because of</u> the long, cold winters <u>and</u> short summers, farming in high
     A   **B**

    latitudes is <u>more difficult</u> <u>than</u> low latitudes. <u>No error.</u>
             C   **D**   **E**

10. When my sister and I were in Los Angeles, we hoped that both of us
                         A B   **C**
    could be a contestant on a quiz show. No error.
              D   **E**

11. After he had broke the vase that his mother had purchased in Europe,
                 A   **B**   **C**
    he tried to buy a new one for his father and her. No error.
                                                D   **E**

12. Some of the people with whom the witness worked were engaged in
                         A   **B**   **C**
    covert activities on behalf of the United States government. No error.
                      D   **E**

13. Because of their cold personalities and hot tempers, neither John
    A   **B**
    Adams nor his son John Quincy Adams were especially successful in
          C   **D**
    politics. No error.
              E

14. Among the reasons for United States participation in World War II
    A   **B**
    were the Japanese attack on the naval base at Pearl Harbor on De-
    C   **D**
    cember 7, 1941. No error.
                    E

15. Some parents make a greater attempt to frighten their children about
                        A   **B**
    the dangers of driving than teaching them safe driving habits.
                         C   **D**
    No error.
    E

16. The high standard of living in Sweden is shown by their statistics
                      A   **B**   **C**
    of life expectancy and per capita income. No error.
    D   **E**

17. The snow leopard <u>is</u> a wild mammal in Central Asia <u>that has</u> large
                 A   **B**

    eyes, a four-foot body, <u>and</u> <u>white and bluish gray in color</u>. <u>No error</u>.
                           C   **D**   **E**

18. Selecting a lifetime vocation, <u>a young person</u> may have to choose
                                      A

    either a vocation that he enjoys <u>and</u> a vocation that will make <u>him</u>
                                  B   **C**

    rich; that choice is perhaps the <u>most important</u> one he will ever make.
                                         D

    <u>No error</u>.
    E

19. Failing a test because the student <u>is</u> nervous <u>is</u> understandable; <u>to fail</u>
                                   A   **B**   **C**

    because <u>he or she</u> did not study is quite another matter. <u>No error</u>.
               D   **E**

20. Although she <u>had grown up</u> in the North and <u>had been</u> neither a slave
                    A   **B**

    <u>or</u> a slave owner, Harriet Beecher Stowe <u>vividly</u> portrayed life on a
    C   **D**

    slave-holding plantation in her famous book. <u>No error</u>.
                                       E

21. The reason Jason failed <u>his</u> speech was <u>because</u> he suffered <u>such</u>
                               A   **B**   **C**

    <u>stage fright</u> <u>that he refused</u> to give his final speech. <u>No error</u>.
                     D   **E**

22. <u>After completing the typing course</u>, he made <u>less</u> errors and typed
                        A   **B**

    <u>more rapidly</u> than <u>anyone else</u> in his office. <u>No error</u>.
       C   **D**   **E**

23. Learning the basic <u>components of good nutrition</u> is <u>important for</u> the
                                A   **B**

    young adult <u>who want</u> <u>to gain independence</u> by living in his or her
                 C   **D**

    own apartment. <u>No error</u>.
                      E

24. Because condominiums offer the advantages of property ownership

    along with those of apartment rental, this has made condominiums
    ‾‾A‾‾‾‾ ‾‾B‾‾   ‾C‾ ‾has‾‾made‾
      A   B   C   D
    popular since the 1970s. No error.
                            ‾‾‾‾‾‾‾
                               E

25. Students who eat every day in the college cafeteria generally tire of
             ‾‾‾   ‾‾‾‾‾‾‾‾‾
              A   B
    the frequent repetitious menu that is provided. No error.
        ‾‾‾‾‾‾‾‾   ‾‾‾‾‾‾‾‾‾‾‾‾ ‾‾‾‾‾‾‾‾
           C   D   E

26. Our understanding on the results of closed adoptions has changed as
        ‾‾‾‾‾‾‾‾‾‾‾‾‾‾   ‾‾‾‾‾‾‾‾‾‾‾
              A   B
    adoptees, birth parents, and adoptive parents have described their
                             ‾‾‾   ‾‾‾‾‾‾‾‾‾‾‾‾‾‾
                              C   D
    experiences. No error.
                ‾‾‾‾‾‾‾‾
                   E

27. If President Andrew Johnson would have been found guilty by the
                              ‾‾‾‾‾‾‾‾‾‾‾‾‾‾‾‾‾‾‾   ‾‾‾‾‾‾
                                      A   B
    United States Senate, he would have been removed from office.
    ‾‾‾‾‾‾‾‾‾‾‾‾‾‾‾‾‾‾‾‾   ‾‾‾‾‾‾‾‾‾‾‾‾‾‾‾‾‾‾‾‾‾ ‾‾‾‾‾‾‾‾‾‾
                                      C   D
    No error.
    ‾‾‾‾‾‾‾‾
       E

28. Perhaps one of the most famous myths about an American President
    ‾‾‾‾‾‾‾   ‾‾‾‾‾‾‾‾‾‾‾‾‾‾‾‾‾‾‾‾‾‾‾
       A   B
    is the cherry tree that George Washington supposedly chopped down.
    ‾‾ ‾‾‾‾‾‾‾‾‾‾‾‾
    C   D
    No error.
    ‾‾‾‾‾‾‾‾
       E

29. The first woman who was appointed by President Ronald Reagan to
                   ‾‾‾ ‾‾‾‾‾‾‾‾‾‾‾‾‾
                    A   B
    the Supreme Court was Sandra Day O'Connor of Arizona. No error.
                     ‾‾‾‾   ‾‾‾‾‾‾‾‾‾‾ ‾‾‾‾‾‾‾‾
                      C   D   E

30. The pilot's maneuver for lowering the altitude at which the plane was
                ‾‾‾‾‾‾‾‾‾‾‾‾‾‾‾‾‾‾‾‾   ‾‾‾‾‾‾‾‾   ‾‾‾
                        A   B   C
    flying resulted in a shaking and shuddering of the cabin. No error.
    ‾‾‾‾‾‾   ‾‾‾‾‾‾‾‾‾‾‾‾‾‾‾‾‾‾‾‾‾‾‾‾   ‾‾‾‾‾‾‾‾
       D   D   E

DIRECTIONS: In each of the following sentences, some portion of the sentence is underlined. Under each sentence are five choices. The first choice has the same wording as the original. The other four choices are reworded. Sometimes the first choice containing the original wording is the best; sometimes one of the other choices is the best. Choose the letter of the best choice. Your choice should produce a sentence which is not ambiguous or awkward and which is correct, clear, and precise.

This is a test of correct and effective English expression. Keep in mind the standards of English usage, punctuation, grammar, word choice, and construction.

EXAMPLE:

When you listen to opera, <u>a person may not appreciate it.</u>

(A)   a person may not appreciate it.

(B)   it may not be appreciated by a person.

(C)   which may not be appreciated by one.

(D)   you may not appreciate it.

(E)   appreciating it may be a problem for you.

---

31.   Wealthy citizens often protest <u>about the building of</u> low-cost housing in the affluent communities where they reside.

(A)   about the building of

(B)   whether they should build

(C)   if builders should build

(D)   the building of

(E)   whether or not they should build

32.   Siblings growing up in a family do not necessarily have equal opportunities to achieve, <u>the difference being their placement in the family, their innate abilities, and their personalities.</u>

(A)   the difference being their placement in the family, their innate abilities, and their personalities.

(B) because of their placement in the family, their innate abilities, and their personalities.

(C) and the difference is their placement in the family, their innate abilities, and their personalities.

(D) they have different placements in the family, different innate abilities, and different personalities.

(E) their placement in the family, their innate abilities, and their personalities being different.

33. Two major provisions of the United States Bill of Rights <u>is freedom of speech and that citizens are guaranteed a trial by jury</u>.

(A) is freedom of speech and that citizens are guaranteed a trial by jury.

(B) is that citizens have freedom of speech and a guaranteed trial by jury.

(C) is freedom of speech and the guarantee of a trial by jury.

(D) are freedom of speech and that citizens are guaranteed a trial by jury.

(E) are freedom of speech and the guarantee of a trial by jury.

34. Poets of the nineteenth century tried <u>to entertain their readers but also with the attempt of teaching them</u> lessons about life.

(A) to entertain their readers but also with the attempt of teaching them

(B) to entertain their readers but also to attempt to teach them

(C) to both entertain their readers and to teach them

(D) entertainment of their readers and the attempt to teach them

(E) both to entertain and to teach their readers

35. The city council decided to remove parking meters <u>so as to encourage</u> people to shop in Centerville.

(A) so as to encourage

(B) to encourage

(C) thus encouraging

(D) with the desire

(E) thereby encouraging

36. Visiting New York City for the first time, <u>the sites most interesting to Megan were</u> the Statue of Liberty, the Empire State Building, and the Brooklyn Bridge.

(A) the sites most interesting to Megan were

(B) the sites that Megan found most interesting were

(C) Megan found that the sites most interesting to her were

(D) Megan was most interested in

(E) Megan was most interested in the sites of

37. Although most college professors have expertise in their areas of specialty, <u>some are more interested in continuing their research than in teaching undergraduate students</u>.

(A) some are more interested in continuing their research than in teaching undergraduate students.

(B) some are most interested in continuing their research rather than in teaching undergraduate students.

(C) some prefer continuing their research rather than to teach undergraduate students.

(D) continuing their research, not teaching undergraduate students, is more interesting to some.

(E) some are more interested in continuing their research than to teach undergraduate students.

38. <u>Whether adult adoptees should be allowed to see their original birth certificates or not</u> is controversial, but many adoptive parents feel strongly that records should remain closed.

(A) Whether adult adoptees should be allowed to see their original birth certificates or not

(B) Whether or not adult adoptees should be allowed to see their original birth certificates or not

(C) The fact of whether adult adoptees should be allowed to see their original birth certificates

(D) Allowing the seeing of their original birth certificates by adult adoptees

(E) That adult adoptees should be allowed to see their original birth certificates

39. <u>Having studied theology, music, along with medicine</u>, Albert Schweitzer became a medical missionary in Africa.

(A) Having studied theology, music, along with medicine

(B) Having studied theology, music, as well as medicine

(C) Having studied theology and music, and, also, medicine

(D) With a study of theology, music, and medicine

(E) After he had studied theology, music, and medicine

40. When the Mississippi River threatens to flood, sandbags are piled along its banks, <u>and they do this to keep its waters from overflowing</u>.

(A) and they do this to keep its waters from overflowing.

(B) to keep its waters from overflowing.

(C) and then its waters won't overflow.

(D) and, therefore, keeping its waters from overflowing.

(E) and they keep its waters from overflowing.

41. <u>Because of the popularity of his light verse</u>, Edward Lear is seldom recognized today for his travel books and detailed illustrations of birds.

(A) Because of the popularity of his light verse

(B) Owing to the fact that his light verse was popular

(C) Because of his light verse, that was very popular

(D) Having written light verse that was popular

(E) Being the author of popular light verse

42. Lincoln's Gettysburg Address, <u>despite its having been very short and delivered after a two-hour oration by Edward Everett</u>, is one of the greatest speeches ever delivered.

(A) despite its having been very short and delivered after a two-hour oration by Edward Everett

(B) which was very short and delivered after a two-hour oration by Edward Everett

(C) although it was very short and delivered after a two-hour oration by Edward Everett

(D) despite the fact that it was very short and delivered after a two-hour oration by Edward Everett

(E) was very short and delivered after a two-hour oration by Edward Everett

43. China, which ranks third in area and first in population among the world's countries also has one of the longest histories.

(A) which ranks third in area and first in population among the world's countries

(B) which ranks third in area and has the largest population among the world's countries

(C) which is the third largest in area and ranks first in population among the world's countries

(D) in area ranking third and in population ranking first among the world's countries

(E) third in area and first in the number of people among the world's countries

44. Leonardo Da Vinci was a man who was a scientist, an architect, an engineer, and a sculptor.

(A) Leonardo Da Vinci was a man who

(B) The man Leonardo Da Vinci

(C) Being a man, Leonardo Da Vinci

(D) Leonardo Da Vinci

(E) Leonardo Da Vinci, a man who

45. The age of 35 having been reached, a natural-born United States citizen is eligible to be elected President of the United States.

(A) The age of 35 having been reached

(B) The age of 35 being reached

(C) At 35, when that age is reached

(D) When having reached the age of 35

(E) When he or she is 35 years old

46. It was my roommate who caught the thief stealing my wallet, which is the reason I gave him a reward.

(A) It was my roommate who caught the thief stealing my wallet, which is the reason

(B) My roommate caught the thief stealing my wallet, which is the reason

(C) Because my roommate caught the thief stealing my wallet,

(D) That my roommate caught the thief stealing my wallet is the reason why

(E) My roommate having caught the thief stealing my wallet,

47. The fewer mistakes one makes in life, the fewer opportunities you have to learn from your mistakes.

(A) The fewer mistakes one makes in life

(B) The fewer mistakes you make in life

(C) The fewer mistakes he or she makes in life

(D) The fewer mistakes there are in one's life

(E) The fewer mistakes in life

48. Although the word *millipede* means one thousand feet, millipedes have no more than 115 pairs of legs that are attached to the segments of their bodies.

(A) that are attached to the segments of their bodies.

(B) each of which are attached to a segment of their bodies.

(C) attaching themselves to segments of their bodies.

(D) whose attachment is to the segments of their bodies.

(E) the attachment of which is to the segments of their bodies.

DIRECTIONS: The following passages are considered early draft efforts of a student. Some sentences need to be rewritten to make the ideas clearer and more precise.

Read each passage carefully and answer the questions that follow. Some of the questions are about particular sentences or parts of sentences and ask you to make decisions about sentence structure, diction, and usage. Some of the questions refer to the entire essay or parts of the essay and ask you to make decisions about organization, development, appropriateness of language, audience, and logic. Choose the answer that most effectively makes the intended meaning clear and follows the requirements of standard written English. After you have chosen your answer, fill in the corresponding oval on your answer sheet.

EXAMPLE:

(1) On the one hand, I think television is bad, But it also does some good things for all of us. (2) For instance, my little sister thought she wanted to be a policemen until she saw police shows on television.

Which of the following is the best revision of the underlined portion of sentence 1 below?

On the one hand, I think television <u>is bad, But it also</u> does some good things for all of us.

(A)   is bad; But it also

(B)   is bad. but is also

(C)   is bad, and it also

(D)   is bad, but it also

(E)   is bad because it also

Questions 49–54 are based on the following passage.

(1) Using Indians to track down and fight other Indians was not a new idea during the conflict between the Whites and the Indians during the mid-1800 Indian Wars during the conquest of the Apaches. (2) The English and the French from early colonial times had exploited traditional intertribal rivalries to their own advantage.

(3) What was a novel idea of the U.S. Army during its war against the Apaches was using an Indian against members of his own tribe. (4) Gen. George Crook believed that the best work would be done by an Indian who had only just been fighting him. (5) Crook had learned that such a

scout would know alot because he would know the fighting habits, the hiding places, and the personalities of the Indians being pursued. (6) This method worked well for Crook and by the end of his career he had used about 500 Apache scouts.

(7) Crook demanded trust from all his troops and, in turn, he gave them his trust. (8) He paid his scouts well and on time, a very important factor. (9) Most importantly, Crook treated all the personnel under his command with dignity and respect. (10) These were good qualities. (11) These qualities no doubt earned Crook the admiration and loyalty of his Indian soldiers. (12) Though, the man himself won their respect. (13) Crook was like few West Point trained officers, for he understood his enemy well. (14) He learned to fight the Indians on their terms, to use the land and terrain to his advantage, and to abandon the textbook examples. (15) He got on a trail, and with his Apache scouts to guide him, he followed his quarry relentlessly.

(16) Crook's faith in his scouts never wavered. (17) Moreover, they gave him no grounds for worry. (18) In the annals of the Indian Wars, the story of Crook and his scouts is unique.

49. Which of the following is the best revision of the underlined portion of sentence 1 below?

Using Indians to track down and fight other Indians was not a new idea during the conflict between Whites and the Indians during the mid-1800 Indian Wars during the conquest of the Apaches.

(A) during the mid-1800 Indian Wars between Whites and Apaches.

(B) during the long years of conflict between Whites and Indians.

(C) during the mid-1800s when Indians and Whites came into conflict in the Indian Wars.

(D) when the Apaches and Whites were engaged in conflict.

(E) when, during the mid-1800 Indian Wars, Whites and Apaches engaged in fighting in the Indian Wars.

50. Which of the following is the best revision of the underlined portion of sentence 3 below?

What was a novel idea of the U.S. Army during its war against the Apaches was using an Indian against members of his own tribe.

(A) The U.S. Army's novel idea during this war

(B) What the U.S. Army had as a novel idea during its war

(C) The U.S. Army had the novel idea during this war

(D) During its war the U.S. Army's novelty

(E) A novelty of the U.S. Army's war during this time

51. Which of the following is the best revision of the underlined portion of sentence 5 below?

Crook had learned that such a scout <u>would know alot because he would know</u> the fighting habits, the hiding places, and the personalities of the Indians being pursued.

(A) would know alot about

(B) would know a lot about

(C) would know

(D) would have a great deal of useful knowledge concerning

(E) would have knowledge of

52. Which of the following is the best way to combine sentences 10, 11, and 12?

(A) Admiring and loyal because of Crook's good qualities, the Indian soldiers gave him their respect.

(B) Although earning the loyalty and admiration of the Indian soldiers, Crook won their respect.

(C) Crook won the Indian soldier's respect, admiration, and loyalty because of his good qualities.

(D) Although these good qualities no doubt earned Crook the admiration and loyalty of his Indian soldiers, the man himself won their respect.

(E) Although the man himself earned respect, these good qualities earned Crook the Indian soldier's admiration and loyalty.

53. In relation to the passage as a whole, which of the following best describes the writer's intention in paragraph 4?

(A) To narrate an important event

(B) To describe the best features of the subject

(C) To persuade readers to take a certain course of action

(D) To provide a conclusion

(E) To provide a summary of the passage

54. Which of the following would be the best way to revise sentence 15?

(A) He got on a trail, with his Apache scouts to guide him, he followed his quarry relentlessly.

(B) He got on a trail, and his Apache scouts guiding him, he followed his quarry relentlessly.

(C) He would get on a trail, and with his Apache scouts to guide him, he followed his quarry relentlessly.

(D) He got on a trail and he followed his quarry relentlessly, with his Apache scouts to guide him.

(E) He would get on a trail, and with his Apache scouts to guide him, would follow his quarry relentlessly.

Questions 55-60 are based on the following passage.

Dear Senator Simon,

(1) I am writing in support of your bill that, if passed, will be instrumental in getting legislation which will put a warning label on violent television programs. (2) Violence needs to be de-glamorized. (3) One must detest and deplore violence of excess and other such excesses in one's viewing choices.

(4) Unfortunately, violence sells. (5) One of the main reasons is because violent shows are easily translated and marketed to other countries. (6) Network executives have actually requested their script writers to include more violence in certain shows with a steady audience, as well as to create new violent shows for the late evening slot just before the news.

(7) The National Institute of Health did a study. (8) In this study children viewed violent scenes. (9) After this, children are more prone to violent acts. (10) Maybe parents will pay more attention to their children's viewing if this labeling system is enacted. (11) Maybe commercial sponsors will hesitate to sponsor programs that are labeled violent, so these programs will diminish in number and children will have fewer such programs to view.

(12) Yes, I think people need to be aware of violent events happening around the world and within our own country. (13) We need to know what is happening in the Balkans, Somalia, South Africa, as well in Los Ange-

les riots and the bombings in New York, are just to name two examples. (14) However, these are real events, not glamorizations.

(15) Please keep up your campaign to get rid of excessive violence!

Sincerely,
Sue Chan

55. Which of the following is the best revision of the underlined portion of sentence 1 below?

I am writing in support of your bill that, if passed, will be instrumental in getting legislation which will put a warning label on violent television programs.

(A) in order to pass legislation in order to put

(B) passing legislation which will require putting

(C) to pass a law that will legislate putting

(D) requiring passage of legislation requiring

(E) for a law requiring

56. In the context of the sentences preceding and following sentence 3, which of the following is the best revision of sentence 3?

(A) One should agree with me that excessive violence should be detested and deplored.

(B) I detest and deplore excessive violence.

(C) You can see that I think wanton violence should be detested and deplored.

(D) Detesting and deploring wanton violence and other such excesses is how I feel.

(E) Excessive violence should be detested and deplored.

57. In relation to the passage as a whole, which of the following best describes the writer's intention in paragraph 2?

(A) To present background information

(B) To contradict popular opinion

(C) To provide supporting evidence

(D) To outline a specific category

(E) To rouse the emotions of the reader

58. Which of the following is the best revision of the underlined portion of sentence 5 below?

One of the main reasons is because violent shows are easily translated and marketed to other countries.

(A) is being that violent shows

(B) being that violent shows are

(C) is that violent shows are

(D) is due to the fact that violent shows seem to be

(E) comes from violent shows containing violence being

59. Which of the following is the best way to combine sentences 7, 8, and 9?

(A) After doing a study, the children viewing violent scenes at the National Institute of Health were more prone to violent acts.

(B) Children viewing violent scenes at the National Institute of Health were more prone to violent acts.

(C) After viewing violent scenes, children at the National Institute of Health were more prone to doing violent acts themselves.

(D) The National Institute of Health did a study proving that after viewing violent scenes, children are more prone to violent acts.

(E) The National Institute of Health did a study proving that children viewing violent scenes are more prone to violent acts.

60. Which of the following would be the best revision of the underlined portion of sentence 13?

We need to know what is happening in the Balkans, Somalia, South Africa, as well in Los Angeles riots and the bombings in New York, are just to name two examples.

(A) as well as in Los Angeles riots, and the bombings in New York just to name two examples.

(B) as well as, to name two examples, the Los Angeles riots and the bombings in New York.

(C) as well as riots in Los Angeles and the bombings in New York.

(D) as well as events such as the riots in Los Angeles and the bombings in New York.

(E) Best as it is.

SAT II: WRITING
TEST 3

ANSWER KEY

1.	(C)	16.	(C)	31.	(D)	46.	(C)
2.	(E)	17.	(D)	32.	(B)	47.	(B)
3.	(C)	18.	(B)	33.	(E)	48.	(A)
4.	(C)	19.	(C)	34.	(E)	49.	(A)
5.	(A)	20.	(C)	35.	(B)	50.	(A)
6.	(E)	21.	(B)	36.	(D)	51.	(C)
7.	(A)	22.	(B)	37.	(A)	52.	(D)
8.	(C)	23.	(C)	38.	(E)	53.	(D)
9.	(D)	24.	(C)	39.	(E)	54.	(E)
10.	(D)	25.	(C)	40.	(B)	55.	(E)
11.	(A)	26.	(A)	41.	(A)	56.	(B)
12.	(E)	27.	(A)	42.	(C)	57.	(A)
13.	(D)	28.	(D)	43.	(A)	58.	(C)
14.	(C)	29.	(E)	44.	(D)	59.	(D)
15.	(D)	30.	(A)	45.	(E)	60.	(D)

DETAILED EXPLANATIONS
OF ANSWERS

Part A: Essay

Sample Essays with Commentary

ESSAY I (Score: 5–6)

Happiness, freedom, and peace of mind are goals that everyone wants in life. Yet they are very abstract and difficult to measure. Happiness is a frame of mind that means we enjoy what we do. Freedom is the ability to do what we want, although it is limited to not doing anything that takes away freedom from other people. Peace of mind is a feeling that we are all right and that the world is a good place. How does one achieve these important goals? They can best be acquired when we try to give them to other people rather than when we try to get them ourselves.

The people who feel happiest, experience freedom, and enjoy peace of mind are most often people who are concentrating on helping others. Mother Theresa of Calcutta is an example. Because she takes care of homeless people and is so busy, she probably doesn't have time to worry about whether she is happy, free, and peaceful. She always looks cheerful in her pictures.

There are other people in history who seem to have attained the goals we all want by helping others. Jane Addams established Hull House in the slums of Chicago to help other people, and her life must have brought her great joy and peace of mind. She gave to the mothers in the neighborhood freedom to work and know that their children were being taken care of; and Jane Addams apparently had the freedom to do what she wanted to help them.

On the other hand, there are people in literature who directly tried to find happiness, freedom, and peace of mind; and they were often miserable. The two people who come to mind are Scrooge and Silas Marner. Scrooge had been selfish in the past, and he wouldn't give anything for the poor. He wasn't a bit happy even at Christmas. Later, when he began helping others, he became happy. Silas Marner was very selfish, hoarding his money and thinking it would make him happy. Only when he tried to make little Eppie happy was he able to be happy, too, even without his stolen money.

If we want to achieve happiness, freedom, and peace of mind, we should get involved in helping others so much that we forget ourselves and find joy from the people we are helping. When we try to give away the qualities we want, we find them ourselves.

ANALYSIS

Essay I has a score range of 5-6. It is well organized, with the opening paragraph serving as the introduction and stating the thesis of the paper in its last sentence. Defining the terms serves as an effective way to introduce the paper. The last paragraph concludes the essay, restating the thesis. The three middle paragraphs support the thesis with specific examples that are adequately explained and have a single focus. Transitions effectively relate the ideas. The sentence structure varies, and the vocabulary is effective. There are no major errors in sentence construction, usage, or mechanics. Although the essay would benefit from some minor revisions, it is well done considering the 20 minute time limit imposed upon the writer.

ESSAY II (Score: 4–5)

I think there is a basic problem in this quotation. I do not think that anyone can give happiness, freedom, or peace of mind to anybody. Those things have to come from inside the person, not from someone else, no matter how hard they try to give them to him. That means that the person trying to make someone else happy, free, and peacefull will be frusterated because he really can't do what he wants to do. And if he is frustrated, he won't be happy, free, and peacefull himself.

I think an example of this in history is when the missionaries went to Oregon in early United States history and tried to help the Indians, and the Indians got smallpox and then killed the missionaries. So no one was happy, free, or had a peacefull mind. That's happened with other missionaries in China and other places, too. It just wasn't possible to give happiness, freedom, and peace of mind to anyone else, and the people giving it often lost it themselves.

I know an example from my own life. My parents have tried very hard to make my little sister happy. They have done everything for her and, I'll tell you, she's so spoiled that nothing makes her happy. When they gave her a new bicycle, she was unhappy because she didn't like the color. I'd think she'd be glad just to have a nice bike. I know they never gave me one as nice as they gave her.

So I really think that whoever said the quotation was not right at all. You can't give happiness, freedom, and peace of mind to someone else at all, so you can't get those qualities by giving them.

ANALYSIS

Essay II has a score range of 4-5. It is organized clearly, with an introduction in the first paragraph, a clear statement of thesis, and a conclusion in the last paragraph. Although a few sentences are not relevant to the topic being discussed, the writer attempts to maintain one focus and to support his position with specific details. Paragraphing is good. The use of "I think" and "I know" weakens the essay, and pronouns without clear antecedents occur throughout the essay. Sentence patterns and vocabulary lack variety, and there are some errors in spelling, usage, and sentence construction. Transitions are also lacking.

ESSAY III (Score: 3–4)

I agree with the idea that you don't get happiness without trying to make other people happy. But I'm not sure that you *always* get happiness when you give it to someone else, you may try to make someone else happy and you're miserable even though you do it.

For instance, I've tried many times to make my grandmother happy. No matter what I do, she complains about me and tells my mother I should do everything different. She didn't even act like she liked my Christmas present last year, and she sure didn't make me happy either. Its just the opposite when you let someone else be free he takes away from your freedom and you don't feel free at all.

So, all in all, I think maybe sometimes you get happiness and freedom when you give it to others but most of the time things just get worse.

ANALYSIS

Essay III has a score range of 3-4. The writer attempts to introduce his topic in the first paragraph, but the thesis is not stated precisely. Although the last paragraph serves as a conclusion, it, too, lacks clarity and singleness of purpose. Paragraph 2 gives a specific illustration to develop the theme, but paragraph 3 lacks specific detail. Although there are some transitional words, the essay rambles with words and ideas repeated. In addition, the essay contains errors in usage, sentence construction, and mechanics.

ESSAY IV (Score: 1–2)

I don't think you can give happiness or piece of mind to anyone maybe you can give freedom. My folks are giving me more freedom now that I useta have, so you can give that to someone else. But nobody knows what makes me happy so I can be happy only if I decide what it is I want and go out and get it for myself. And then I'll have piece of mind, too.

Happiness don't come much but I'm happyest when I'm with a bunch of kids and we are having fun together. That's what kids like being together with other kids. but nobody gives me that kind of happiness I have to find a bunch of kids I like and than be with them. And thats real freedom, too, but nobody gave it to any of us. My folks think they can make me happy by giving me gifts but usually I don't like what they give me, and there idea of going for a ride or eating together isn't my idea of being happy.

ANALYSIS

Essay IV has a score range of 1-2. The writer states the thesis in the first sentence and maintains a consistent position, but fails to have an introductory paragraph; and there is no conclusion at all. The writer does give some specific details but rambles, failing to use the details effectively to support his thesis. In addition, there are serious errors in sentence construction like the run-on sentence in the beginning of the paper. There are also major problems with spelling, usage, and mechanics.

Part B: Multiple-Choice

1. **(C)** As you read the sentence, you should recognize the choice (C) presents an error in comparison. The comparison of two bridges requires the comparative form "longer." All of the other choices are acceptable in standard written English. Choice (A), the interrogative adjective "Which," introduces the question; choice (B), "is," agrees with its singular subject "bridge"; choice (D), "or," is a coordinating conjunction joining the names of the two bridges.

2. **(E)** The correct response to this question is choice (E). All labeled elements are choices acceptable in standard written English. Choice (A), "of proteins," is a prepositional phrase that modifies the word "function"; in choice (B), the pronoun "they "is plural to agree with its antecedent, "proteins," and the verb "come" is also plural to agree with its subject, "they"; choice (C), "plant or animal sources," is idiomatic; and Choice (D), "is," is singular to agree with its singular subject, "function."

3. **(C)** The error is choice (C), "I," which is in the nominative case. Because the words "Janice" and "I" serve as indirect objects in the sentence, the correct pronoun is the first person objective form, "me." Choice (A), "Recognizing," is a participle introducing an introductory participial phrase modifying "teacher;" choice (B), "had worked," is a verb in the past perfect tense because the action in the phrase was completed before the action in the main clause occurred; choice (D), "tomorrow," is an adverb modifying the verb "could give."

4. **(C)** The error occurs at choice (C), where the preposition "from" is idiomatic after the word "different." Although some experts insist upon the use of "from" after the adjective "different," others accept the use of "different than" in order to save words. An example would be "different than you thought"; the use of "from" would require the addition of the word "what." Choice (A), "According to," is a preposition correctly introducing a prepositional phrase; choice (B), "has," is third person singular to agree with its subject "branch"; and choice (D), "those," is a plural pronoun to agree with its antecedent "powers."

5. **(A)** Choice (A) should be a gerund in the present perfect form (having "been studied") to indicate that the action expressed by the gerund occurred before the relationship was reported. Choice (B), "preceding ten

years," is idiomatic. Choice (C), "having," is a gerund introducing the phrase "having heart attacks" which is the object of the preposition "of"; choice (D), the past tense passive verb "was reported," is singular to agree with its subject, "relationship."

6.   **(E)**   Your answer should be choice (E), indicating that this sentence contains no error in standard written English. Choice (A), "demonstrates," is present tense third person singular to agree with its subject, "book"; choice (B), "was expected," uses the third person singular form of "to be" to agree with its subject "each;" choice (C), the infinitive "to use," is idiomatic after the passive verb "was expected"; and choice (D), "his or her," is singular to agree with its antecedent, the indefinite pronoun "each," and provides gender neutrality.

7.   **(A)**   You should recognize in choice (A) that the idiomatically acceptable preposition to follow "aversion" is "to." The other choices in the sentence are acceptable in standard written English. Choice (B), "for him," is a prepositional phrase modifying "activity;" choice (C), "one," is a pronoun appropriate to refer to its antecedent "activity;" and choice (D), "that," is a relative pronoun introducing a restrictive adjective subordinate clause modifying "one."

8.   **(C)**   Choice (C) contains the error because the subject of the verb "show" is "story," a singular noun that calls for the third person singular verb, "shows." The rest of the sentence represents correct usage. Choices (A) and (B), "those" and "their," are plural pronouns that agree with the antecedent "pioneers"; choice (D), "us," is in the objective case because it is the indirect object in the sentence.

9.   **(D)**   Choice (D) presents an error in comparison, appearing to compare "farming" with "low latitudes" when what is intended is a comparison of "farming in high latitudes" with "farming in low latitudes." The corrected sentence reads: "Because of the long, cold winters and short summer growing season, farming in high latitudes is more difficult than farming in low latitudes." The other choices all represent appropriate usage in standard written English. Choice (A), "Because of," is idiomatically correct as a preposition; choice (B), "and," is a coordinating conjunction joining the nouns "winters" and "summers." Choice (C), "more difficult," is the comparative form appropriate to compare two items.

10. **(D)** The error is in choice (D). The word "contestant" is a predicate nominative in the subordinate noun clause, and it must agree in number with the plural subject of the clause, the pronoun "both," to which it refers. The noun clause should, therefore, read: "that both of us could be contestants on a quiz show." Choice (A), "I," is part of the compound subject of the introductory adverb clause and is, correctly, in the nominative case. Choice (B), "were," is plural to agree with its compound subject. Choice (C), "we," is plural to agree with its compound antecedent, "sister and I," and is in the nominative case because it is the subject of the verb "hoped."

11. **(A)** The error is in choice (A). The auxiliary verb "had" calls for the past participle form of the verb "break," which is "broken." All of the other choices are acceptable in standard written English. Choice (B), "that," is the correct relative pronoun to follow "vase" and introduce the subordinate adjective clause; choice (C), "had purchased," is the past perfect form of the verb to indicate action completed in the past before the action of the verb in the main clause; choice (D), "her," is the object of the preposition "for."

12. **(E)** This sentence contains no error in standard written English. Choice (A), the prepositional phrase "with whom," introduces an adjective clause modifying the word "people." The relative pronoun "whom" is in the objective case because it serves as the object of the preposition "with." The simple past tense "worked" is appropriate for choice (B); choice (C), "were engaged," is plural to agree with its subject "some"; choice (D) is an idiomatic expression replacing the preposition "for."

13. **(D)** Your reading of the sentence should indicate that choice (D), "were," presents an error in subject-verb agreement. A compound subject joined by "or" or "neither . . . nor" calls for a verb that agrees in number with the second part of the compound subject, which is, in this case, singular. The correct choice is the verb "was." The other answers represent correct usage. Choice (A), "Because of," is idiomatic; choices (B) and (C) are correlative conjunctions.

14. **(C)** Again the error is one of agreement of the subject and verb. Choice (C), "were," is plural; because its subject is "attack," not "reasons," which is the object of the preposition "among" and therefore cannot be the subject of the sentence, the verb should be the singular "was." Choice (A), "Among," introduces a prepositional phrase; choice (B) is an

idiomatically acceptable prepositional phrase to modify the noun "reasons;" choice (D), "naval base," poses no error in usage.

15. **(D)** Your analysis of this sentence should disclose an error in parallelism in choice (D). "Teaching" should be replaced by "to teach," an infinitive parallel with "to frighten." Both infinitives modify the noun "attempt." The other choices all represent standard usage in written English. Choice (A), "greater," is the comparative form of the adjective, correctly used to compare two items; choice (B), "their," is a plural possessive pronoun agreeing in number with its plural antecedent, "parents"; and choice (C), "than," is idiomatic to introduce the second part of the comparison.

16. **(C)** You should recognize that the possessive pronoun in choice (C), "their," is not the appropriate pronoun to use in referring to a country. Choice (A), "of living," and choice (D), "of life expectancy," are both idiomatically acceptable prepositional phrases; choice (B), "is shown," is passive and agrees in number with its singular subject, "standard."

17. **(D)** Choice (D), "white and bluish gray in color," is the third in a series of objects of the verb "has." The error lies in its lack of parallelism with the other two objects, "eyes" and "body." Corrected, the sentence reads: "The snow leopard is a wild mammal in Central Asia that has large eyes, a four-foot body, and a white and bluish gray color." The other choices are all acceptable in standard written English. Choice (A), "is," is singular to agree with its subject "leopard." Choice (B), "that has," is composed of the relative pronoun "that" referring to the noun "mammal," and the verb "has," that agrees with its subject in number. Choice (C), "and," is a coordinating conjunction correctly used to join the three objects of the verb.

18. **(B)** You should recognize that choice (B), "and," is not the correct correlative conjunction to follow "either." The correct word is "or." The other choices all represent acceptable choices in standard written English. Choice (A), "a young person," is correctly placed immediately after the introductory participial phrase that modifies it; choice (C), "him," is singular to agree with its antecedent "person" and objective because it is the object of the verb "make." Choice (D), "most important," is in the superlative form because the comparison involves more than two choices.

19. **(C)**   Choice (C), "to fail," is incorrect in standard written English. The sentence contains two parallel ideas that should be expressed with the same grammatical form. Because "Failing" is a gerund, the "infinitive" to "fail" should be replaced with "failing" to make the construction parallel. Choice (A), "is," agrees in number with its subject, "student"; choice (B), "is," agrees in number with its subject, "Failing"; choice (D) is singular to agree with its antecedent, "student," and indicates no sexual preference.

20. **(C)**   You should recognize that choice (C), "or," is in error because the correlative conjunction that should follow "neither" is "nor." All other choices are correct. Choice (A), "had grown up," is idiomatically acceptable and it and choice (B), "had been," are in the past perfect tense to indicate that the actions occurred before the action mentioned in the main clause; choice (D), "vividly," is an adverb correctly modifying the verb "portrayed."

21. **(B)**   As you read the sentence, you should recognize that choice (B) is incorrect because "that" is the relative pronoun that should introduce a noun clause following "reason"; another option would be to revise the sentence by omitting the words "The reason," but that is not an option provided on this test. Choice (A), "his," is the correct possessive pronoun to refer to "Jason." Choice (C), "such stage fright," is idiomatic and choice (D) is the relative pronoun, subject, and verb of an adjective clause modifying "fright."

22. **(B)**   Your recognition that the word "less" is used with a singular noun and the word "fewer" is appropriate before a plural noun will lead you to locate the error in choice (B). Choice (A) is an introductory participial phrase, correctly followed by the pronoun it modifies. Choice (C) is the comparative adverb, the correct choice to compare two people ("anyone else" is singular), and choice (D) is idiomatic as a singular indefinite pronoun.

23. **(C)**   You should recognize that the verb "want" in choice (C) does not agree with its subject "who," a pronoun that is singular to agree with its antecedent, "adult." The word ordering used in choices (A), (B), and (D) are all idiomatic in standard written English.

24. **(C)**   As you read the sentence, you should recognize that the pronoun "this" in choice (C) does not have a clear antecedent in the sentence.

The other choices are all correct in standard written English. Choice (A), "along with," is idiomatic and serves as one preposition. Choice (B), "those," has as its antecedent "advantages" and choice (D), "has made," is in the present perfect tense because the action began in the past and continues into the present.

25. **(C)** You should find the error at choice (C), where the adverb "frequently" is needed to modify the adjective "repetitious; frequent" is an adjective and does not correctly modify another adjective. Choice (A), the pronoun "who," correctly refers to its antecedent "Students"; choice (B), the adverb "generally," modifies the verb; and choice (D) is a relative pronoun "that" and its verb, "is provided," that comprise the adjective clause modify "menu."

26. **(A)** Choice (A) is not idiomatic in standard written English; the word "understanding" should be followed by "of," not "on." All of the other choices are correct. The verb in choice (B), "has changed," agrees in number with its singular subject, "understanding," and is in the present perfect tense to show action that occurred in the past and continues to the present; choice (C), "and," is the coordinating conjunction joining members of a series; and choice (D), "have described," agrees in number with its compound subject and is also in the present perfect tense.

27. **(A)** The error is in choice (A), where correct usage calls for "had" instead of "would have" following an introductory adverb clause beginning with "if." All of the other choices are correct. Choice (B), the prepositional phrase "by the United States Senate," modifies the adjective "guilty"; choice (C), "would have," is correct in the main clause following the "if" clause; and choice (D), "from office," is a prepositional phrase modifying the verb.

28. **(D)** You should recognize the error in choice (D), "the cherry tree," which is decidedly "not" a myth in itself; to make the sentence correct, you must insert a noun or pronoun to serve as a predicate nominative following the linking verb "is." Otherwise, the choices are correct in standard written English. "Perhaps," choice (A), is an adverb and is idiomatic. Choice (B), "about an American President," is a prepositional phrase modifying "myths"; and choice (C), "is," agrees in number with its subject, "one."

29. **(E)**　This sentence contains no error in standard written English. Choice (A), "who," agrees in number with its antecedent and is in the nominative case because it serves as the subject of the subordinate adjective clause. Choice (B), "was appointed," is singular to agree with its subject "who," the antecedent of which is singular. Choice (C), "was," is singular to agree with its subject "woman"; and choice (D), "of Arizona," is an adjective clause.

30. **(A)**　The error occurs in choice (A), where "maneuver for lowering" is not idiomatic in standard English; "to lower" should follow "maneuver." The other choices are correct. Choice (B), "at which," introduces the adjective clause and the pronoun "which" has as its antecedent "altitude." Choice (C), the verb "was flying," correctly agrees in number with its subject "plane"; and choice (D), "shaking and shuddering," is composed of two gerunds that are the compound object of the preposition "in."

31. **(D)**　Because the verb "protest" can be transitive and have a direct object, choice (D) avoids awkward wordiness and use of the unnecessary preposition "about." Choices (B) and (E) include unnecessary words and uses the pronoun "they" that has no clear antecedent; choice (C) is also unnecessarily wordy and contains the repetitious words, "builders should build."

32. **(B)**　Choice (B) best shows the causal relationship between sibling opportunities and their placement in the family, their abilities, and their personalities, and retains the subordination of the original sentence. Choices (A) and (E) provide dangling phrases. Choice (C) with its use of the coordinating conjunction "and" treats the lack of opportunity and its cause as if they are equal ideas and does not show the causal relationship between them, and choice (D) results in a run-on sentence.

33. **(E)**　Only choice (E) corrects the two major problems in the sentence, the lack of subject-verb agreement and the lack of parallelism. In choices (A), (B), and (C), the verb "is" does not agree with its plural subject, "provisions." Choices (A) and (D) have unlike constructions serving as predicate nominatives, the noun "freedom" and the clause "that citizens are guaranteed a trial by jury." Choice (E) correctly uses the plural verb "are" to agree with the plural subject, and the predicate nominative is composed of two parallel nouns, "freedom" and "guarantee."

34. **(E)**   The errors found in the original sentence, choice (A), involve parallelism and redundancy. Choice (E) uses the parallel infinitives "to entertain" and "to teach" as direct objects and eliminates the repetition created in use of both "tried" and "attempt" in the original sentence. Choices (B) and (C) provide parallel construction, but choice (B) retains the redundancy and choice (C) incorrectly splits the infinitive "to entertain;" although choice (D) provides parallelism of the nouns "entertainment" and "attempt," the redundancy still remains, and the word order is not idiomatic.

35. **(B)**   Choice (B) adequately conveys the reason for removal of the parking meters with the least wordiness. Choices (A) and (D) contain unnecessary words; choices (C) and (E) have dangling participial phrases.

36. **(D)**   Choice (D), in which "Megan" correctly follows the phrase, conveys the meaning with the least wordiness. The problem with choice (A) is the introductory participial phrase; it must be eliminated or followed immediately by the word modified. Choice (B) does not solve the problem of the dangling phrase; choices (C) and (E) add words unnecessary to the meaning of the sentence.

37. **(A)**   The given sentence is acceptable in standard written English. Each of the alternate choices introduces a problem. Choice (B) uses the superlative form of the adjective, "most interested," when the comparative form "more interested" is correct for the comparison of two options; choices (C) and (E) introduce a lack of parallelism and choice (D) is not idiomatic.

38. **(E)**   The noun clause in choice (E) is idiomatically acceptable. The use of "Whether" in choices (A) and (B) leads the writer to add "or not," words that contribute nothing to the meaning and result in awkwardness of construction. In choice (C), "the fact of whether," is not idiomatic, and choice (D) with its awkward gerund phrase is also not idiomatic.

39. **(E)**   This sentence presents two problems, namely use of a preposition instead of a coordinating conjunction to join the objects of the participle "having studied" and failure to show a time relationship. Choice (E) corrects both problems. Choice (B) simply replaces the preposition "along with" by "as well as"; choice (C) unnecessarily repeats the conjunction "and" rather than using the quite appropriate series construction. None of the choices (A), (B), (C), or (D) correctly shows the time relationship.

40. **(B)**   This sentence contains the ambiguous pronoun "they," for which there is no antecedent and fails to show the relationship of the ideas expressed. Choice (B) eliminates the clause with the ambiguous pronoun and correctly expresses the reason for the sandbag placement. Choice (C) suggests that the two clauses joined by "and" are equal and does not show the subordinate relationship of the second to the first. Choice (D) introduces a dangling phrase with a coordinating conjunction, "and," that suggests the joining of equals, and choice (E) retains both errors from the original sentence.

41. **(A)**   This sentence is correct in standard written English. Choices (B) and (C) introduce unnecessary words that add nothing to the meaning and make the sentence awkward and wordy; choices (D) and (E) do not correctly show relationship.

42. **(C)**   Choice (C) shows the relationship accurately and eliminates the awkward gerund construction as the object of the preposition "despite." The adjective clause in choice (B) fails to show the relationship of the original sentence; choice (D) introduces the superfluous words "the fact that." Choice (E) inappropriately places the qualifying information in equal and parallel construction to the main idea of the sentence.

43. **(A)**   This sentence is correct in standard written English. Choices (B) and (C) lose the strength of the parallelism in choice (A). Choice (D), although containing parallel construction, is idiomatically awkward with its participial phrases. Choices (B), (C), and (E) all exhibit wordiness.

44. **(D)**   The original sentence, choice (A), contains the obvious and redundant words "was a man who." Choices (B), (C), and (E) are also unnecessarily verbose. Choice (D) makes the statement in the most direct way possible and represents correct standard usage.

45. **(E)**   Choice (E) eliminates the awkward participial phrase with its passive verb, and, in direct fashion, clearly shows the desired relationship. Choices (A), (B), and (D) retain the awkward construction; choice (C) is repetitious, wordy, and not idiomatic.

46. **(C)**   The error in this sentence involves the use of the pronoun "which," that refers not to a single antecedent but to the entire main clause in the sentence. A pronoun should have a single noun or pronoun as its antecedent. Choice (C) most economically shows the causal relationship

of the original sentence and effectively eliminates the pronoun altogether. Although choice (B) eliminates unnecessary words, the basic problem remains; choice (D) is also wordy and repetitive; and choice (E) is not idiomatic.

47. **(B)**   The problem in this sentence involves the need for consistent pronoun use and for parallel construction. Because the portion of the sentence not underlined uses the pronouns "you" and "your," the first part of the sentence must also use the second person pronoun. Choice (B) alone accomplishes that consistency and yet retains parallel construction.

48. **(A)**   This sentence contains no error in standard written English. Each of the possible revisions makes no real improvement, and choice (B) adds an error in subject-verb agreement. Choice (C) creates confusion in pronoun reference with the addition of "themselves," and choices (D) and (E) are not idiomatic.

49. **(A)**   Choice (A) is the best condensation of the wordy portion. Choice (B) and choice (D) omit the time period. Choice (C) is redundant, repeating the "conflict" idea twice. Choice (E) is almost as wordy and repetitive as the original.

50. **(A)**   Choice (A) reduces wordiness through two means: deleting a subordinate clause by eliminating "What" and deleting a prepositional phrase by converting it to a possessive. Choice (B) keeps the subordinate clause. Choice (C) creates an incorrect sentence structure. Choice (D) trivializes the serious conflicts by using the word "novelty," which has light connotations. Choice (E) changes the focus of the action from the Army.

51. **(C)**   Choice (C) is the best reduction of the wordy original. Choice (A) uses "alot" and choice (B) uses "a lot," both of which are not formal usage to mean "much." Choice (D) is almost wordier than the original. Choice (E) is a bit stiff for the tone of the article.

52. **(D)**   Choice (D) presents the ideas correctly and concisely. Choices (A) and (C) use the awkward phrase "because of." Choice (B) sounds as if the first part of the sentence is unrelated to the last part. Choice (E) repeats the verb "earned" twice.

53. **(D)**   Paragraph 4 is a conclusion (D), winding up the main idea, the good relationship between Crook and Indian soldiers. Choice (A) is not correct as there is no specific incident given. Choice (B) could be a second choice, but the best features of the subject are more fully discussed earlier in the paper. Choice (C) has no bearing on this essay. Choice (E) could be a choice if there were a recounting of the main points, but the major ideas of the last paragraph are the faith Crook and the Apaches had in one another and the uniqueness of their relationship.

54. **(E)**   The past progressive tense is best, as it expresses Crook's use of the scouts as a common occurrence, not as a single event, which may be implied by the past tense in the original. (A) eliminates "and" which further confuses the sentence and does not help the verb problem. (B) makes it sound even more like a singular occurrence. (C) changes only the first verb to the progressive. (D) is not incorrect, but does not clarify the sentence any, and lets the verb tense stand.

55. **(E)**   Choice (E) is the clearest and most concise rewording of the sentence portion. Choice (A) repeats the phrase, "in order to," and choice (D) contains repetition of "requiring." Choice (B) and choice (C) both contain unnecessary wordiness in the clauses beginning with "which will" and "that will."

56. **(B)**   Choice (B) keeps the first person voice and states the main point using parallel structure and concise language. Choices (A), (C), and (D) are still excessively wordy; in addition, choice (A) changes the voice to "one." Choice (E), while somewhat more concise, uses passive voice; since this letter is a call to action, passive voice weakens the argument and intent of the letter.

57. **(A)**   Paragraph 2 provides background information, choice (A), for the reason there is so much violence on television. Choice (B) is incorrect as the argument in paragraph 2 is not a contradiction to anything. Choice (C) would be correct if the paragraph contained support for the main argument. While the paragraph does give some specifics, choice (D), the evidence cannot be considered as categorizing anything. Choice (E) incorrectly implies that the paragraph is written in an emotionally charged manner.

58. **(C)**   Although choice (C) employs two forms of the verb "to be," it is the best wording. Choices (A) and (B) both use the weak phrase "being

that" and create fragments. Choice (D) is far too wordy and uses the weak wording "seem to be"; use of the word "seem" makes the writer appear uncertain and tentative, not precise. Choice (E) is still too wordy, using the phrase "shows containing violence" instead of the more concise phrase "violent shows."

59. **(D)** Choice (D) is the most concise combination, one which clearly shows time sequence and cause-and-effect. Choice (A), because it has a misplaced modifier, implies that the children conducted the study. Choices (B) and (E) imply that the children were prone to violence only while they were viewing the violent acts, a slight distortion of the correct finding. Choice (C) subtly suggests that only the children at the Institute were affected by this condition, with the implication that other children are not. This failure to indicate an extension of the findings subtly distorts the original meaning.

60. **(D)** (D) would be the best revision; the phrase "are just to name two examples," besides being grammatically incorrect, is unnecessary, and the structure of (D) sets up the parallel best. (B) is the next best, but "to name two examples" is awkward and unnecessary. (A) and (C) are not specific about any particular riots (these would at least need the article "the" as in (B) and (D).

SAT II: Writing

Practice Test 4

SAT II: WRITING
TEST 4

Part A: Essay

TIME: 20 Minutes

DIRECTIONS: You have 20 minutes to plan and write an essay on the topic below. You may write only on the assigned topic.

Make sure to give specific examples to support your thesis. Proofread your essay carefully and take care to express your ideas clearly and effectively.

Write your essay on the lined pages at the back of the book.

ESSAY TOPIC:

The end justifies the means.

ASSIGNMENT: Do you agree or disagree with the statement? Support your opinion with specific examples from history, current events, literature, or personal experience.

Part B: Multiple-Choice

(Answer sheets appear in the back of this book.)

TIME: 40 Minutes
                60 Questions

DIRECTIONS: Each of the following sentences may contain an error in diction, usage, idiom, or grammar. Some sentences are correct. Some sentences contain one error. No sentence contains more than one error.

If there is an error, it will appear in one of the underlined portions labeled A, B, C, or D. If there is no error, choose the portion labeled E. If there is an error, select the letter of the portion that must be changed in order to correct the sentence.

EXAMPLE:

He drove <u>slowly</u> and <u>cautiously</u> in order to <u>hopefully</u> avoid having an
                   A   **B**   **C**

<u>accident</u>. <u>No error</u>.
       D   **E**

---

1.   Each campus appointed <u>their</u> own committee to apply the <u>findings of</u>
                                              A   **B**

      the city-wide survey concerning ways <u>in which</u> the school district <u>can</u>
                                                                    C   **D**

      save money. <u>No error</u>.
                            E

2.   When <u>I</u> asked Gary and John what would be <u>good</u> for dinner, the
                A   **B**

      boys said they <u>could care less</u> <u>about eating</u> liver for the main dish
                                  C   **D**

      with spinach for a vegetable. <u>No error</u>.
                                                        E

3.   John will be <u>liable for</u> damages to Mrs. Simon's car because he was
                            A

fascinated by his new red truck and driving so fast that he failed to
  B   C

conform to a law limiting the speed of any vehicle within the city
  D

limits. No error.
    E

4. I have seen, more than anything else, that self-esteem is a problem in
   A   B   C   D

   many people of all ages and nationalities. No error.
                  E

5. Mr. Burgess made sure the ten-year-olds were accommodated with
                    A

   quarters for a video games party; afterwards, he declined to say how
                       B

   much the event cost him but allowed as how it was more than he
              C

   had expected. No error.
    D   E

6. This afternoon's boating accident having turned out differently
            A   B

   through the efforts of Jack Williams, a fellow vacationer who knows
                     C

   CPR, so the little girl has survived. No error.
     D   E

7. Three hundred years ago John Milton protested against laws which
       A   B

   required a government official to approve of any manuscript before it
              C D

   was published. No error.
        E

8. Frequently called the "Fourth Estate," journalists have rapidly
      A   B

   developed into powerful people, influencing public opinion and gov-
    C

   ernment policy that has a bearing on the course of history. No error.
         D   E

9. Totaling <u>more than expected</u>, the groom's wedding expenses
             A

 <u>included</u> hiring a limousine for the trip to the airport after the wed-
   B

 ding, <u>buying gifts</u> for his groomsmen, and <u>a tuxedo</u> for the ceremony.
       C   **D**

 <u>No error</u>.
   E

10. <u>Our viewing</u> these photographs of Dad standing in front of the throne
      A

 at Macchu Pichu <u>brings</u> back pleasant memories for <u>we</u> children,
              B   **C**

 reminding us <u>of the need for</u> more family get-togethers. <u>No error</u>.
          D   **E**

11. Finally confessing to the <u>theft of</u> money collected for a class movie,
                A

 Jules said <u>he only</u> stole money once in his life and <u>his</u> conscience
        B   **C**

 would not allow <u>him</u> to enjoy spending it. <u>No error</u>.
         D   **E**

12. If <u>a person</u> is a criminal, <u>he</u> should be punished for <u>it</u>; unfortunately,
    A   **B**   **C**

 many criminals are <u>never</u> caught. <u>No error</u>.
         D   **E**

13. An intriguing habit many hawks have <u>is bringing</u> a fresh green
                        A

 branch <u>daily</u> to line the nest <u>during the season</u> in which <u>they</u> are
     B   **C**   **D**

 mating and rearing their young. <u>No error</u>.
                   E

14. Hawks and owls can be seen <u>more frequent</u> in populated areas than
                   A

 <u>most people</u> <u>suppose</u>, and it is <u>possible</u> to hear screech owls at night
   B   **C**   **D**

 when the adult birds feed their chicks. <u>No error</u>.
                        E

15. The grass was <u>growing over</u> the curb and the oak tree had a branch
             A

    hanging almost <u>to</u> the ground, so we decided to trim <u>it</u> before the
             B   **C**

    neighbors became <u>annoyed with us</u>. <u>No error</u>.
             D   **E**

16. Charles Draper developed the <u>theory of</u> and invented the <u>technology</u>
             A   **B**

    <u>for</u> inertial navigation, a guidance system <u>which</u> does not <u>rely on</u>
    C   **C**   **D**

    external sources. <u>No error</u>.
             E

17. Inertial navigation is a system of navigation <u>employed</u> in submarines
                                     A

    when <u>they are</u> underwater, missiles used <u>for</u> defense purposes, air-
           B   **C**

    craft, and <u>to get</u> man to the moon in the Apollo exploration series.
             D

    <u>No error</u>.
    E

18. Much <u>to</u> <u>everyone's</u> surprise, the company president, <u>known for</u> his
           A   **B**   **C**

    intelligence and good business judgment, <u>and enjoying</u> a hobby of
                                     D

    sky diving. <u>No error</u>.
             E

19. <u>They</u> are very <u>grateful the city</u> has <u>set up</u> a special fund which <u>helps</u>
    A   **B**   **C**   **D**

    <u>pay</u> for electric bills of the elderly and the handicapped. <u>No error</u>.
    E (pay)   **E**

20. <u>In order to</u> stay cool during the summer months, Americans <u>not only</u>
    A   **B**

    are using ceiling fans, but they are also using devices <u>to add humidity</u>
                                                     C

    to the air in <u>particularly</u> arid climates such as Arizona. <u>No error</u>.
             D   **E**

21. <u>After seeing</u> the technique demonstrated on television, Janie baked
      A

    homemade bread for the first time yesterday, <u>and her</u> brother thought
                                             B

    it tasted <u>good,</u> an opinion everyone <u>agreed with</u>. <u>No error</u>.
           C   **D**   **E**

22. Although not <u>so</u> prevalent as they once were, <u>hood</u> ornaments still
            A   **B**

    exist, <u>some of which</u> are quite distinctive, <u>such as</u> the symbol for
           C   **D**

    Mercedes-Benz and Jaguar. <u>No error</u>.
                          E

23. If I <u>were</u> that tourist, I would not <u>argue with</u> those two members of
       A   **B**

    the Guardia Civil because, although they are <u>speaking politely</u>, it is
                                              C

    obvious they are <u>becoming angry</u>. <u>No error</u>.
                   D   **E**

24. Mr. Burns is fully <u>aware of</u> statistics proving the <u>harmful</u> conse-
                  A   **B**

    quences of smoking; <u>irregardless</u>, he <u>persists</u> in his habit. <u>No error</u>.
                 C   **D**   **E**

25. David was not capable <u>to win</u> the singles tennis match because he
                 A

    <u>had been</u> injured <u>in</u> a game last week and the doctor prohibited him
      B   **C**

    <u>from</u> playing for two weeks. <u>No error</u>.
    D   **E**

26. <u>In spite of</u> the doctor's orders, David is playing tennis today because
      A

    he is <u>one of those</u> athletes who <u>are</u> determined to play, no matter what
          B   **C**

    the <u>coach and she</u> say. <u>No error</u>.
       D   **E**

27. Although <u>unequal in</u> ability compared to other team members, Wilt
            A

    <u>practices</u> his free throws every <u>afternoon</u> so he would become a
     B   **C**

    <u>member of</u> the varsity squad. <u>No error</u>.
     D   **E**

28. If you <u>would have</u> listened to me <u>carefully</u>, you would have heard me
         A   **B**

    <u>advise against</u> your <u>subscribing to</u> the magazine of that ultra-conser-
      C   **D**

    vative political group. <u>No error</u>.
                E

29. A graduating high school senior who <u>wants to attend</u> a university
                A

    must <u>attend to</u> many details, such as taking the SAT or ACT, sending
      B

    an official transcript to the university, <u>arranging for</u> a dormitory
             C

    room, <u>and etc</u>. <u>No error</u>.
       D   **E**

30. <u>Running</u> errands for upperclassmen, pushing pennies, and being
     A

    <u>thrown in</u> mud holes are all <u>factors of</u> being hazed <u>as</u> a freshman.
      B   **C**   **D**
    <u>No error</u>.
     E

DIRECTIONS: In each of the following sentences, some portion of the sentence is underlined. Under each sentence are five choices. The first choice has the same wording as the original. The other four choices are reworded. Sometimes the first choice containing the original wording is the best; sometimes one of the other choices is the best. Choose the letter of the best choice. Your choice should produce a sentence which is not ambiguous or awkward and which is correct, clear, and precise.

This is a test of correct and effective English expression. Keep in mind the standards of English usage, punctuation, grammar, word choice, and construction.

EXAMPLE:

When you listen to opera, <u>a person may not appreciate it.</u>

(A)   a person may not appreciate it.

(B)   it may not be appreciated by a person.

(C)   which may not be appreciated by one.

(D)   you may not appreciate it.

(E)   appreciating it may be a problem for you.

31. The new secretary proved herself <u>to be not only capable and efficient but also a woman who was adept</u> at working under pressure and handling irate customers.

   (A) to be not only capable and efficient but also a woman who was adept

   (B) not only to be capable or efficient but also a woman who was adept

   (C) not only to be capable and efficient but also a woman who was adept

   (D) to be not only capable and efficient but also adept

   (E) to be not only capable and efficient but also an adept woman

32. Hunting, if properly managed and carefully controlled, can cull excess animals, thereby producing a healthier population of wild game.

    (A) Hunting, if properly managed and carefully controlled

    (B) Managing it wisely, carefully controlled hunting

    (C) Managed properly hunting that is carefully controlled

    (D) Properly and wisely controlled, careful hunting

    (E) If properly managed, hunting, carefully controlled

33. In spite of my reservations, I agreed on the next day to help her put up new wallpaper.

    (A) I agreed on the next day to help her put up new wallpaper.

    (B) I agreed on the next day to help put up her new wallpaper.

    (C) I agreed to help her put up new wallpaper on the next day.

    (D) I, on the next day, agreed to help her put up new wallpaper.

    (E) I agreed to, on the next day, help her put up new wallpaper.

34. We saw many of, though not nearly all, the existing Roman ruins along the Mediterranean coastline of Africa.

    (A) We saw many of, though not nearly all, the existing Roman ruins

    (B) We saw many, though not nearly all, of the existing Roman ruins

    (C) Seeing many, though not nearly all, of the existing Roman ruins

    (D) Having seen many of, though not nearly all, the existing Roman ruins

    (E) Many of, though not nearly all, the existing Roman ruins we saw

35. The horned owl is a carnivore who hunts a diversity of creatures, like hares, grouse, and ground squirrels.

    (A) The horned owl is a carnivore who hunts a diversity of creatures, like

    (B) The horned owl, a carnivore who hunts a diversity of creatures like

(C) A hunting carnivore, the horned owl likes a diversity of creatures

(D) The horned owl likes a diversity of carnivorous creatures, such
as

(E) The horned owl is a carnivore who hunts a diversity of creatures,
such as

36. In many of his works Tennessee Williams, <u>of whom much has been
written,</u> has as main characters drifters, dreamers, and those who are
crushed by having to deal with reality.

(A) of whom much has been written

(B) of who much has been written

(C) of whom much has been written about

(D) about him much having been written

(E) much having been written about him

37. The world history students wanted to know <u>where the Dead Sea was
at and what it was famous for</u>.

(A) where the Dead Sea was at and what it was famous for.

(B) where the Dead Sea is at and for what it is famous.

(C) where the Dead Sea is located and why it is famous.

(D) at where the Dead Sea was located and what it was famous for.

(E) the location of the Dead Sea and what it is famous for.

38. Literary historians <u>cannot help but admit that they do not know</u>
whether poetry or drama is the oldest form of literature.

(A) cannot help but admit that they do not know

(B) cannot admit that they do not admit to knowing

(C) cannot help admitting that they do not know

(D) cannot help but to admit that they do not know

(E) cannot know but admit that they do not

39. Getting to know a person's parents <u>will often provide an insight to</u> his personality and behavior.

    (A) will often provide an insight to

    (B) will often provide an insight into

    (C) will often provide an insight for

    (D) will provide often an insight for

    (E) often will provide an insight with

40. Upon leaving the nursery, Mr. Greene, together with his wife, <u>put the plants in the trunk of the car they had just bought</u>.

    (A) put the plants in the trunk of the car they had just bought.

    (B) put in the plants to the trunk of the car they had just bought.

    (C) put into the trunk of the car they had just bought the plants.

    (D) put the plants they had just bought in the trunk of the car.

    (E) put the plants into the trunk of the car.

41. The way tensions are increasing in the Middle East, some experts <u>are afraid we may end up with a nuclear war</u>.

    (A) are afraid we may end up with a nuclear war.

    (B) being afraid we may end up with a nuclear war.

    (C) afraid that a nuclear war may end up over there.

    (D) are afraid a nuclear war may end there.

    (E) are afraid a nuclear war may occur.

42. <u>Whether Leif Erickson was the first to discover America or not</u> is still a debatable issue, but there is general agreement that there probably were a number of "discoveries" through the years.

    (A) Whether Leif Erickson was the first to discover America or not

    (B) That Leif Erickson was the first to discover America

    (C) That Leif Erickson may have been the first to have discovered America

(D) Whether Leif Erickson is the first to discover America or he is not

(E) Whether or not Leif Erickson was or was not the first discoverer of America

43. <u>People who charge too much are likely to develop</u> a bad credit rating.

(A) People who charge too much are likely to develop

(B) People's charging too much are likely to develop

(C) When people charge too much, likely to develop

(D) That people charge too much is likely to develop

(E) Charging too much is likely to develop for people

44. The museum of natural science has a special exhibit of gems and minerals, <u>and the fifth graders went to see it on a field trip.</u>

(A) and the fifth graders went to see it on a field trip.

(B) and seeing it were the fifth graders on a field trip.

(C) when the fifth graders took a field trip to see it.

(D) which the fifth graders took a field trip to see.

(E) where the fifth graders took their field trip to see it.

45. <u>When the case is decided, he plans appealing</u> if the verdict is unfavorable.

(A) When the case is decided, he plans appealing

(B) When deciding the case, he plans appealing

(C) After the case is decided, he is appealing

(D) After deciding the case, he is planning to appeal

(E) When the case is decided, he plans to appeal

46. <u>We decided there was hardly any reason for his allowing us</u> to stay up later on weeknights.

(A) We decided there was hardly any reason for his allowing us

(B) We, deciding there was hardly any reason for his allowing us,

(C) Deciding there was hardly any reason, we allowed

(D) We decided there were none of the reasons for him to allow us

(E) For him to allow us there was hardly any reason we decided

47. At this time <u>it is difficult for me agreeing with your plan of having everyone</u> in the club working on the same project.

    (A) it is difficult for me agreeing with your plan of having everyone

    (B) I find it difficult to agree to your plan of having everyone

    (C) for my agreement with your plan is difficult for everyone

    (D) an agreement to your plan seems difficult for everyone

    (E) finding it difficult for me to agree to your plan of having everyone

48. When the Whites hired a contractor to do remodeling on their home, he <u>promised to completely finish the work inside of three months</u>.

    (A) promised to completely finish the work inside of three months.

    (B) promised to complete the work within three months.

    (C) completely promised to finish the work inside of three months' line span.

    (D) promising to completely finish the work in three months.

    (E) completely finished the work within three months.

DIRECTIONS: The following passages are considered early draft efforts of a student. Some sentences need to be rewritten to make the ideas clearer and more precise.

Read each passage carefully and answer the questions that follow. Some of the questions are about particular sentences or parts of sentences and ask you to make decisions about sentence structure, diction, and usage. Some of the questions refer to the entire essay or parts of the essay and ask you to make decisions about organization, development, appropriateness of language, audience, and logic. Choose the answer that most effectively makes the intended meaning clear and follows the requirements of standard written English. After you have chosen your answer, fill in the corresponding oval on your answer sheet.

EXAMPLE:

(1) On the one hand, I think television is bad, But it also does some good things for all of us. (2) For instance, my little sister thought she wanted to be a policemen until she saw police shows on television.

Which of the following is the best revision of the underlined portion of sentence 1 below?

On the one hand, I think television <u>is bad, But it also</u> does some good things for all of us.

(A) is bad; But it also

(B) is bad. but is also

(C) is bad, and it also

(D) is bad, but it also

(E) is bad because it also

Questions 49–54 are based on the following passage.

(1) Actually, the term "Native Americans" is incorrect. (2) Indians migrated to this continent from other areas, just earlier then Europeans did. (3) The ancestors of the Anasazi—Indians of the four-state area of Colorado, New Mexico, Utah, and Arizona—probably crossed from Asia into Alaska. (4) About 25,000 years ago while the continental land bridge still existed. (5) This land bridge arched across the Bering Strait in the last Ice Age. (6) About A.D. 500 the ancestors of the Anasazi moved onto the Mesa Verde a high plateau in the desert country of Colorado. (7) The Wetherills, five brothers who ranched the area, is generally given credit

for the first exploration of the ruins in the 1870s and 1880s. (8) There were some 50,000 Anasazi thriving in the four-corners area by the 1200s. (9) At their zenith A.D. 700 to 1300, the Anasazi had established widespread communities and built thousands of sophisticated structures—cliff dwellings, pueblos, and kivas. (10) They even engaged in trade with Indians in surrounding regions by exporting pottery and other goods.

49. Which of the following best corrects the grammatical error in sentence 7?

   (A) The Wetherills, a group of five brothers who ranched in the area, is generally given credit for the first exploration of the ruins in the 1870s and 1880s.

   (B) The Wetherills, five brothers who ranched in the area, are generally given credit for the first exploration of the ruins in the 1870s and 1880s.

   (C) The Wetherills are generally given credit for the first exploration of the ruins in the 1870s and 1880s, five brothers who ranched in the area.

   (D) The Wetherills, generally given credit for the first exploration of the area, is five brothers who ranched in the area.

   (E) Best as it is.

50. Which of the following sentences would best fit between sentences 9 and 10 of the passage?

   (A) Artifacts recovered from the area suggest that the Anasazi were artistic, religious, agricultural, classless, and peaceful.

   (B) By 12,000 to 10,000 B.C., some Indians had established their unique cultures in the southwest.

   (C) The Navaho called their ancestors the Anasazi, the Ancient Ones.

   (D) I think it is unfortunate that such a unique and innovative culture should have disappeared from the country.

   (E) Before Columbus reached the New World, the Anasazi had virtually disappeared.

51. Which of the following is an incomplete sentence?

    (A) 4   (D) 7

    (B) 5   (E) 10

    (C) 6

52. Which of the following best corrects the underline portion of sentence 9?

    <u>At their zenith A.D. 700 to 1300</u>, the Anasazi has established widespread communities and built thousands of sophisticated structures—cliff dwellings, pueblos, and kivas.

    (A) At their zenith which was from A.D. 700 to 1300

    (B) At their zenith B.C. 700 to 1300

    (C) At their zenith, from A.D. 700 to 1300,

    (D) At their zenith, being A.D. 700 to 1300,

    (E) At their zenith, of A.D. 700 to 1300,

53. Which of the following would be the best way to punctuate sentence 6?

    (A) About A.D. 500, the ancestors of the Anasazi moved onto the Mesa Verde a high plateau, in the desert country of Colorado.

    (B) About A.D. 500 the ancestors of the Anasazi moved, onto the Mesa Verde: a high plateau in the desert country of Colorado

    (C) About A.D. 500 the ancestors of the Anasazi moved onto the Mesa Verde: a high plateau, in the desert country of Colorado.

    (D) About A.D. 500, the ancestors of the Anasazi moved onto the Mesa Verde, a high plateau in the desert country of Colorado.

    (E) Best as it is.

54. Which of the following sentences contains a spelling/grammatical error?

    (A) 1   (D) 10

    (B) 2   (E) 5

    (C) 3

Questions 55–60 are based on the following passage.

(1) A growing number of businesses are providing day care facilities for the children of their employees. (2) Some companies charge a standard fee, but most provide the day care free or at a nominal cost. (3) These care programs provide services that continue through the early teens of the children. (4) If they should help with day care at all is what many companies are trying to decide. (5) In the event parents need to work overtime, centers are even open on weekends, and some companies <u>showing</u> special initiative in building company loyalty of each employee by making arrangements for special field trips to zoos and museums. (6) Is this kind of care really necessary? (7) Should businesses really be in the business of day care.

(8) Experts in the field cite many advantages for this system. (9) Therefore, loyalty to the company is built, so morale climbs. (10) Studies show that when a company helps its employees blend parent and worker roles, absenteeism and tardiness drop. (11) In addition, workers feel the company has taken more of a personal interest in them. (12) Most companies also provide various health care programs for their employees. (13) Turnover becomes a much less significant factor for managers. (14) Human resource managers also estimate that every $1 spent on these programs returns $2 or more in increased productivity.

55. Which of the following best improves the underlined portion of sentence 3?

    These care programs provide services that <u>continue through the early teens of the children.</u>

    (A) continue, through the early teens, of the children.

    (B) continue through the children and their early teens.

    (C) continue through the children's early teens.

    (D) continue on through the early teens of the children.

    (E) Best as it is.

56. Which of the following would be a better way to structure sentence 4?

    (A) What many companies are trying to decide is if they should help with day care at all.

(B) Unsure if they should help with day care at all, many companies are trying to decide.

(C) Many companies, unsure if they should help with day care at all, are trying to decide.

(D) Many companies are trying to decide if they should help with day care at all.

(E) Many companies are trying to help with day care at all.

57. Which of the following would be an acceptable substitution for the underlined word in sentence 5?

(A) show   (D) A and B.

(B) have been showing   (E) A, B, and C.

(C) have shown

58. Which of the following contains a punctuation error?

(A) Sentence 1   (D) Sentence 10

(B) Sentence 3   (E) None of these.

(C) Sentence 7

59. Which of the following sentences is irrelevant in the second paragraph and should be eliminated?

(A) 8   (D) 14

(B) 10   (E) None of these.

(C) 12

60. Which of the following best improves the sequence of ideas in the second paragraph?

(A) Reverse the order of sentences 8 and 9.

(B) Place sentence 13 before sentence 9.

(C) Delete sentence 11.

(D) Place sentence 9 after sentence 11

(E) Delete sentence 8.

SAT II: WRITING
TEST 4

ANSWER KEY

1. (A)	16. (E)	31. (D)	46. (A)
2. (C)	17. (D)	32. (A)	47. (B)
3. (D)	18. (D)	33. (C)	48. (B)
4. (E)	19. (A)	34. (B)	49. (B)
5. (C)	20. (B)	35. (E)	50. (A)
6. (A)	21. (D)	36. (A)	51. (A)
7. (B)	22. (A)	37. (C)	52. (C)
8. (D)	23. (E)	38. (C)	53. (D)
9. (D)	24. (C)	39. (B)	54. (B)
10. (C)	25. (A)	40. (D)	55. (C)
11. (B)	26. (E)	41. (E)	56. (D)
12. (C)	27. (B)	42. (B)	57. (E)
13. (B)	28. (A)	43. (A)	58. (C)
14. (A)	29. (D)	44. (D)	59. (C)
15. (C)	30. (C)	45. (E)	60. (D)

DETAILED EXPLANATIONS OF ANSWERS

Part A: Essay

Sample Essays with Commentary

ESSAY I (Score: 5–6)

The primary figure associated with the philosophy of "the end justifies the means" is Machiavelli. His treatise, *The Prince*, is a study in cynicism. He outlines methods a sensible prince will take in order to maintain a stable, and thus prosperous, state: military conquest, bribery, large (rather than minor) insults and threats, and so on. During the Elizabethan times, his infamous reputation earned him the dubious honor of having his Christian name be a synonym for the devil; however, Machiavelli's methods are studied and employed by many leaders.

The military establishment has always employed somewhat less than total honesty in order to win. The Greeks are a notable example of a people who accepted bribery and trickery as an honorable battle tactic. Themistocles sent his personal slave with a message that the Greek general secretly supported the Persian invaders and the retreating Greeks could easily be trapped in the narrow waters at the exit to the Bay of Salamis. The Persians deployed their troops accordingly, and the devastating defeat of Xerxes at Salamis is a textbook study in military brilliance. Giving false intelligence to the enemy and concealing one's own numbers, position, and plans are only intelligent tactics: wars are not won with honesty.

Politics is another arena for less than honorable dealings. Spies ferret out secrets useful in applying leverage to another nation's position. Russia and the United States maintain a constant stream of information about each other through the use of secret intelligence; even supposed allies such as the United States and Israel spy on each other. A recent survey of Americans showed politicians are considered less trustworthy than used car dealers. However, compromising his ideals is inherent in the politician's job: a person who never bends or looks the other way will never be a chairman of the military or budget committee.

Even a "gung-ho" patriot can be excused his methods if he is effective in getting the job done. During the Iran-Contra hearings it became painfully obvious that the intent of the law was circumvented, but Oliver North has emerged a national hero. His testimony, as well as the testimony of others, shows him to have been a "can-do" kind of person, one who can even supply within two days a ship for the CIA that the government agency could not attain for itself through normal channels.

The American public overlooks the methods if the person achieves goals no one else can—or will. Machiavelli and Themistocles knew the business of statesmanship and war. So do modern government officials. They are all judged by their accomplishments.

ANALYSIS

Essay I has a score range of 5-6. With fluid transition of ideas, depth of thought, and good vocabulary, it is the strongest of the four essays. This essay has a clear thesis in the introductory paragraph, three body paragraphs with a specific focus for each, and a conclusion that sums up the main points without exactly repeating the thesis or topic sentences. Each body paragraph begins with a clear topic sentence which is supported either with an extended example or with several examples. There is a good variety of sentence length and structure. Although not perfect, this essay shows clarity and purpose. The wording is often quite effective.

ESSAY II (Score: 4–5)

In spite of what people may say, might does not make right, and the end does not justify the means. Just because a person is more powerful or more sneaky, he does not have the right to force his views on others. Other people can get hurt.

Literature is full of examples of bad leaders who used bad methods. Shakespeare presents several examples. *Julius Caesar,* a tragedy, is a story about how an assassination destroys a kingdom. Claudius is a king who kills his brother and marries his sister-in-law in *Hamlet. Macbeth* also becomes king although assassinating the rightful king, Duncan. Both Claudius and Macbeth are destroyed and their kingdoms thrown into turmoil. Assassination, though it gets some people the power they crave, hurts many others. Many people die besides the one who is assassinated. In *Antigone* by Sophocles, Creon wishes to retain power and condemns Antigone to death. Creon condemns her because she puts the laws of religion above the laws of the state. Creon learns too late that his power and his methods will not assure him a peaceful kingdom.

Moving into more recent times, politics provides many examples. Richard Nixon's fanatic supporters, nicknamed "the plumbers," wanted to re-elect Nixon to another term as president. Nixon was reelected, but the methods used were not good. A building was broken into, a psychiatrist's records were made public, and untrue rumors were spread about opponents. These bad methods hurt many people and they hurt America's reputation. Leaders of some South American and African nations use torture and secret police squads in order to stay in power. Some individuals drop out of sight, and the family never knows if that person is alive or dead. In order to stay in power, politicians should not use illegal or sneaky methods.

Politicians and kings are political leaders who should be a role model for the rest of the people they govern. A government can only be as good as its leader. A weak or bad leader makes for a weak or a bad government. A chain is only as strong as its weakest link. When people in a position of power see their leader using dishonest methods in order to stay in power, they either lose respect for him, or worse, they imitate his methods.

ANALYSIS

Essay II has a score range of 4-5. It is developed in a logical, organized manner. The opening paragraph has a thesis, each body paragraph deals with a different aspect of the topic, and the last paragraph concludes. The two body paragraphs have many specific examples, but the transitions are abrupt. This essay is weakened by the simple sentence structure in places and by the lack of variety in vocabulary. Too many words are repeated. The writer uses passive voice, one cliché in the introduction, and another cliché in the conclusion.

ESSAY III (Score: 3–4)

A person should always be honest and never break the law or hurt people. You should be able to trust people. And depend on them to help you.

I don't like cheaters. Cheating is a real problem in my school. The popular kids have answers to a lot of the teacher's tests. Why don't the teachers know or do something about it? I have even heard that in college lots of fraternities and sororities have files of old tests from college professors. There is a lot of it in all schools, even law school and medical school. Yes, cheating can get you a good grade on a test, but I sure don't want to be operated on by a doctor who cheated his way through medical school. Or have a lawyer who cheated in law school.

Politicians are people everyone expects that are dishonest. They make all kinds of deals with each other, so no one can keep all of their campaign promises. Then, they vote themselves big, fat raises. Which all of us have to pay for with higher taxes. Any company working for the government can cut itself in on the corruption. If they know the right people. Screwdrivers and toilet seats have been sold to the government for hundreds of dollars, and they can be bought cheap in the hardware store. And we get higher taxes.

America is not helped by people who cheat and who are not truthful.

ANALYSIS

Essay III has a score range of 3-4. It has an organization of thesis paragraph, two body paragraphs, and a conclusion. However, the introduction and the conclusion sound a bit too moralistic and "preachy," as well as being brief. The sentence structure is a problem because there are too many simple sentences; there are also several fragments. The writer of this essay uses contractions, slang, and an informal tone. There are some grammar errors, including shifts in voice.

ESSAY IV (Score: 1–2)

It doesn't matter what anyone says. If a person can win, that's all that matters. Lombardi said once that winning is everything.

When I look around, the best grades are the ones who cheat. With cheat sheets or look at a smart student's paper. Even the so-called honor students have ways to cheat. They know good grades look good and make their parents happy. They will get into the right university. Where they will probably cheat in college, make good grades, and then get a good job. They know its important to get a good job they can support a family and have money to spend for things

Athletes know its important to win. The coaches teach a student how to use their elbows and hurt another player in a basketball game. Steroids are taken by pro athletes. Especially weightlifters and football players. If you don't, one doesn't stand a chance to beat other teams. A team that doesn't win isn't very popular. It feels good to win.

ANALYSIS

Essay IV has a score range of 1-2. The paper has a controlling purpose of sorts stated in the opening paragraph, two body paragraphs, and a conclusion. However, the introduction has a poor tone and is not well developed; the conclusion is one sentence tacked onto the last paragraph. There are too many generalities and not enough specifics in the two body paragraphs. Vocabulary is limited and there are many contractions. There are problems with spelling, usage, and wording. The paper has several fragments.

Part B: Multiple-Choice

1.   **(A)**   "Campus" is a singular noun; therefore, the pronoun referring to "campus" should be "its" so that the pronoun will agree with its antecedent. Choices (B), "findings of," and (C), "in which," both have prepositions appropriately used. Choice (D), "can," is a helping verb in the correct tense.

2.   **(C)**   Choice (C) should read, "could not care less." A person using this expression is indicating his total lack of interest in something; to say, "I could care less" indicates some interest, so the correct expression is "I could not care less." Choice (A) is the correct subject pronoun; choice (B), "good," is the adjective form used to follow the linking verb "be" and choice (D) is a gerund used as the object of a preposition.

3.   **(D)**   The idiom is "conform with" a law; something or someone will "conform to" an environment. Choices (A) and (B) are correctly used idioms. Choice (C) is the proper form of the adjective.

4.   **(E)**   Choice (A), "have seen," is the present perfect tense, which is used to make a statement about something occurring in the past but continuing into the present. The speaker has observed the problem of lack of self-esteem, but this problem has not stopped in the present time. Choice (B) is a comparative form, and "else" of choice (C) is necessary when comparing one thing with the group of which it is a member or part. (The observation about self-esteem is but one of several observations the speaker has made.) Choice (D) has a preposition to indicate relationship between "problem" and "people."

5.   **(C)**   "Allowed as how" is used sometimes in speaking, but the proper expression should be "allowed that." "Accommodated with," choice (A), is an idiom used to indicate "to supply with." Choice (B) is an infinitive phrase followed by a subordinate clause as the direct object. Choice (D), "had expected," is the past perfect tense to indicate previous past action: Mr. Burgess's estimate of the cost was made before the actual event.

6.   **(A)**   As this sentence reads, it is a fragment. "Having" should be eliminated, leaving "turned out" as the main verb in the proper tense. Choice (D), "so," is a coordinating conjunction relating two events of

cause-and-effect; therefore, both main clauses should be independent. Choice (B) is the adverb form modifying the verb "turned out," and choice (C), "who," is the nominative form serving as the subject of "knows."

7. **(B)** "Protested against" is redundant; "protested" is sufficient. "Ago" in choice (A) is an adjective used following the noun "years" or as an adverb following "long." Choice (C) is a correct idiom. Choice (D), "any," is an adjective.

8. **(D)** Two subjects joined by "and" require a plural verb; "public opinion and government policy" should be completed by "have." Choice (A), "called," is a participle modifying "journalists." Choice (B), "rapidly," is an adverb modifying choice (C), which is a correct idiom.

9. **(D)** The expression should read, "renting (or buying) a tuxedo," in order to complete the parallelism following choice (B) "included": "hiring a limousine" and "buying gifts," choice (C). Choice (A) is a correct expression which can also be phrased, "more than he expected." if greater clarity is desired.

10. **(C)** The object pronoun "us" should follow the preposition "of." In choice (A), "viewing" is a gerund used as the subject and therefore requires the possessive adjective "our." Choice (B) is the verb. Choice (D) is a correct idiom.

11. **(B)** The modifier "only" is misplaced. To place this word before "stole" indicates that stealing is a minor problem; also, the meaning of the sentence clearly indicates Jules has stolen money one time, so the sentence should read, "stole money only once." Choice (A) is a correct preposition; choice (C) is a possessive pronoun modifying "conscience"; and choice (D) is an object pronoun as the object of "allow."

12. **(C)** There is no antecedent for "it." Choice (A), "a person," is the subject to which "he" in choice (B) refers. "Never" in choice (D) is a correctly placed adverb. The sentence should include a phrase such as "a crime" to serve as the antecedent of "it," or the phrase "for it" could be deleted.

13. **(B)** The adverb "daily" is misplaced and should be placed with "is bringing," choice (A), or with "habit." Choice (C) is a prepositional phrase, and choice (D) is a subject pronoun for the subordinate clause.

14. **(A)** The adverb form, "frequently," should be used to modify the verb. Choices (B) and (C) are a correct subject-verb combination. The adjective form, "possible," of choice (D) follows the linking verb "is."

15. **(C)** The antecedent for "it" is unclear because "it" can refer to the grass or to the branch. Choice (A), "growing over," and choice (B), "to," are correct pronouns. Choice (D) is a correct idiom because we become "annoyed with" people but "annoyed at" things or situations.

16. **(E)** The sentence is correct as written. Choices (A) and (B) are a compound structure and are in proper parallel form. Choice (C) has a clear reference to "system." Choice (D) is a correct idiom.

17. **(D)** The preposition "in" has three objects: "submarines," "missiles," and choice (D) which must be made parallel to the previous two nouns. Choice (A) is a participle modifying "navigation." Choice (B) is a part of a subordinate clause modifying "submarines." Choice (C) is a correct preposition.

18. **(D)** This sentence is a fragment made by the conjunction "and" linking "enjoying" with "known," the participial adjective of choice (B); "and" should be eliminated and "enjoying" changed to "enjoys" to be the subject of "president." Choice (A) is an idiom. Choice (B) is the correct possessive form to complete the idiom.

19. **(A)** There is no antecedent for this pronoun, although it is implied that the elderly and the handicapped are the logical ones to be grateful. Choice (B) and (D) are elliptical constructions, "grateful [that] the city" and "helps [to] pay." Choice (C) is a verb.

20. **(B)** This sentence is not parallel. Two actions are mentioned, connected by "not only" and "but also." The sentence should read, "not only are Americans . . . but also they are." Choices (A) and (C) contain properly-used infinitives. Choice (D), "particularly," is the adverb form modifying the adjective, "arid."

21. **(D)** Sentences should not end with a preposition; the sentence should read, "an opinion with which everyone agreed." Choice (A) is a gerund as the object of a preposition. Choice (B) is an appropriate conjunction; and choice (C), "good," is the positive form of the adjective to follow the linking verb "tasted."

22. **(A)** The expression should read, "as prevalent as" for the proper comparison. Choice (B) is a noun used as an adjective. Choice (C), "some of which," has clear reference to "ornaments." Choice (D), "such as," is correct to mean, "for example."

23. **(E)** Choice (A) is subjunctive mood to indicate a condition contrary to fact. Choice (B) is a correct idiom. Choice (C) uses the adverb "politely" to modify "speaking," and choice (D) uses the adjective "angry" to follow the linking verb "becoming."

24. **(C)** "Irregardless," an incorrect expression, is a combination of "irrespective" and "regardless." (Taking into account the prefix and the suffix of "irregardless," the combination would mean, "not, not regarding," and so would be redundant.) Usually, "regardless" is used, although "irrespective" is also correct. The idioms in choices (A) and (D) are correct. Choice (B) is an adjective.

25. **(A)** The idiom should be "capable of winning." The verb in choice (B) indicates the prior action of two past actions; the prepositions in choices (C) and (D) are correct.

26. **(E)** Choice (A) is a correct expression. Choice (B) uses an indefinite pronoun as the predicate nominative, and "those" as the object of a preposition. The verb in (C), "are," is plural because a plural verb must be used in a subordinate clause following the phrase "one of those." Choice (D) uses the nominative form of the pronoun as the subject of "say."

27. **(B)** The verb should be in the past tense, "practiced," as signaled by "would become." Choice (A) is a correct idiom. Choice (C) is one word as used in this sentence. Choice (D) contains a correct preposition.

28. **(A)** In the prior of two past actions, the verb should be past perfect: "had listened" comes before "would have heard." Choice (B), "carefully," is an adverb modifying "would have heard." Choices (C) and (D) are correct idioms.

29. **(D)** The expression "and etc." is redundant; it would mean "and, and." In this case, "etc." or "and so on" would be acceptable. Choice (A) is an infinitive; choice (B) and choice (C) are correct idioms.

30. **(C)** A "factor" is something which contributes toward a result. This phrase could be reworded to read, "are part of being hazed as a freshman" or "are part of freshman hazing." Choice (A) is a gerund parallel to the others: "pushing" and "being." Choices (B) and (D) are correct.

31. **(D)** The conjunction "not only . . . but also" must be properly placed to indicate which qualities are being discussed and to maintain proper parallelism. Choice (D) contains three adjectives to follow the verb "to be": "capable and efficient" and "adept." Choices (A), (B), (C), and (E) are not parallel. In addition, choices (B) and (C) have "to be" after the conjunction, and this construction would require another verb after the second conjunction, "but also."

32. **(A)** This sentence contains two concepts, proper management and careful control. In choice (A) these two concepts are concisely worded and appear in parallel form. Choice (B) has no noun for "Managing" to modify. Choice (C) would be acceptable with the addition of commas to set off the introductory phrase. Choice (D) mangles the concepts, and the wording in choice (E) is poor.

33. **(C)** Choice (A) is a "squinting" modifier: it is unclear if "on the next day" tells when "I agreed" or when "to put up." Choice (B) does not clarify this problem. Choice (D) unnecessarily splits the subject and the verb, and choice (E) unnecessarily splits an infinitive.

34. **(B)** The interrupter, "though not nearly all," should be placed so as not to split important parts of the sentence. Choices (A), (D), and (E) are incorrect because the interrupter splits a preposition and its object. Choices (C) and (D) will produce a fragment because the subject "we" is missing.

35. **(E)** To mean "for example," the expression "like" is incorrect; the correct usage is "such as." Therefore, choices (A) and (B) are incorrect. Choices (C) and (D) incorrectly use "likes" as a verb, thereby changing the intent of the sentence.

36. **(A)** Choice (A) correctly uses the object pronoun "whom" to follow the preposition "of." Choice (B) uses the wrong pronoun. Choice (C) inserts an extraneous preposition "about" that has no object. Choice (D) is awkward wording; choice (E) is also poor wording, especially with the pronoun "him" so far away from its antecedent.

37. **(C)**   Choice (C) clearly and simply deals with the location and the fame of the Dead Sea. It is incorrect to use a preposition with no object in order to end a sentence. Choices (A), (D), and (E) are incorrect because they end with "famous for." Also, in the phrase, "where the Dead Sea is at," the word *at* is redundant; it is sufficient to write "where the Dead Sea is." Therefore, choices (A) and (B) are incorrect. Finally, since the Dead Sea still exists, the verbs must be in the present tense.

38. **(C)**   The phrase "cannot help" should be followed by a gerund, not by "but." Choice (C) follows "cannot help" with the gerund "admitting." Choices (A) and (E) are incorrect because they follow "cannot help" with "but." The wording of choice (B), "cannot admit," and choice (E), "cannot know," twists the meaning of the sentence.

39. **(B)**   The correct idiom is to have an insight into a situation or person. While "to" in choice (A) is close in meaning, it is not exact; "for" and "with" of choices (C), (D), and (E) are unacceptable. The location of "often" in choice (D) is poor, and the location of "often" in choice (E) makes no significant change in the meaning.

40. **(D)**   It is obvious that the Greenes have just purchased plants: "Upon leaving the nursery." The location of the modifying phrase, "they had just brought," should be carefully placed in the sentence so it clearly modifies "plants" and not "car." Choice (D) has the modifying phrase immediately following "plants," and the meaning is clear. The wording of choices (A), (B), and (C) makes the reader think the car has just been purchased. Choice (E) omits the concept "they had just bought."

41. **(E)**   Choice (E) retains the central idea while eliminating the wording problems of the other choices. There is no antecedent for "we" in choices (A) and (B). Also, the phrase "end up" is redundant; "up" should be eliminated. Therefore, choice (C) is incorrect. Choice (D) introduces a new concept of "war may end over there," an idea clearly not intended by the original.

42. **(B)**   Choice (B) clearly and precisely states the issue of debate. Choice (C) is eliminated because it is too wordy and not the precise issue under debate. The correlative conjunctions, "whether . . . or," should be followed by parallel structures. Choice (A) follows "Whether" with a subject-verb combination not seen after "not." Choice (D) is parallel but in

the wrong tense. Choice (E) has "Whether or not" run together and uses poor wording in the rest of the sentence.

43. **(A)** Choice (A) has both correct agreement and clear reference. Choice (B) has a subject-verb agreement problem, "charging . . . are." Choice (C) produces a fragment. It is unclear in choice (D) who will have the bad credit rating, and the wording of choice (E) has the obvious subject, "people," in a prepositional phrase.

44. **(D)** Choice (D) correctly presents the fifth grade field trip in a subordinate clause modifying "exhibit." Choices (A) and (B) have the coordinating conjunction "and," but the first part of the sentence is not equal in meaning or importance to the second part of the sentence. Choice (C) introduces "when" with no antecedent. Choice (E) uses "where" as the subordinating conjunction, but it is too far from its antecedent and is not the important idea of the sentence.

45. **(E)** In choice (E) the present infinitive is correctly used to express an action following another action: "plans to appeal." Choices (A) and (B) use the wrong form, "appealing." Choice (C) uses the wrong tense, "is appealing." Choice (D) sounds as if the same person is deciding the case and appealing the case.

46. **(A)** Choice (A) has clear wording. Choice (B) is a fragment because it puts the verb in the nonessential phrase. Choices (C), (D), and (E) produce twisted wording. Choice (C) has no object for the verb "allowed" and sounds as if the speakers were allowed to stay up later. Choice (E) needs commas and sounds as if the speakers decided to stay up later.

47. **(B)** Choice (B) plainly states the subject and the verb, "I find." Choices (A) and (E) have the subject in a prepositional phrase, "for me." Choice (E) produces a fragment. Choice (C), a fragment, has no subject because both potential subjects are in prepositional phases: "agreement" and "plan." Choices (C) and (D) imply "everyone" as the main subject.

48. **(B)** Choice (B) avoids the split infinitive and the incorrect expression, "inside of." Choices (A) and (D) split the infinitive "to finish" with the adverb "completely." Choice (C) uses "inside of," an expression that is incorrect to use because it is redundant ("of" should be deleted) and because it should not be used with measuring time. Choice (E) erroneously

changes the idea and would employ two verbs in simple past tense: "hired" and "finished."

49. **(B)** "The Wetherills" is plural, and the verb must agree. Choice (B) correctly changes "is" to "are"; the rest of the sentence is fine. (A) adds the singular "a group" which may make the verb "is" seem right, though it still modifies "The Wetherills" and must agree accordingly. (C) corrects the verb problem, but misplaces the clause "five brothers who ranched in the area" at the end of the sentence where it is unclear. (D) fails to correct the verb disagreement and places the clause at the end of the sentence, which alters the sense.

50. **(A)** Choice (A) best continues the topic of sentence 9, which concerns the cultural achievements of the Anasazi, and provides a nice transition toward the final sentence. (B) concerns an entirely different historical epoch, and is clearly irrelevant. (C) may fit somewhere in this essay, but not between sentences 9 and 10, where this new fact would seem obtrusive. (D) introduces the personal voice of the author which is contrary to the expository tone in the passage thus far, and which would not fit between the factual content of sentences 9 and 10. (E) would be a good topic sentence for a new paragraph, but would not be good here.

51. **(A)** Sentence 4 is a dependent prepositional clause and would be best added onto sentence 3.

52. **(C)** The years of the Anasazi's zenith are best set off by commas and turned into a prepositional phrase, and of the two choices which do this, (C) uses "from," which is more appropriate than (D) "being." Without the punctuation, choice (A) is awkward; if the phrase were set off by commas, it would be acceptable, though (C) is more concise. (B) is just wrong; from the context of the passage it is clear that the Anasazi thrived in the years A.D and not B.C.

53. **(D)** Choice (D) best utilizes commas which clarify the sense of the sentence. Choice (A) places the second comma incorrectly. (B) and (C) both utilize a colon, and each has an unnecessary comma. Choice (E) is correct as written.

54. **(B)** Sentence 2 uses "then," a temporal reference, instead of "than," which should be used for the comparison in this sentence.

55. **(C)**   "Children's early teens" is much neater and clearer than "the early teens of the children." (A) introduces unnecessary punctuation. (B) is nonsensical ("continue through the children"). (D) adds "on" which does nothing but further convolute the original sentence.

56. **(D)**   (D) makes a clear and simple sentence out of the clumsy original. The structures of (A), (B), and (C) duplicate the confusions of the original.

57. **(E)**   "Showing" in the original sentence is clearly wrong, and any of these three forms would be acceptable.

58. **(C)**   Sentence 7 is a rhetorical question, like sentence 6, and needs a question mark.

59. **(C)**   Sentence 12 introduces a new issue in the middle of the paragraph and would best be eliminated.

60. **(D)**   The idea in sentence 9 about company morale and employee loyalty would be best placed in support of the ideas in sentence 11, that the workers feel that the company has taken interest in them. "Therefore" sets up a logical relation which is not present between sentence 8 and 9.

SAT II: Writing

Practice Test 5

SAT II: WRITING
TEST 5

Part A: Essay

TIME: 20 Minutes

DIRECTIONS: You have 20 minutes to plan and write an essay on the topic below. You may write only on the assigned topic.

Make sure to give specific examples to support your thesis. Proofread your essay carefully and take care to express your ideas clearly and effectively.

Write your essay on the lined pages at the back of the book.

ESSAY TOPIC:

Television often causes the viewer to lose touch with reality and become completely passive and unaware. Like other addictions, television provides a pleasurable escape route from action to inaction.

ASSIGNMENT: Do you agree or disagree with this statement? Support your opinion with specific examples from history, current events, literature, or personal experience.

Part B: Multiple-Choice

(Answer sheets appear in the back of this book.)

TIME: 40 Minutes
60 Questions

DIRECTIONS: Each of the following sentences may contain an error in diction, usage, idiom, or grammar. Some sentences are correct. Some sentences contain one error. No sentence contains more than one error.

If there is an error, it will appear in one of the underlined portions labeled A, B, C, or D. If there is no error, choose the portion labeled E. If there is an error, select the letter of the portion that must be changed in order to correct the sentence.

EXAMPLE:

He drove <u>slowly</u> and <u>cautiously</u> in order to <u>hopefully</u> avoid having an
        A   **B**   **C**

<u>accident</u>. <u>No error</u>.
  D   **E**   Ⓐ Ⓑ ● Ⓓ Ⓔ

---

1. If anyone <u>plans</u> to visit Yosemite National Park, <u>you</u> should allow
          A   **B**

    several days <u>to see</u> all <u>of the sites</u>. <u>No error</u>.
            C   **D**   **E**

2. It is <u>important</u> that medications <u>and</u> cleaning preparations <u>be stored</u> in
          A   **B**   **C**

    places that are <u>inaccessible from</u> young children. <u>No error</u>.
                  D   **E**

3. Although he worked very <u>slow</u>, he was <u>meticulously</u> careful, and his
                        A   **B**

    report of the findings of his studies <u>was</u> always very <u>accurate</u>.
                                  C   **D**

    <u>No error</u>.
     E

4. The man <u>giving</u> the radio news <u>is</u> a commentator <u>who</u> radio listeners
       A   B   C

   <u>have heard</u> for many years. <u>No error</u>.
       D   E

5. <u>Although</u> she is <u>older</u> than <u>anyone else</u>, she looks very young <u>for her</u>
      A   B   C   D

   age. <u>No error</u>.
        E

6. A large crowd <u>gathered</u> on the <u>president's</u> lawn and <u>shouting</u> their
                     A   B   C

   protests about the <u>dismissal of</u> Professor Maxwell. <u>No error</u>.
                          D   E

7. The sign in the ice cream parlor read, "Because we make our ice

   cream <u>fresh</u> <u>daily</u>, the variety <u>of flavors</u> <u>change</u> regularly." <u>No error</u>.
          A   B   C   D   E

8. Although <u>it provided</u> a dangerous way of life, whaling was once
              A

   <u>an important vocation</u> in New England seaports because whale oil
      B

   <u>was used</u> for lamps, candles, soap, and <u>as a lubricant</u>. <u>No error</u>.
      C   D   E

9. He ate <u>greedily</u> because he was <u>literally</u> starved to death after he
             A   B

   <u>had been lost</u> in the woods <u>for two days</u>. <u>No error</u>.
      C   D   E

10. Of all the important contributions to history that he <u>might have made</u>,
                                                             A

    John Montagu, the Earl of Sandwich, is <u>better</u> known for a lunch of
                                               B

    meat between two slices of bread <u>that permitted</u> him <u>to continue</u> his
                                         C   D

    gambling while he ate. <u>No error</u>.
                              E

11. <u>When</u> Rutgers <u>had beaten</u> Princeton in the first intercollegiate college
    A   **B**

football game in America, the 25-man teams <u>made</u> goals by <u>kicking a</u>
                                        C   **D**

<u>round ball</u> under the cross bars. <u>No error.</u>
                          E

12. He was one of those <u>kind</u> of people <u>who</u> never feel <u>good</u> about
                        A   **B**   **C**

<u>themselves</u>. <u>No error.</u>
  D   **E**

13. After he <u>had been sent</u> to bed, the little boy <u>snuck</u> <u>downstairs</u> and <u>lay</u>
          A   **B**   **C**   **D**

down on the kitchen floor. <u>No error.</u>
                      E

14. Although Walt Disney's cartoon, *Snow White and the Seven Dwarfs,*

<u>was originally shown</u> in 1937, most of today's young people hadn't
           A

had <u>no chance</u> <u>to see</u> it until <u>its</u> 1987 revival. <u>No error.</u>
    B   **C**   **D**   **E**

15. Although Gilbert Stuart, whose portraits of George Washington

<u>are recognized</u> <u>by most Americans</u>, and his daughter Jane <u>were</u> both
     A   **B**   **C**
American painters, the father is the <u>most famous</u> of the two. <u>No error.</u>
                              D   **E**

16. If it <u>were</u> <u>me</u> <u>who</u> had to work that hard, I <u>would complain</u> to the
      A **B**   **C**   **D**
manager. <u>No error.</u>
       E

17. Everyone thought it was <u>really tragic</u> when the child <u>fell</u> down the
                         A   **B**

well <u>that</u> <u>should of been</u> sealed off years before. <u>No error.</u>
   C   **D**   **E**

18. Only five days <u>after the surrender</u> of General Lee to General Grant
　　　　　　　　　　　A

　　　<u>signalled</u> the end of the Civil War, Abraham Lincoln <u>has been shot</u>
　　　B　　　　　　　　　　　　　　　　　　　　　　　　　　**C**

　　　while he <u>was attending</u> a play at Ford's Theatre. <u>No error.</u>
　　　　　　　　D　　　　　　　　　　　　　　　　　　　**E**

19. The majority of parents <u>are concerned</u> about the <u>effects</u> <u>of watching</u>
　　　　　　　　　　　　　　　A　　　　　　　　**B**　　**C**

　　　too much television upon the development of <u>their</u> children. <u>No error.</u>
　　　　　　　　　　　　　　　　　　　　　　D　　　　　　**E**

20. Whenever anyone who <u>is</u> a toy collector <u>thinks</u> about Theodore
　　　　　　　　　　　　A　　　　　　　　**B**

　　　Roosevelt, <u>they usually remember</u> that one of the <u>most popular</u> toys,
　　　　　　　　　　C　　　　　　　　　　　　　　　**D**

　　　the teddy bear, was named for him. <u>No error.</u>
　　　　　　　　　　　　　　　　　　E

21. Horses <u>named</u> Gato del Sol, Sunny's Halo, and Swale <u>have been</u>
　　　　　　A　　　　　　　　　　　　　　　　　　　　**B**

　　　<u>a winner</u> of the Kentucky Derby in <u>recent years</u>. <u>No error.</u>
　　　C　　　　　　　　　　　　　**D**　　　**E**

22. After he <u>had felt</u> the excruciating pain in his chest, he <u>had laid</u> <u>down</u>
　　　　　　A　　　　　　　　　　　　　　　　　　**B**　　**C**

　　　for a while before he <u>arose</u> and called an ambulance. <u>No error.</u>
　　　　　　　　　　　　D　　　　　　　　　　　　　　**E**

23. Because the attendants on the airplane were <u>busily</u> serving lunch
　　　　　　　　　　　　　　　　　　　　　A

　　　to the passengers, <u>he</u> did not notice <u>immediately</u> when the child
　　　　　　　　　　B　　　　　　**C**

　　　<u>traveling alone</u> began to cry. <u>No error.</u>
　　　D　　　　　　　　　**E**

24. <u>Irregardless</u> of how <u>well</u> he did on his practice test, he was afraid <u>that</u>
　　　A　　　　　　**B**　　　　　　　　　　　　　　　　**C**

　　　he <u>would fail</u> the final examination. <u>No error.</u>
　　　　D　　　　　　　　　　　　**E**

25. Although Henry Ward Beecher was a <u>moderately</u> famous American
    A
    clergyman <u>who</u> supported the abolitionists, his sister, Harriet Beecher
    B
    Stowe, became <u>better</u> known than <u>him</u> after she wrote *Uncle Tom's*
    C   D
    Cabin. <u>No error</u>.
    E

26. She felt <u>really</u> <u>bad</u> because the child's balloon <u>burst</u> immediately after
    A   B   C
    she <u>had purchased</u> it. <u>No error</u>.
    D   E

27. By the time that election day <u>comes</u>, the candidate <u>will have shaken</u>
    A   B
    <u>more</u> hands than he <u>ever</u> imagined. <u>No error</u>.
    C   D   E

28. Because I <u>never</u> had <u>any</u> athletic skill, the captain found it easy to
    A   B
    choose <u>between</u> <u>her and I</u>. <u>No error</u>.
    C   D   E

29. The circumstances <u>about</u> the disappearance of the Lindbergh baby
    A
    <u>were</u> very <u>suspicious</u> and <u>frightening</u>. <u>No error</u>.
    B   C   D   E

30. <u>Keeping one's weight under control</u> <u>is</u> <u>more difficult</u> at college
    A   B   C
    <u>than home</u>. <u>No error</u>.
    D   E

DIRECTIONS: In each of the following sentences, some portion of the sentence is underlined. Under each sentence are five choices. The first choice has the same wording as the original. The other four choices are reworded. Sometimes the first choice containing the original wording is the best; sometimes one of the other choices is the best. Choose the letter of the best choice. Your choice should produce a sentence which is not ambiguous or awkward and which is correct, clear, and precise.

This is a test of correct and effective English expression. Keep in mind the standards of English usage, punctuation, grammar, word choice, and construction.

EXAMPLE:

When you listen to opera, <u>a person may not appreciate it.</u>

(A)   a person may not appreciate it.

(B)   it may not be appreciated by a person.

(C)   which may not be appreciated by one.

(D)   you may not appreciate it.

(E)   appreciating it may be a problem for you.

---

31. <u>Eating chips of dried paint</u>, lead poisoning is a serious illness of children who live in old houses.

  (A) Eating chips of dried paint

  (B) Having eaten chips of dried paint

  (C) Because of eating chips of dried paint

  (D) Chips of dried paint being eaten

  (E) Because they may eat chips of dried paint

32. The French architect Pierre Charles L'Enfant was hired to plan the United States capital <u>although he and President Washington had a disagreement</u>, L'Enfant's plan was used in the design of Washington, D.C.

  (A) although he and President Washington had a disagreement

  (B) and, although he and President Washington had a disagreement

(C) who had a disagreement with President Washington, but

(D) although having had a disagreement with President Washington

(E) he and President Washington had a disagreement

33. While trying to reduce cholesterol, <u>you should eat lentils in casse-roles, salads, and soups, the reason being that lentils</u> provide an excellent source of protein.

(A) you should eat lentils in casseroles, salads, and soups, the reason being that lentils

(B) lentils should be eaten in casseroles, salads, and soups, the reason being that lentils

(C) you should eat lentils in casseroles, salads, and soups because lentils

(D) eating lentils in casseroles, salads, and soups will

(E) you should eat lentils in casseroles, salads, and soups which

34. <u>Being that the first Library of Congress had been destroyed in the War of 1812,</u> Congress purchased the personal library of Thomas Jefferson to replace it.

(A) Being that the first Library of Congress had been destroyed in the War of 1812,

(B) Although the first Library of Congress was destroyed in the War of 1812,

(C) The first Library of Congress, having been destroyed in the War of 1812, was restored because

(D) The first Library of Congress was destroyed in the War of 1812, so

(E) Having destroyed the first Library of Congress in the War of 1812,

35. The fewer people you tell your secret to, <u>there are fewer people to divulge it to others.</u>

(A) there are fewer people to divulge it to others.

(B) there will be fewer people to divulge it to others.

    (C) there being fewer people to divulge it to others.

    (D) the fewer people there are to divulge it to others.

    (E) the fewer people can divulge it to others.

36. Lisbon, Portugal, is a large city <u>whose history goes back</u> to ancient Greek and Roman times.

    (A) whose history goes back

    (B) which history goes back

    (C) the history of which goes back

    (D) its history goes back

    (E) who's history goes back

37. The young entertainer gets unusual opportunities <u>due to the fact that he is a man whose</u> father is famous.

    (A) due to the fact that he is a man whose

    (B) due to the fact that he is a man who's

    (C) due to the fact that his

    (D) because he is a man whose

    (E) because his

38. Because it was cracking, London Bridge was taken down in <u>1967, and they rebuilt it in Lake Havasu City, Arizona</u>.

    (A) 1967, and they rebuilt it in Lake Havasu City, Arizona.

    (B) 1967 and rebuilt in Lake Havasu City, Arizona.

    (C) 1967, being rebuilt in Lake Havasu City, Arizona.

    (D) 1967, and in lake Havasu City, Arizona, they rebuilt it.

    (E) 1967, they rebuilt it in Lake Havasu City, Arizona.

39. The instinctive habits of a beaver <u>is that he cuts down trees, stores food, and builds dams and lodges</u>.

    (A) is that he cuts down trees, stores food, and builds dams and lodges.

(B) is the cutting down of trees, storage of food, and dam and lodge building.

(C) are the cutting down of trees, the storing of food, and the building of dams and lodges.

(D) are having cut down trees, storing food, and building dams and lodges.

(E) are trees being cut down, food being stored, and dams and lodges being built.

40. Bolivia, a South American country named for Simon Bolivar, who was a leader in freeing the Latin American colonies from Spain, having a climate in which rainfall is seasonal.

(A) having a climate in which rainfall is seasonal.

(B) the climate of which has seasonal rainfall.

(C) has a climate in which rainfall is seasonal.

(D) and it has a climate in which rainfall is seasonal.

(E) the rainfall is seasonal in its climate.

41. Brutus participated in the plot to assassinate Caesar despite the fact that he was pardoned for treason.

(A) despite the fact that he was pardoned for treason.

(B) despite the fact that Brutus had been pardoned by Caesar for treason.

(C) despite the pardoning of Brutus by Caesar of treason.

(D) although he was pardoned for treason.

(E) although Caesar had pardoned Brutus for treason.

42. Prisoners in Venice crossed from prison to the Doges' Palace on the Bridge of Sighs and then they were tried to determine if they were to be executed or freed.

(A) and then they were tried

(B) before they were tried

(C) and after that they were tried

(D) and then being tried

(E) and then a trial took place

43. Polo horses, <u>which are usually 60 to 64 inches in height and 850 to 1000 pounds in weight</u>, must be trained to tolerate having clubs swung near their heads.

(A) which are usually 60 to 64 inches in height and 850 to 1000 pounds in weight

(B) which are usually 60 to 64 inches high and weigh 850 to 1000 pounds

(C) which are usually 60 to 64 inches high and 850 to 1000 pounds in weight

(D) the height of which is usually 60 to 64 inches and the weight usually 850 to 1000 pounds

(E) who's height and weight are usually 60 to 64 inches and 850 to 1000 pounds respectfully

44. <u>Having a large elastic pouch under its bill, the pelican uses it</u> as a scoop to catch fish.

(A) Having a large elastic pouch under its bill, the pelican uses it

(B) The pelican uses the large elastic pouch under its bill

(C) The pelican, having a large elastic pouch under its bill, uses it

(D) Because it has a large elastic pouch under its bill, the pelican uses it

(E) Having a large elastic pouch under its bill, it is used by the pelican

45. Pigeons have been bred for thousands of years <u>not only to provide food but also carry messages</u>.

(A) not only to provide food but also carry messages.

(B) to not only provide food but also carry messages.

(C) to provide not only food but also to carry messages.

(D) to provide not only food but also message carrying.

(E) not only to provide food but also to carry messages.

46. According to a recent study by the Census Bureau, the more education anyone gets, <u>the more money you will make</u>.

    (A) the more money you will make.

    (B) the more money will be made.

    (C) the most money you will make.

    (D) the more money he will make.

    (E) the more money he will have made.

47. Father Junipero Serra, who was a Franciscan missionary sent from Spain to Mexico, <u>where he taught and worked among the Indians</u> and then founded many missions in California that later became cities.

    (A) where he taught and worked among the Indians

    (B) there he taught and worked among the Indians

    (C) he taught and worked among the Indians

    (D) taught and worked among the Indians

    (E) teaching and working among the Indians

48. He went to the meeting eager to explain his point of view <u>but with some fear of public speaking</u>.

    (A) but with some fear of public speaking.

    (B) but afraid to speak in public.

    (C) but having fear that he would have to speak in public.

    (D) fearing public speaking.

    (E) but fearing public speaking.

DIRECTIONS: The following passages are considered early draft efforts of a student. Some sentences need to be rewritten to make the ideas clearer and more precise.

Read each passage carefully and answer the questions that follow. Some of the questions are about particular sentences or parts of sentences and ask you to make decisions about sentence structure, diction, and usage. Some of the questions refer to the entire essay or parts of the essay and ask you to make decisions about organization, development, appropriateness of language, audience, and logic. Choose the answer that most effectively makes the intended meaning clear and follows the requirements of standard written English. After you have chosen your answer, fill in the corresponding oval on your answer sheet.

EXAMPLE:

(1) On the one hand, I think television is bad, But it also does some good things for all of us. (2) For instance, my little sister thought she wanted to be a policemen until she saw police shows on television.

Which of the following is the best revision of the underlined portion of sentence 1 below?

On the one hand, I think television <u>is bad. But it also</u> does some good things for all of us.

(A)   is bad; But it also

(B)   is bad. but is also

(C)   is bad, and it also

(D)   is bad, but it also

(E)   is bad because it also

Questions 49–54 are based on the following passage.

(1) Polar bears, so named because they lived near the North Pole, are called "Nanook" by the Eskimo. (2) Living along the cold waters and ice floes of the Arctic Ocean, some polar bears spend time along the coastal areas of northern Canada, Alaska, Norway, Siberia, and Greenland, although some bears live on the islands of the Arctic Ocean and never come close to the mainland. (3) Most of these areas lie north of the Arctic circle and about 85% of Greenland is always covered with ice. (4) To protect them from the arctic cold and ice, polar bears have water-repellant fur and

a pad of dense, stiff fur on the soles of their snowshoe-like feet. (5) In addition, the bears have such a thick layer of fat that infrared photos show no detectable heat, except for their breath.

(6) Polar bears are the largest land-based carnivores. (7) Because their fur is white with a tinge of yellow, they are difficult to spot on ice floes, their favorite hunting ground. (8) Polar bears have a small head, a long neck, and a long body, so they make efficient swimmers. (9) Polar bears have no natural enemy except man. (10) Increased human activity in the Arctic region has put pressure on polar bear populations. (11) The Polar Bear Specialist Group was formed to conserve and manage this unique animal. (12) An increase in the number of polar bears is due to cooperation between five nations. (13) In 1965, there were 8,000 to 10,000 bears reported, but that population is estimated at 25,000 at the present.

49. Which of the following best expresses the author's intentions in the first paragraph?

   (A) To celebrate his/her fondness for polar bears

   (B) To describe some of the wildlife of Alaska

   (C) To provide a basic account of some of the polar bear's primary habits

   (D) To prove that mammals can live comfortably in unfavorable conditions

   (E) To show why polar bears are not suited to the Arctic region.

50. Which of the following verbs is used in an inappropriate tense?

   (A) "lived" in sentence 1

   (B) "Living" in sentence 2

   (C) "is covered" in sentence 3

   (D) "conserve" in sentence 11

   (E) None of these.

51. Which of the following sentences is not necessary to the first paragraph, and would be best eliminated?

   (A) Sentence 1   (D) Sentence 4

   (B) Sentence 2   (E) Sentence 5

   (C) Sentence 3

52. Which of the following would be the best way to improve the structure of sentence 5?

    (A) In addition, except for their breath, the bears have such a thick layer of fat that infrared photos show no detectable heat.

    (B) The bears have such a thick layer of fat that, in addition, infrared photos show no detectable heat except for their breath.

    (C) Except for their breath, infrared photos show no detectable heat, the bears have such a thick layer of fat.

    (D) The bears have, in addition, such a thick layer of fat that, except for their breath, infrared photos show no detectable heat.

    (E) Best as it is.

53. Which of the following sentences would best fit the writer's plan of development, and would fit between sentences 6 and 7?

    (A) Full-grown polar bears may be about nine feet long and weigh between 1,000 and 1,600 pounds.

    (B) These bears have keen eyesight and are not sensitive to snow blindness.

    (C) In the winter the female polar bear enters a cave in an iceberg and gives birth to one or two cubs.

    (D) Polar bears can swim great distances with a speed of approximately six miles an hour.

    (E) Polar bears are often a popular attraction in city zoos; even Atlanta boasts a healthy polar bear.

54. How would sentences 9, 10, and 11 be properly combined to better effect?

    (A) Polar bears have no natural enemy, except man: increased human activity in the Arctic region has put pressure on polar bear populations, while the Polar Bear Specialist Group was formed to conserve and manage this unique animal.

    (B) Since polar bears have no natural enemy except man, the Polar Bear Specialist Group has formed to conserve and manage this unique animal because increased human activity in the Arctic region has put pressure on polar bear populations.

(C) Polar bears have no natural enemy except man, and though increased human activity in the Arctic region has put pressure on polar bear populations, the Polar Bear Specialist Group was formed to conserve and manage this unique animal.

(D) Polar bears have no natural enemy except man, and since increased human activity in the Arctic region has put pressure on polar bear populations, the Polar Bear Specialist Group was formed to conserve and manage this unique animal.

(E) None of these.

Questions 55–60 are based on the following passage.

(1) In the poem "The Raven" by Edgar Allen Poe, a man has nodded off in his study after reading "many a quaint and curious volume of forgotten lore." (2) His mood is melancholy. (3) He is full of sorrow. (4) He is grieving for "the lost Lenore."

(5) When he hears the tapping at his window, he lets in a raven. (6) The raven perches on the bust of Pallas Athena, a goddess often depicted with a bird on her head by the Greeks who believed that birds were heralds from the dead. (7) At first, the man thinks the bird might be a friend but one who would leave soon, but the raven says, "Nevermore," an affirmation which makes the man smile. (8) However, the bird's repetition of "Nevermore" leads the speaker to the realization that Lenore will never return, the bird becomes an omen of doom and is called "evil" by the mournful speaker. (9) He becomes frantic, imploring the raven to let him know if there is comfort for him or if he will ever again hold close the sainted Lenore. (10) To both questions, the bird replies, "Nevermore." (11) Shrieking with anguish, the bird is ordered to leave, but it replies, "Nevermore." (12) At the end of the poem, the man's soul is trapped in the Raven's shadow "that lies floating on the floor" and "shall be lifted—nevermore."

(13) Thus, the bird evolves into an ominous bird of ill omen. (14) Some argue that the bird deliberately drives the speaker insane. (15) While others feel the bird is innocent of any premeditated wrong doing, and I think the bird doesn't do anything but repeat one word. (16) One thing is certain, however. (17) The poem's haunting refrain is familiar, one which students of American literature will memorize and forget "nevermore."

55. Which of the following is the best way to combine sentences 2, 3, and 4?

(A) He is melancholy and sorrowful and grieving for "the lost Lenore."

(B) He is grieving for "the lost Lenore," full of melancholy and sorrow.

(C) Melancholy and sorrowful, he is grieving for "the lost Lenore."

(D) Melancholy and full of sorrow, he is grieving for "the lost Lenore."

(E) Full of a melancholy mood and sorrow, he is grieving for "the lost Lenore."

56. Which of the following is the best revision of the underlined portion of sentence 8 below?

However, the bird's repetition of "Nevermore" leads the speaker to the realization that Lenore will never return, the bird becomes an omen of doom and is called "evil" by the mournful speaker.

(A) realize the following—Lenore will never return, the bird is evil and an omen of doom.

(B) the realization of Lenore's failure to return, the evil and omen of doom of the bird.

(C) realize that Lenore will never return, so the bird, called "evil" by the mournful speaker, becomes an omen of doom.

(D) the realization that Lenore will never return, the bird becomes an omen of doom and is called "evil" by the mournful speaker.

(E) the Lenore will never return, that the bird is an omen of doom, and that the bird should be called "evil."

57. Which is the best revision of the underlined portion of sentence 11 below?

Shrieking with anguish, the bird is ordered to leave, but it replies, "Nevermore."

(A) the bird is ordered to leave but replies

(B) the man orders the bird to leave, but it

(C) the order is given for the bird to leave, but it

(D) the bird, ordered to leave,

(E) the man orders the bird to leave and

58. In relation to the passage as a whole, which of the following best describes the writer's intention in the second paragraph?

(A) To show specific examples of supernatural effects

(B) To argue that the bird has evil intent

(C) To convince the reader to read the poem

(D) To analyze the progression of ideas in the literature

(E) To describe the appearance of the bird

59. In the context of the sentences preceding and following sentence 15, which of the following is the best revision of sentence 15?

(A) Only repeating one word, others feel the bird is innocent of any premeditated wrongdoing.

(B) Innocent and not doing anything, the bird repeats one word.

(C) Innocent of any premeditated wrongdoing, the bird does not do anything.

(D) One may argue that, innocent of any premeditated wrongdoing, the bird does not do anything but repeat one word.

(E) Others feel the bird is innocent of any premeditated wrongdoing because it does not do anything but repeat one word.

60. Which of the following would be a better way to end the passage, combining sentences 16 and 17?

(A) One thing is certain, however: the poem's haunting refrain is a familiar one which students of American literature will memorize and forget "nevermore."

(B) One thing is certain, however, that the poem's haunting refrain is familiar, one which students of American literature will memorize and forget "nevermore."

(C) One thing is certain, however; the poem's haunting refrain is familiar, one which students of American literature will memorize and forget "nevermore."

(D) One thing is certain, however: the poem's haunting refrain is familiar, one which students of American literature will memorize and forget "nevermore."

(E) One thing that is certain is that the poem's haunting refrain is familiar, one which students of American literature will memorize and forget "nevermore."

SAT II: WRITING
TEST 5

ANSWER KEY

1. (B)	16. (B)	31. (E)	46. (D)
2. (D)	17. (D)	32. (B)	47. (D)
3. (A)	18. (C)	33. (C)	48. (B)
4. (C)	19. (E)	34. (D)	49. (C)
5. (E)	20. (C)	35. (E)	50. (A)
6. (C)	21. (C)	36. (A)	51. (C)
7. (D)	22. (B)	37. (E)	52. (E)
8. (D)	23. (B)	38. (B)	53. (A)
9. (B)	24. (A)	39. (C)	54. (D)
10. (B)	25. (D)	40. (C)	55. (C)
11. (B)	26. (E)	41. (E)	56. (C)
12. (A)	27. (E)	42. (B)	57. (B)
13. (B)	28. (D)	43. (A)	58. (D)
14. (B)	29. (A)	44. (B)	59. (E)
15. (D)	30. (D)	45. (E)	60. (D)

DETAILED EXPLANATIONS
OF ANSWERS

Part A: Essay

Sample Essays with Commentary

ESSAY I (Score: 5–6)

In the past thirty years, television has become a very popular pasttime for almost everyone. From the time the mother places the baby in his jumpseat in front of the television so that she can relax and have a second cup of coffee until the time the senior citizen in the retirement home watches Vanna White turn the letters on "Wheel of Fortune," Americans spend endless hours in front of the "boob tube." I believe that television can become an addiction that provides an escape from the problems of the world and from facing responsibility for your own life.

When my mother was a little girl, what did children do to entertain themselves? They played. Their games usually involved social interaction with other children as well as imaginatively creating entertainment for themselves. They also developed hobbies like woodworking and sewing. Today, few children really know how to play with each other or entertain themselves. Instead, they sit in front of the television, glued to cartoons that are senseless and often violent. Even if they watch educational programs like "Sesame Street," they don't really have to do anything but watch and listen to what the answer to the question is.

Teenagers, also, use television as a way of avoiding doing things that will help them mature. How many kids do much homework anymore? Why not? Because they come home from work tired and relax in front of the television. Even if they watch a controversial program about some problem in the world like AIDS or the war in the Middle East, they don't usually do anything about it.

In addition, young mothers use television to escape their problems. The terrible woes of the people on the soap operas make their problems seem less important. This means that they don't need to solve their own problems.

Although it may seem as if television is really great for older people, I think even my grandma would have more fun if she had more interests rather than just watching quiz shows. I know she has blotted out the "real world" when she expects us to act like the Cosby kids when she comes to visit.

In conclusion, I believe that television really can become an addiction that allows people of all ages to avoid facing their own problems and lose themselves in the problems of other people.

ANALYSIS

Essay I has a score range of 5-6. It has a traditional structure; the first paragraph introduces the topic, even suggesting the chronological organization of the essay. Each of the next four paragraphs has a clear topic sentence and details that develop it. The concluding paragraph, although only one sentence in length, restates the main idea. The essay is, therefore, clearly unified around the writer's opinion, which the writer tries to prove in a logical fashion. The writer effectively employs transitional words to relate the main ideas, varied sentence structure, and controlled vocabulary. Although the writer misspells *pastime*, uses the colloquial word *kids*, and has some problem with parallelism, repetition, and pronoun usage, the essay is well written considering the 20-minute time limit.

ESSAY II (Score: 4–5)

I do not agree with the given statement. I think that instead of being bad for people, television not only does not blot out the real world but, instead, gives the person watching it a chance to experience the real world, even places he can't possibly go and may never get a chance to go.

For instance, I've learned a lot about the Vietnam War by watching TV. For a while, I heard things about it, about how some of the veterans didn't feel as if they were welcomed right when they came back from that war. I didn't understand what was the matter. Then they built a special memorial in Washington for the veterans that didn't come back. Since then, I have seen a lot of programs that showed what went on in Vietnam, and I've heard Vietnam vets talk about what happened to them. I think that that war has become very real to me because of TV.

Television educates us about the dangers of growing up in America today. I've seen good programs about the dangers of using drugs, about teenage pregnancy and what happens if you try to keep the baby, about eating too much cholesterol (That doesn't matter to me yet, but my dad needs to watch that!), and also anorexia. These are things we all need to know about, and TV has told about them so we know what to do.

I really am convinced that television brings the real world into your house. I think us kids today know a lot more about the real world than our grandparents did who grew up without television.

ANALYSIS

Essay II has a score range of 4-5. It is competently written. The writer takes one position and develops it. The first paragraph provides a clear introduction, and paragraphs two and three develop the thesis. Generalized examples are provided. The final paragraph concludes the essay. The essay contains some problems in correct usage, colloquial words like *kids*, and a lack of specific, concrete examples. (What, specifically, did the writer learn about the Vietnam War?) Sentences lack variety in length and construction, with many beginning with the pronoun "I." Ideas are not always clearly related to each other. The theme contains unnecessary repetition and errors in pronoun use.

ESSAY III (Score: 3–4)

On the one hand, I think television is bad, But it also does some good things for all of us. For instants, my little sister thought she wanted to be a policeman until she saw police shows on TV. Then she learned how dangerous it is and now she wants to be an astronaut. I guess she didn't watch the Challenger explode often enough to scare her out of that.

But the bad thing about television programs are the ideas it puts in kids heads. Like violent things happen on television, and little kids see it and don't know that other people hurt when they are hit, battered up, beat, shot, ect. Then the kids go out and try to knock their friends around and think if they are strong and handsome that they can get their own way whatever happens. Even parents sometimes have trouble controling their own kids because of too much TV. Of course that's partly because the parents watch too much too when they should of been taking care of the kids they necklected them watching television.

So I think that television has both it's good and it's bad points. I'd hate to see us get rid of it all together, but I wonder if I'll let my kids watch it when I have them. It sometimes puts bad ideas in their heads.

ANALYSIS

Essay III has a score range of 3-4. The failure of the writer of this essay, to take one opinion and clearly develop it, weakens the essay. The writer does try to give specific examples, but the details in the introductory paragraph would be more appropriate later in the essay. The apparent topic sentence of the second paragraph suggests a discussion of the results of children's watching television, but the writer discusses the parents' viewing in the same paragraph. The last sentence of the conclusion repeats the idea of the topic sentence of the second paragraph. The writer does not express his ideas in precise fashion ("Even parents sometimes have trouble controling (sic) their own kids because of too much TV.") or provide clear relationships between them. The essay also contains colloquialisms and errors in pronoun use, spelling, use of the apostrophe, and sentence construction.

ESSAY IV (Score: 1–2)

I get really upset when someone says they don't think we should watch television. Us students learn a lot more from television than whats in a lot of our classes in school. I've even learned stuff from the comertials they show the best way to clean house or the best kinds of car to buy right now I wouldn't have no idea what to get my sister for her birthday if I hadn't of seen it on television and said to myself, "Sally'd love one of those!"

If no one watched television, can you just think about how much crime there would be because kids would be board and would have to get excitment somewheres else than in his own living room where the TV set is.

There's also educational television with shows that ask questions and see if you know any answers. That's where I learned a lot of stuff about the world and everything.

ANALYSIS

Essay IV has a score range of 1-2. The writer of this essay digresses from the emphasis of the assigned topic in his effort to defend the watching of television. Although he has a clearly stated opinion, he falls to develop it in a logical, unified fashion. There is no clear introduction; the second paragraph, only one sentence in length, is not properly developed; and the paper is lacking a conclusion. In addition, the language of this essay is not exact, and the ideas are not developed with specific examples. For example, what "stuff" has he learned from educational television? The essay contains serious problems in grammar and usage such as double negatives, run-on sentences, errors in pronoun reference and case, misspelled words, and errors in idiom.

Part B: Multiple-Choice

1. **(B)**   As you read the sentence, you should recognize that choice (B) presents a shift of pronoun. The correct choice of pronoun to refer to the antecedent, the indefinite pronoun "anyone," is "he or she." Choice (A), "plans," is third-person singular to agree with its subject "anyone"; choice (C), "to see," is an infinitive introducing an adverb phrase; and choice (D), "of the sites," is a prepositional phrase modifying "all."

2. **(D)**   Choice (D), "inaccessible from," is idiomatically incorrect. The preposition that should follow "inaccessible" is "to." Choice (A), "important," is a predicate adjective modifying the subject "it"; choice (B) is a coordinating conjunction correctly joining the nouns "medications" and "preparations"; and choice (C), "be stored," is the subjunctive form, correctly used in a "that" clause expressing a requirement or recommendation.

3. **(A)**   You should recognize that choice (A) calls for the adverb "slowly" to modify "worked" rather than the adjective "slow." Choice (B), "meticulously," is an adverb modifying the adjective "careful"; choice (C), "was," is third-person singular to agree with the singular subject "report"; and choice (D) is the predicate adjective "accurate" that modifies the subject of the clause, "report."

4. **(C)**   Choice (C) calls for the objective form, "whom," because the relative pronoun is the object of the verb "have heard." Choice (A), "giving," is a participle introducing a participial phrase modifying the subject "man"; choice (B), "is," agrees in number with its subject "man"; and choice (D), "have heard," is a verb in the present perfect tense that correctly expresses action that occurred in the past and continues into the present.

5. **(E)**   All labeled elements of this sentence are choices acceptable in standard written English. Choice (A), "although," is a subordinating conjunction introducing a subordinate clause; choice (B), "older," is the comparative form of the adjective, appropriate for the comparison of the singular "she" to the singular indefinite pronoun "anyone else"; choice (C), "anyone else," is idiomatically correct; and choice (D) is an adverb prepositional phrase modifying the adjective "young."

6. **(C)** The problem with this sentence is parallel structure. Choice (C) "shouting" is a present participle while choice (A) is a simple past tense. Choice (C) should be changed to "shouted" so the tenses will be the same. Choice (B) "president's" is a correct possessive; and choice (D) is idiomatically correct.

7. **(D)** The verb at choice (D) must agree with its subject, "variety," and, therefore, needs to be the singular form, "changes." Choice (A), "fresh," is an adjective describing the noun "ice cream"; choice (B), "daily," is an adverb modifying the verb "make"; and choice (C), "of flavors," is an adjective prepositional phrase modifying the noun "variety."

8. **(D)** You should recognize that the word arrangement and punctuation place the prepositional phrase "as a lubricant" as the fourth object of the preposition "for"; the phrase is not parallel to the preceding noun objects. By inserting an "and" between "candles" and "soap" and eliminating the comma after "soap," you revise this sentence by providing parallel phrases after the verb. Choice (A), "it provided," is correct as pronoun subject, referring to "whaling," and verb of the introductory adverb clause; choice (B) is a predicative nominative, "vocation," and its modifier; the passive verb "was used," choice (C), is past tense and agrees in number with its subject, "oil."

9. **(B)** The error is one of diction. The word "literally," choice (B), is an adverb that means that the action of the verb really occurred; clearly the subject did not "really" die of starvation if he was able to eat. Choice (A), "greedily," is an adverb appropriately describing how "he" ate; choice (C), the past perfect verb, "had been lost," is correct to refer to an action that occurred before the action of the main verb; and choice (D), "for two days," is an adverb prepositional phrase modifying the verb "had been lost."

10. **(B)** You should recognize an error in comparison in choice (B). Because the writer is comparing more than two contributions that Montagu might have made, the adverb should be the superlative form, "best." Choice (A), "might have made," is the correct form for the conditional verb in a "that" clause; choice (C), "that permitted," is the subject "that," referring to the antecedent "lunch," and the verb of the adjective subordinate clause; and choice (D), the infinitive "to continue," is idiom-

atically correct to introduce a noun phrase that serves as direct object of the verb "permitted."

11. **(B)** You should recognize in choice (B) an error in verb tense. The past perfect, "had beaten," would be appropriate only if the action occurred before the action of the verb in the main clause. Because the two actions occurred simultaneously, the simple past tense form, "beat," is correct. Choice (A), "When," is a subordinating conjunction correctly introducing a subordinate clause; choice (C), "made," is in the simple past tense and agrees in number with its subject, "teams"; choice (D), "kicking a round ball," is an idiomatically correct phrase serving as object of the preposition "by."

12. **(A)** You should know that the noun "kind" must agree in number with the adjective preceding it; therefore, in choice (A), the word "kinds" should replace the singular "kind" to agree with the plural adjective "those." Choice (B), "who," introduces the subordinate adjective clause and is in the nominative case because it serves as subject in the clause; choice (C), "good," is the correct predicate adjective to modify "who" when the meaning is "satisfactory"; and choice (D), "themselves," is a reflexive pronoun referring to "who."

13. **(B)** The error is in choice (B), where the correct past tense form of the verb "sneak" is "sneaked," not "snuck." Choice (A), "had been sent," is correct in the past perfect form because the action was completed before the action of the main clause; choice (C), "downstairs," is an adverb modifying the verb; and choice (D), "lay," is the correct past tense form of the verb "lie."

14. **(B)** The given sentence contains a double negative. The "no" in choice (B) should be replaced by "any" or "a" following the negative verb and adverb, "hadn't." Choice (A) is a past tense passive verb, "was shown," and adverb, "originally," in idiomatic word order; choice (C), "to see," is an infinite introducing an adjective phrase modifying "chance"; choice (D), "its," is a possessive pronoun referring to "cartoon."

15. **(D)** You should recognize that the error occurs in choice (D), where the correct adjective to compare two people is the comparative form, "more famous." Choice (A), "are recognized," is correct in the present passive form and is plural to agree with its subject, "portraits"; choice (B), "by most Americans," is an adverb prepositional phrase in

idiomatic word order; and choice (C), "were," agrees in number with its compound subject, "Gilbert Stuart" and "daughter" and is correct in the past tense.

16. **(B)** You should recognize that the nominative case pronoun, "I," is needed as predicate nominative following the linking verb, "were," in choice (B). Choice (A), the subjunctive form "were," is correct to show condition contrary to fact; choice (C), "who," is a relative pronoun serving as subject of the subordinate adjective clause it introduces and, therefore, is correct in the nominative case; choice (D) "would complain," uses the auxiliary "would" to express condition.

17. **(D)** The error in choice (D) is one of diction. The auxiliary verb for the present perfect tense is "have'; "of" is a preposition and does not belong in a verb phrase. Choice (A), the adverb "really" and the predicate adjective "tragic," is idiomatically correct; choice (B), the verb "fell," is correct in the simple past tense; and choice (C), "that," is a relative pronoun that introduces the subordinate adjective clause modifying its antecedent, "well."

18. **(C)** The correct tense to indicate action that occurred once in the past is the simple past passive form "was shot"; the present perfect form with the auxiliary "has" would be appropriate for action from the past that continues into the present. Choice (A), "after the surrender," is idiomatically correct as the subordinating conjunction, article modifier, and subject of the adverb subordinate clause; choice (B), "signalled," is a verb in the past tense that agrees in number with "surrender" and is appropriate for an action that occurred once in the past; and choice (D), "were attending," is the past progressive verb showing an action that continued for a period of time in the past.

19. **(E)** All choices in this sentence are correct in standard written English. The passive verb, "are concerned," choice (A), is plural to agree with its subject, the collective noun "majority" that is plural in meaning; choice (B), the noun "effects," represents correct diction; choice (C), "of watching" is a preposition with a gerund serving as its object; and choice (D), "their," is a plural possessive pronoun agreeing in number with its antecedent, "majority."

20. **(C)** The error is at choice (C), where the singular "he" or "she" is correct to refer to its singular antecedent, the indefinite pronoun "anyone,"

and where the verb "remember" must also be changed to the singular form "remembers" to agree with its subject. Choice (A), "is," agrees with its singular subject "who"; choice (B), "thinks," agrees with its singular subject "anyone"; and choice (D), "most popular," is the superlative form of the adjective, correct to compare more than two toys.

21. **(C)** You should recognize that the problem in the sentence is that the predicate nominative, "winner," does not agree in number with the subject, "Horses." It must be replaced by "winners" and the article "a" must be eliminated. Choice (A), "named," is correct as a participle introducing a phrase that modifies "Horses"; "have been," choice (B), is in the present perfect tense, correct for a verb expressing action that occurred in the past and continued over a period of time; and choice (D), "recent years," is idiomatically correct as the object of a preposition and its adjective modifier.

22. **(B)** The error here occurs with the verb form of "lie" in choice (B); the past perfect tense calls for the past participle, with is "lain." The past perfect verb, "had felt," is correct in form and tense in choice (A); choice (C), "down," is an adverb idiomatic as modifier of "had lain"; and choice (D), "arose," is the past tense form of the verb "arise."

23. **(B)** Choice (B) contains a pronoun, "he," that does not have an antecedent in the sentence. A correction would replace the pronoun with a noun. Choices (A) and (C), "busily" and "immediately," are the correct forms of adverbs modifying "were serving" and "did notice," respectively, and their placement is idiomatic; and choice (D) is the participle "traveling" that modifies "child" and the adverb "alone," also idiomatic in wording.

24. **(A)** You should recognize that choice (A), "Irregardless," presents an error in diction. The suffix "less" makes the word "regard" negative; therefore, the correct word is "regardless." Choice (B), "well," is appropriate because an adverb is needed to modify the verb "did"; choice (C) is the proper conjunction to introduce the adverb subordinate clause modifying "afraid"; and choice (D), "would fail," correctly uses the past tense of the auxiliary verb "will" (to indicate possibility) with the present tense plural of the verb "fail."

25. **(D)** As you read the sentence, you should recognize that the error is in choice (D). The pronoun is the subject of the elliptical adverb clause,

"than he (was known)" and must, therefore, be in the nominative case rather than in the objective case. Choice (A) is an adverb correctly modifying the adjective "famous"; choice (B), the relative pronoun "who," correctly refers to its antecedent, "clergyman," and is in the nominative case as subject of the subordinate clause it introduces; and choice (C) is the comparative form of the adverb "well," indicating comparison of two people.

26. **(E)**　All choices in this sentence are correct in standard written English. Choice (A), "really," is an adverb that modifies the adjective "bad"; choice (B), "bad," is a predicate adjective modifying the subject, "She," and following the linking verb "felt"; choice (C), "burst," is the correct past tense form of the verb "burst"; and choice (D), "had purchased," is appropriate in the past perfect tense because it expresses an action that occurred before other actions or states of being expressed in the sentence.

27. **(E)**　This sentence contains no errors in standard written usage. Choices (A) and (B) correctly combine the present tense, "comes," with the future perfect tense, "will have shaken," to express action to be completed at a future time. Choice (C), "more," is the comparative form of the adjective "much," correct to compare two circumstances, the number of hands he shook with the number of hands he imagined he would shake; and choice (D), "ever," is an adverb correctly modifying "imagined."

28. **(D)**　You should recognize that the preposition "between" has a compound object; therefore, in choice (D) both pronouns must be in the objective case, "her and me." Choice (A), "never," is an adverb modifying the verb "had," and its placement is idiomatic; choice (B), "any," is an adjective modifying "skill," again placed idiomatically; and choice (C), "between, "is the appropriate preposition to refer to two people.

29. **(A)**　Choice (A), "about," is not idiomatically correct following the noun "circumstances"; correct prepositions to follow "circumstances" are "of, surrounding," or "concerning." Choice (B), "were," is a plural verb that agrees with its plural subject, "circumstances"; and choices (C) and (D) are predicate adjectives modifying the subject.

30. **(D)**　The error in this sentence is that the lack of parallelism in the comparison results in ambiguity. Choice (D), "than home," should read either "than it is at home" or "than at home." Choice (A), "Keeping one's

weight under control" is an idiomatically correct introductory gerund phrase used as a subject; choice (B), "is," agrees in number and person with the subject; and choice (C), "more difficult," is the comparative form of the adjective, correct for comparison of two situations.

31. **(E)**   This sentence starts with a dangling participial phrase that must be followed by the noun or pronoun that it modifies or be eliminated from the sentence altogether. Choice (E) correctly replaces the phrase with a subordinate clause that shows the causal relationship between the eating of paint chips and lead poisoning. Choices (B), (C), and (D) are also dangling phrases and create the same basic problem as the phrase in the original sentence.

32. **(B)**   Only choice (B) corrects the run-on sentence in this exercise in an acceptable fashion by adding the conjunction "and" to join the two sentences. Choice (C) corrects the run-on but poses the problem of the relative pronoun "who" that does not follow its antecedent; choice (D) retains the run-on and adds an awkward participial phrase; and choice (E) results in two run-on errors.

33. **(C)**   Choice (C) retains the pronoun "you" after the participial phrase that modifies it but eliminates the wordy dangling phrase, "the reason being that"; the revision expresses clearly the causal relationship. Choices (B) and (D) leave the introductory phrase dangling; and choice (E) results in an unclear antecedent for the pronoun "which" and fails to show the causal relationship.

34. **(D)**   Only choice (D) corrects the opening independent clause while retaining the original meaning of the sentence. Choice (A) is incorrect because "Being" is both an unattached participle and an improper conjugation of "to be," which must always be used as the main verb. Choices (B) and (E) are idiomatically incorrect and change the meaning. (E) also contains an unattached participle. Choice (C) is excessively wordy.

35. **(E)**   The problem here is one of parallel construction; choice (E) completes the comparison in parallel fashion and avoids the wordiness of choice (D). Choice (B) unnecessarily changes the tense but does not eliminate the problem; and choice (C) replaces the second clause with a dangling phrase.

36. **(A)**   This sentence is correct in standard written English because "whose," a possessive relative pronoun, is appropriate to refer to a city. Choice (B) eliminates the required possessive pronoun and is not idiomatically correct; choice (C) is wordy and awkward; choice (D) results in a run-on sentence; and choice (E) replaces the possessive pronoun with the contraction that means "who is."

37. **(E)**   The problem is one of wordiness, and choice (E) correctly shows relationship and eliminates words that add nothing to the meaning of the sentence. Each of the other choices retains unnecessary words.

38. **(B)**   The original sentence is wordy and includes the use of the pronoun "they," for which there is no antecedent. Choice (B) replaces the independent clause with the second part of a compound predicate that is parallel to the predicate in the preceding clause. Choice (C) adds a dangling participial phrase; choice (D) retains the original "they" without an antecedent as well as the unnecessary use of the pronoun "it"; and choice (E) results in a run-on sentence.

39. **(C)**   Choice (C) correctly replaces the singular verb "is" with the plural form "are" to agree with the plural subject, "habits"; in addition, it replaces with parallel gerund phrases the awkward noun clause that serves as predicate nominative. Choices (A) and (B) retain the incorrect singular verb "is"; choice (D) inappropriately changes the gerund to the present perfect form; and choice (E) equates the habits with trees, food, and dams and lodges rather than with the beaver's activities.

40. **(C)**   The words in this exercise result in a sentence fragment, not a complete sentence. Only choice (C) provides a predicate for the subject, "Bolivia." Choice (B) replaces the dangling phrase with a subordinate clause; choices (D) and (E) add main clauses but leave the subject, "Bolivia," without a predicate.

41. **(E)**   The problem with the original sentence is the ambiguity of "he." Choice (D) does not clarify whether Brutus or Caesar was pardoned. Choices (B) and (C) solve the problem, but each sentence is excessively wordy. Only choice (E) clarifies the meaning economically.

42. **(B)**   Choice (B) best shows the temporal relationship by making the second clause subordinate. The other choices do not show the relationship clearly; and, in addition, choice (D) contains a dangling participial phrase.

43. **(A)**   The sentence is correct in standard written English. Choices (B), (C), and (D) introduce problems in parallelism; and choice (E) is awkward, uses the contraction for "who" is instead of the possessive pronoun "whose," and confuses "respectfully" with "respectively."

44. **(B)**   Choice (B) eliminates unnecessary words and the use of the pronoun "it" without a clear antecedent. All of the other choices retain the vague and ambiguous use of "it." In addition, choice (E) begins with a dangling participial phrase.

45. **(E)**   Only choice (E) provides the correct parallel construction in which each major element appearing after "not only" has a parallel element after "but also." Each of the other choices has a lack of parallelism, and choice (B), in addition, unnecessarily splits the infinitive "to provide."

46. **(D)**   The original sentence contains a shift of pronoun from third person "anyone" to second person "you." Only choice (D) provides consistency in pronoun number without using an inappropriate tense, as in choice (E). Use of the passive voice in choice (B) loses parallelism in construction; and choice (C) retains the incorrect "you."

47. **(D)**   This exercise is a sentence fragment, not a complete sentence. The subject has no verb but is followed by two subordinate clauses. To correct this sentence, eliminate the subordinating conjunction, "where," and the subject of the subordinate clause, "he," to provide a predicate for the subject, "Father Junipero Serra." Choice (D) accomplishes what is necessary. Choices (B) and (C) result in run-on sentences; and choice (E) substitutes a verbal phrase for the necessary predicate and does not solve the problem of the fragment.

48. **(B)**   The given sentence does not provide parallelism in construction. The conjunction "but" joins the adjective "eager" with a prepositional phrase. Choice (B) correctly provides the adjective "afraid" followed by an infinitive phrase parallel with "eager to explain his point of view." The verbal phrases in the other choices do not result in parallel construction; in addition, choice (C) is a dangling phrase.

49. **(C)**   The passage basically describes some of the polar bear's basic traits. Its tone is detached and factual, like an entry in an encyclopedia. Therefore, the writer's personal feeling is not the issue as in choice (A). The paragraph is describing one example of Alaskan wildlife, so (C) is

insufficient. (D) is inaccurate because the passage does not seem to set out to "prove" anything. Choice (E) contradicts the focus of the entire passage.

50. **(A)**　Polar bears continue to live near the North Pole, so the past tense is inappropriate.

51. **(C)**　Sentence (C) digresses from the main topic, which is the polar bear and its habits, to a geological account of the Arctic region in general. This is irrelevant to the progression of this passage, and would best be eliminated.

52. **(E)**　Sentence 5 is best as it is; the punctuation is correct and the modifiers are properly placed. (D) would be the next best choice; it is technically correct, though more clumsy than the original. (A), (B), and (C) all scramble the sense of an otherwise clear sentence.

53. **(A)**　Choice (A) is best because it continues the physical description of the polar bear. (B) is not wholly irrelevant, as it deals with the bears' eyesight, but it would be best placed elsewhere. (C) and (E) introduces new subjects. (D), like (B), is somewhat relevant, but would be best placed elsewhere.

54. **(D)**　Choice (D) combines the two sentences best using commas to separate the thoughts. Choice (A) introduces a colon which may work, if the end of the sentence were altered. "While" in the last portion of the sentence, though, is absolutely wrong. (B), as it stands, would best be changed back to two sentences. Choice (C) is similar to (A) insofar as "though" confuses the relationship between the two ideas.

55. **(C)**　Choice (C) correctly and smoothly combines the two adjectives while providing sentence variety. Choice (A) is not parallel; "grieving" is not parallel with the other two adjectives. In choice (B), the adjectives appear to modify the dead Lenore. In choices (D) and (E), the ideas of melancholy and grief are not stated in concise parallel structure.

56. **(C)**　Choice (C) is the most concise expression of the major ideas. Choice (A) is too abrupt and states that the bird "is evil" instead of being "called 'evil.'" Choice (B) contains awkward wording: "the realization of" and "the evil and omen of doom of the bird." The wording of choice (D) creates a run-on sentence. Choice (E) incorrectly twists the idea of evil.

57. **(B)** Choice (B) correctly identifies who is doing what. Choices (A) and (C) do not indicate the man as the subject. Choice (D) implies the bird is shrieking with anguish, and choice (E) implies the man is shrieking with anguish as well as replying.

58. **(D)** This essay is an analysis of Poe's narrative poem "The Raven," and as such shows the progression of ideas in that poem. Choices (A) and (B) might be plausible, but there is too much ambiguity for the events to be classified as supernatural or the bird's intent as clearly evil. Choice (E) is not fully developed in the paper. Choice (C) might be a logical choice, but it is not the outstanding intent.

59. **(E)** Choice (E) correctly uses the cause-and-effect construction; in addition, this choice uses a transition word at the beginning of the sentence in order to indicate contrast of ideas. Choice (A) employs a misplaced modifier which implies the "others" are repeating the "one word." Choices (B) and (C) leave out a transition word and present as fact what is considered opinion. Choice (D) is too formal and also omits the transition word.

60. **(D)** The colon is the most appropriate way to unify the closing thoughts into a single sentence. (A) also utilizes the colon, but the elimination of the comma to create the phrase "is a familiar one" is more clumsy than the original. (B) adds a comma between the two sentences, which creates a run-on. (C) uses a semicolon which is inappropriate. (E), "that is certain is that," both loses the necessary sense of "however," as well as creates an unnecessarily long and convoluted sentence.

SAT II: Writing

Practice Test 6

SAT II: WRITING TEST 6

Part A: Essay

TIME: 20 Minutes

DIRECTIONS: You have 20 minutes to plan and write an essay on the topic below. You may write only on the assigned topic.

Make sure to give specific examples to support your thesis. Proofread your essay carefully and take care to express your ideas clearly and effectively.

Write your essay on the lined pages at the back of the book.

ESSAY TOPIC:

Polls of American youth suggest they want high paying jobs, not necessarily satisfying careers. This reflects the current cultural value implied in the popular media that money is the key which opens the golden door to satisfaction, unlike the traditional value of work for its own reward.

ASSIGNMENT: Do you agree or disagree with this statement? Support your opinion with specific examples from history, current events, literature, or personal experience.

Part B: Multiple-Choice

(Answer sheets appear in the back of this book.)

TIME: 40 Minutes
         60 Questions

DIRECTIONS: Each of the following sentences may contain an error in diction, usage, idiom, or grammar. Some sentences are correct. Some sentences contain one error. No sentence contains more than one error.

If there is an error, it will appear in one of the underlined portions labeled A, B, C, or D. If there is no error, choose the portion labeled E. If there is an error, select the letter of the portion that must be changed in order to correct the sentence.

EXAMPLE:

He drove <u>slowly</u> and <u>cautiously</u> in order to <u>hopefully</u> avoid having an
       A   **B**   **C**

<u>accident</u>. <u>No error</u>.
   D   **E**
                                      (A) (B) ● (D) (E)

---

1.   If the selection of the <u>President of the United States</u> <u>was</u> <u>solely</u> the
                                A   **B**   **C**

   responsibility of a handful of people, we <u>would</u> have an oligarchy,
                                         D

   not a democratic republic. <u>No error</u>.
                          E

2.   Writer Tom Wolfe says that many Americans <u>flaunt</u> religion by
                                           A

   <u>worshipping</u> art, <u>contributing</u> their money not to their church or syna-
       B   **C**

   gogue but to the <u>arts</u>. <u>No error</u>.
                D   **E**

3.   The reason <u>astronomers</u> study quasars, small <u>quasi-stellar</u> objects, is
               A   **B**

because they might provide clues to the origin of the universe.
  C   D

No error.
E

4.   English essayist Francis Bacon proposed a system of reasoning re-
                                    A

ferred to as induction, and is a quasi-scientific method involving the
                     B   C

collecting and inventorying of a great mass of observations from
                D

nature. No error.
        E

5.   Due to her pride in African-American culture, Zora Neale Hurston
     A

wrote in the 1920's that she was "the only Negro in the United
  B   C

States" without an Indian chief for a grandfather. No error.
             D   E

6.   People from the Middle East and Latin America stand more closely
              A   B

to each other when holding a conversation than in the United States.
          C   D

No error.
E

7.   Distinguished psychiatrist Karen Horney claiming that the distrust
                                A   B

between the sexes cannot be explained away as existing only in indi-
                                    C

viduals because of psychological forces that exist in men and women.
        D

No error.
E

8.   An ethnic American, for example, an Asian-American, who becomes
                                  A

an academic exists by definition in a culture separate from their non-
                                         B

academic roots <u>and, therefore,</u> has difficulty <u>reestablishing</u> ties to the
              C   **D**

ethnic community. <u>No error.</u>
                    E

9. Curiously, there <u>are</u> <u>more</u> teachers of the English language in Russia
                     A **B**

   <u>than there are</u> students of the <u>Russian language</u> in the United States.
         C   **D**

   <u>No error.</u>
    E

10. <u>Although</u> philosopher George Santayana assumed that the material
    A

   world was the source of <u>thought,</u> he believed that all <u>that</u> was worth-
                         B   **C**

   while in human experience <u>has</u> developed from the imagination.
                         D

   <u>No error.</u>
    E

11. To find the time <u>during which</u> our view of the natural world <u>came to</u>
                 A   **B**

   <u>be</u> expressed as an orderly mathematical model, we must <u>refer back</u>
                                                 C

   to the <u>1600s</u> when Rene Descartes proposed a clockwork model of
          D

   the universe. <u>No error.</u>
              E

12. Gregor Mendel, the famous <u>monk</u> and early <u>geneticist,</u> studied not
                            A   **B**

   only the <u>color</u> of the peas, but also <u>observed</u> the shapes of the seed.
            C   **D**

   <u>No error.</u>
    E

13. Many government officials <u>distrust</u> the people <u>who</u> they <u>serve;</u> there-
                         A   **B**   **C**

   fore, these officials arrogate decision-making power <u>to themselves.</u>
                                                 D

No error.
  E

14. Lamenting the demise of the familiar essay, Joseph Wood Krutch
    A   B
    wrote that no modern "live-wire" magazine editor would never pub-
                                                             C
    lish nonfiction articles unless they were factual, polemical, or repor-
                                        D
    torial. No error.
            E

15. Judith Martin, writing as "Miss Manners," thinks Americans have
                    A
    etiquette problems because we believe people should behave "natu-
    B   C   D
    rally." No error.
            E

16. Spaniard Santiago Ramon y Cajal's 1904 book on the human nervous
                              A
    system, still recognized as the most important single work in
            B
    neurobiology, infers that neuron interconnections are highly struc-
    C   D
    tured. No error.
           E

17. Filmmakers like Italian Federico Fellini, whose autobiographical 8 1/2
                                              A
    explores the artist's creative dysfunction, helps define motion pic-
                 B   C
    tures as art because of the exploration of ideas and images rather than
                                                                    D
    the exploitation of movie stars and popular novels. No error.
                                                        E

18. By answering the charges against communism in the second section
       A
    of "The Communist Manifesto," Karl Marx is able to exactly clarify
                                                         B

what communism is and what it promises. No error.
  C   D   E

19. Wolfgang Mozart <u>claimed</u> to compose an entire piece of music in his
                         A

    head all at once before he <u>actually</u> wrote it <u>travelling in a carriage</u> as
                                  B   C

    if the writing down of the composition <u>were</u> a mechanical act.
                                        D

    No error.
    E

20. Saying that <u>bullfighting</u> is not a sport but a tragedy, <u>there is</u> danger
              A   B

    for the man <u>but certain death</u> for the animal, <u>writes Ernest</u>
                    C   D

    Hemingway in a 1932 book. No error.
                          E

21. Young and old <u>alike</u> have long considered <u>such</u> novels as *Treasure*
               A   B

    Island and *Alice in Wonderland* <u>to be</u> <u>a classic</u> of children's literature.
                                    C   D

    No error.
    E

22. Between 50 <u>to</u> 53 percent of eligible Americans <u>voted</u> in the last
              A   B

    seven <u>Presidential</u> elections; <u>the rest</u> did not. No error.
              C   D   E

23. Everybody seems <u>quick</u> to <u>assert</u> <u>their</u> rights; very few <u>seem</u> quick to
                     A   B   C   D

    acknowledge their responsibilities. No error.
                               E

24. Reading the ancient classics by <u>such</u> writers as Homer, Plato, Virgil,
                              A

    and Ovid, until recently standard in the college curriculum, <u>are</u> once
                                                B

    <u>again</u> an <u>integral</u> part of an undergraduate's education. <u>No error</u>.
    C   D   E

25. Recent studies <u>suggesting</u> <u>that</u> dinosaurs have the "<u>right-sized</u>" brains
               A   **B**   **C**

    for reptiles of <u>their</u> body size. <u>No error</u>.
                   D   **E**

26. <u>As far as</u> the beginning of life on land, Rachel Carson <u>says</u> that an
    A   **B**

    <u>arthropod</u> first <u>crept out</u> on shore some 350 million years ago.
    C   **D**

    <u>No error</u>.
    E

27. <u>Because of</u> <u>triple-digit</u> inflation in some countries, maintaining a liv-
    A   **B**

    ing standard is difficult; and <u>they</u> must have <u>either</u> big salary in-
                                 C   **D**

    creases or a lower standard of living. <u>No error</u>.
                                   E

28. <u>Throughout</u> the election campaign, the President <u>maintains</u> that
    A   **B**

    <u>people</u> were <u>better off</u> than they were before he was elected. <u>No error</u>.
    C   **D**   **E**

29. Anne Frank <u>says</u> <u>in her diary</u> that <u>nobody</u> would want to read her
              A   **B**   **C**

    thoughts, but she had nothing to <u>loose</u> by writing them down.
                                 D

    <u>No error</u>.
    E

30. A recent educational study <u>reports</u> that high school students <u>are</u>
                          A   **B**

    <u>not only</u> ignorant of the past but also <u>indifferent</u> to historical dates
    C   **D**

    and chronology. <u>No error</u>.
                   E

DIRECTIONS: In each of the following sentences, some portion of the sentence is underlined. Under each sentence are five choices. The first choice has the same wording as the original. The other four choices are reworded. Sometimes the first choice containing the original wording is the best; sometimes one of the other choices is the best. Choose the letter of the best choice. Your choice should produce a sentence which is not ambiguous or awkward and which is correct, clear, and precise.

This is a test of correct and effective English expression. Keep in mind the standards of English usage, punctuation, grammar, word choice, and construction.

EXAMPLE:

When you listen to opera, <u>a person may not appreciate it.</u>

(A)   a person may not appreciate it.

(B)   it may not be appreciated by a person.

(C)   which may not be appreciated by one.

(D)   you may not appreciate it.

(E)   appreciating it may be a problem for you.

31. <u>In Harry Golden's "vertical Negro plan," he suggests</u> facetiously that a solution to the perceived problem of sit-ins in the 1950s would be to provide stand-up desks—with no seats—in the public schools.

   (A) In Harry Golden's "vertical Negro plan," he suggests

   (B) In his "vertical Negro plan" he suggests

   (C) Harry Golden's "vertical Negro plan" suggests

   (D) In the "vertical Negro plan" Harry Golden suggests

   (E) In his satiric "vertical Negro plan" Harry Golden suggests

32. A famous basketball player's reason for his uncanny ability to shoot hook shots accurately is that he has a <u>sense of where you are on the court.</u>

   (A) sense of where you are on the court.

   (B) sense of where he is on the court.

(C) sense of where you were on the court.

(D) sense of where he was on the court.

(E) sense of where the court was in relation to his position on it.

33. Both Huckleberry Finn and Holden Caulfield wanted <u>to be a free person</u>, unburdened by social inconveniences.

(A) to be a free person

(B) each to be free persons

(C) to be free persons each one

(D) to be free persons

(E) to be free people

34. The student thought that the professor was <u>an absent-minded kind of stereotype</u>.

(A) an absent-minded kind of stereotype.

(B) the typical absent-minded professor type.

(C) typically like the kind of stereotyped absent-minded professor.

(D) an absent-minded professor type.

(E) stereotypically absent-minded.

35. Through photosynthesis, trees and plants absorb carbon <u>dioxide and they in the same complex and complicated process</u> release oxygen into the atmosphere.

(A) dioxide and they in the same complex and complicated process

(B) dioxide and in the same complex process

(C) dioxide, and they in the same complicated process

(D) dioxide, and they in the same complex process

(E) dioxide; they in the same complex and complicated process

36. <u>When the President reaped political benefit from a television documentary critical of him in its script, it proved that the pictures showing him being "Presidential" outweighed the words.</u>

(A) When the President reaped political benefit from a television documentary critical of him in its script, it proved that the pictures showing him being "Presidential" outweighed the words.

(B) When the President reaped political benefit from a television documentary critical of him only in its script, it went to prove that the pictures showing him being "Presidential" outweighed the words.

(C) Proving that the pictures showing him being "Presidential" outweighed the words, the President reaped political benefit from a television documentary critical of him in its script.

(D) Proving that the pictures of the President being "Presidential" outweighed the words, the President reaped political benefit from a television documentary critical of him only in the words, not in the pictures.

(E) Proving that the pictures which showed the President being "Presidential" outweighed the words, the President reaped political benefit from a television documentary that was, nonetheless, critical of him only in the words.

37. Former slave Harriet Tubman, whose participation in the Underground Railroad made her famous, <u>does not appear on E.D. Hirsch's list</u> of "What Literate Americans Know."

(A) does not appear on E.D. Hirsch's list

(B) did not appear on E.D. Hirsch's list

(C) had not appeared on E.D. Hirsch's list

(D) was not on E.D. Hirsch's list

(E) never appeared on E.D. Hirsch's list

38. <u>Having command of realism, subtlety, as well as drawing</u>, Mary Cassatt earned a belated reputation as a great American painter.

(A) Having command of realism, subtlety, as well as drawing

(B) Having command of realism, subtlety, and her drawing ability

(C) By being in command of both realism and subtlety and also drawing

(D) With her command of realism and subtlety and being able to draw

(E) Because of her command of realism, subtlety, and drawing

39. In primitive culture, myth fulfills an indispensable function: <u>the ex-pression, enhancement, and codification of belief, and makes it</u> a vital ingredient of human civilization.

    (A) the expression, enhancement, and codification of belief, and makes it

    (B) it expresses, enhances, and codifies belief, which makes it

    (C) the expression, enhancement, and codification of belief, which makes myth

    (D) the expression, enhancement, and codification of belief, making it

    (E) it expresses, enhances, and codifies belief, and this, in turn, makes it

40. <u>The claim that the goal of teaching basic science is</u> to convey the scientific method is to make the same formalistic mistake as to claim that the goal of teaching reading is to understand reading strategies.

    (A) The claim that the goal of teaching basic science is

    (B) The claim that teaching basic science is the goal

    (C) To claim that the goal of teaching basic science is

    (D) Claiming that the goal of teaching basic science is

    (E) The claiming that the goal of basic science teaching is

41. <u>Being anatomically indistinguishable from the grizzly, the Alaskan brown bear nonetheless differs from the grizzly by its often larger size</u>.

    (A) Being anatomically indistinguishable from the grizzly, the Alaskan brown bear nonetheless differs from the grizzly by its often larger size.

    (B) Although the two are indistinguishable anatomically, it is never-theless a point of difference that the Alaskan brown often grows larger than the grizzly bear.

(C) Simply because the Alaskan brown bear is often larger than the grizzly does not in any way diminish the fact that they are anatomically indistinguishable.

(D) Indistinguishable anatomically, the Alaskan brown bear only differs from the grizzly because it is often larger than the grizzly.

(E) Even though the two are anatomically indistinguishable, the Alaskan brown bear often grows larger than the grizzly.

42. Novelist Richard Wright wrote that he was influenced by books, which were the windows to his world, he specifically cited Fyodor Dostoevsky, George Moore, James Joyce, and D.H. Lawrence.

   (A) his world, he specifically cited

   (B) his world; specifically he cites

   (C) his world; he specifically cited

   (D) his world, and he specifically cites

   (E) his world, for example he cited

43. The earth's land masses comprise of tectonic plates which often shift and slide over each other, the result being to cause earthquakes.

   (A) other, the result being to

   (B) other to

   (C) other; the result being to

   (D) other; with the result being to

   (E) other, with the result being to

44. Literary scholars are beginning to take notice of women and ethnic writers because they provide new insights, write with unusual style, and another part of culture is examined.

   (A) write with unusual style, and another part of culture is examined.

   (B) unusual written style is used, and another part of culture is examined.

   (C) writing with unusual style and examining another part of culture.

(D) write with unusual style, and examine another part of culture.

(E) unusual written style is used, and examine another part of culture.

45. The word "boycott" was originally the last name of an English land agent in Ireland who was ostracized in <u>1880 because he refused to reduce rents</u>.

(A) 1880 because he refused to reduce rents.

(B) 1880 for refusing to reduce the prevailing rent at the time.

(C) 1880 being that he refused to reduce rents.

(D) 1880 being that he refused to reduce the current prevailing rents.

(E) 1880 because of his refusal to reduce rents.

46. <u>In Virginia Woolf's essay titled "The Death of the Moth," it</u> says that nothing and nobody have a chance against death.

(A) In Virginia Woolf's essay titled "The Death of the Moth," it

(B) In the essay by Virginia Woolf titled "The Death of the Moth," it

(C) Virginia wrote an essay titled "The Death of the Moth," it

(D) In "The Death of the Moth," an essay by Virginia Woolf, it

(E) Virginia Woolf's essay, "The Death of the Moth"

47. <u>The more we use machines</u>, the more human beings live at odds with their environment.

(A) The more we use machines

(B) The more they use machines

(C) The more machines are used by us

(D) As our use of machines is increased

(E) As we add to our use of machines

48. Many politicians believe in "ad hominem" arguments, <u>meaning that one attacks</u> the person, not the issue.

(A) meaning that one attacks

(B) meaning that they attack

(C) which attack

(D) the meaning of which is that one attacks

(E) attacking

DIRECTIONS: The following passages are considered early draft efforts of a student. Some sentences need to be rewritten to make the ideas clearer and more precise.

Read each passage carefully and answer the questions that follow. Some of the questions are about particular sentences or parts of sentences and ask you to make decisions about sentence structure, diction, and usage. Some of the questions refer to the entire essay or parts of the essay and ask you to make decisions about organization, development, appropriateness of language, audience, and logic. Choose the answer that most effectively makes the intended meaning clear and follows the requirements of standard written English. After you have chosen your answer, fill in the corresponding oval on your answer sheet.

EXAMPLE:

(1) On the one hand, I think television is bad, But it also does some good things for all of us. (2) For instance, my little sister thought she wanted to be a policeman until she saw police shows on television.

Which of the following is the best revision of the underlined portion of sentence 1 below?

On the one hand, I think television <u>is bad, But it also</u> does some good things for all of us.

(A) is bad; But it also

(B) is bad. but is also

(C) is bad, and it also

(D) is bad, but it also

(E) is bad because it also

Questions 49–54 are based on the following passage.

(1) A French composer, the bolero inspired Anton Ravel to create the ballet *Bolero*. (2) The sister of the legendary Russian dancer Vaslav Nijinsky choreographed the ballet created by Ravel. (3) A popular and

well-known folk dance in Spain, the bolero as we know it is credited to Anton Bolsche and Sebastian Cerezo around the mid-1700s. (4) Although no one has actually seen the ballet, the music from *Bolero* has retained immense popularity and is performed on a regular basis throughout the world.

(5) The center and driving force of it is a snare drum. (6) The percussionist begins by playing a rhythmic pattern lasting two measures and six beats, the rhythm of the bolero dance, as quietly as possible. (7) At the beginning, other instruments pick up the rhythm as the frenzy builds. (8) The first flute then introduces the melody, the second important part of *Bolero*; different instruments play individual parts, such as the clarinet, bassoon, and piccolo. (9) The buildup of the music occurs in two ways: the individual musicians play their instrument louder and louder, and more and more instruments beginning to play together. (10) For most of the 15 to 17 minutes of the performance, *Bolero* is played in a relenting harmony of C Major. (11) The end is signaled by a brief shift to E Major and then a strong return to C Major.

49. Which of the following revisions would best improve sentence 1?

   (A) The bolero inspired Anton Ravel to create the ballet *Bolero*, a French composer.

   (B) The bolero, a French composer, inspired Anton Ravel to create the ballet *Bolero*.

   (C) The bolero inspired Anton Ravel, a French composer, to create the ballet *Bolero*.

   (D) The bolero inspired Anton Ravel to create the ballet, a French composer, *Bolero*.

   (E) Best as is.

50. Which of the following would best replace "it" in sentence 5?

   (A) this musical composition

   (B) the folk dance

   (C) them

   (D) Anton Bolsche and Sebastian Cerezo

   (E) None of these.

51. Which of the following best improves the underlined portion of sentence 8?

The first flute then introduces the melody, the second important part of *Bolero*; <u>different instruments play individual parts, such as the clarinet, bassoon, and piccolo.</u>

(A) the clarinet, bassoon and piccolo and other different instruments play individual parts.

(B) different instruments, such as the clarinet, bassoon and piccolo, play individual parts.

(C) individual parts are played by the clarinet, bassoon and piccolo, as well as other different instruments.

(D) different instruments play different parts, like the clarinet, bassoon and piccolo.

(E) Best as it is.

52. Which of the following verbs is used incorrectly?

(A) "inspired" in sentence 1

(B) "credited" in sentence 3

(C) "pick up" in sentence 7

(D) "beginning" in sentence 9

(E) "signaled" in sentence 11

53. Which of the following corrections should be made?

(A) Change "choreographed" to "composed" in sentence 2.

(B) Change "retained" to "remained" in sentence 4.

(C) Change "individual" to "total" in sentence 9.

(D) Change "relenting" to "unrelenting" in sentence 10.

(E) None of these.

54. Which of the following would be the best way to punctuate sentence 11?

(A) The end, is signaled by a brief shift, to E Major and then a strong return to C Major.

(B) The end is signaled, by a brief shift to E Major, and then a strong return, to C Major.

(C) The end is signaled by a brief shift to E Major, and then a strong return to C Major.

(D) The end is signaled by a brief shift, to E Major, and then a strong return, to C Major.

(E) Best as is.

Questions 55–60 are based on the following passage.

(1) Dena may die soon. (2) For 21 years, all Dena has ever known is captivity. (3) How would you like to spend your entire life in captivity? (4) Even though Dena is not a human, but an orca, a killer whale, like in the movie *Orca*, don't you think Dena deserves to be released from her natural habitat? (5) Orcas are much too intelligent and too delicate to be confined in tanks. (6) Dena's owners claim that she is displaying geriatric signs normal for an orca 25 years old, Sea Habitat, Inc. (7) Orcas are not meant to be caged, no matter how kind the jailer who holding the keys.

(8) We don't know enough about orcas and how they interact. (9) Who are we to confine a species that may be as intelligent as humans? (10) True, Dena may be rejected by her original pod, members of which stayed together for life. (11) Maybe she is too old to live much longer. (12) However, we should at least allow Dena to die with dignity in her natural surroundings. (13) And, if Dena succeeds in surviving in the wild, maybe we can pressure other zoos and marine institutions around the world to release these beautiful animals back to the wild, where they can live longer, healthier lives. (14) I urge everyone to write a letter to their local senator and congressman demanding the return of all orcas to the oceans of the earth.

55. Which of the following phrases is unnecessary and should be eliminated?

(A) "For 21 years" in sentence 2

(B) "like in the movie *Orca*" in sentence 4

(C) "may be as intelligent as humans" in sentence 9

(D) "to the oceans of the earth" in sentence 14

(E) None of these.

56. Which of the following corrects the underlined portion of sentence 4?

Even though Dena is not a human, but an orca, a killer whale, like in the movie *Orca*, don't you think <u>Dena deserves to be released from her natural habitat?</u>

(A) Dena deserved to be released from her natural habitat?

(B) Dena deserves from her natural habitat to be released?

(C) Dena deserves to be released under her natural habitat?

(D) Dena deserves to be released into her natural habitat?

(E) None of these.

57. Which of the following best corrects Sentence 6?

(A) Dena's owners, Sea Habitat, Inc., claim she is displaying geriatric signs normal for an orca 25 years old.

(B) Since they are Dena's owners, Sea Habitat, Inc. claim she is displaying geriatric signs normal for an orca 25 years old.

(C) Sea Habitat, Inc., Dena's owners, claim she is displaying geriatric signs normal for an orca 25 years old.

(D) Choices (A), (B), and (C).

(E) Choices (A) and (C) only.

58. Which of the following, if used between sentences 10 and 11, best develops the main idea of the second paragraph?

(A) Another problem to be overcome is training Dena to hunt live fish, instead of depending on being fed dead fish by her human captors.

(B) As a matter of fact, it is now against the law to capture orcas in the wild and sell them to zoos.

(C) As we all know, the breeding of captive orcas has not been successful.

(D) This issue has recently been made famous by the movie *Free Willy*.

(E) Since orcas live an average of 20–30 years, Dena should not be released because she is clearly too old to adapt to the wild.

59. Which of the following verbs are used incorrectly?

    (A) "deserves" in sentence 4

    (B) "holding" in sentence 7

    (C) "stayed" in Sentence 10

    (D) Choices (B) and (C) only.

    (E) Choices (A), (B), and (C).

60. Which of the following best punctuates sentence 8?

    (A) We don't know enough, about orcas, and how they interact.

    (B) We don't know enough, about orcas and how they interact!

    (C) We don't know enough about orcas, and how they interact.

    (D) We don't know enough: about orcas and how they interact.

    (E) Best as is.

SAT II: WRITING
TEST 6

ANSWER KEY

1.	(B)	16.	(D)	31.	(C)	46.	(E)
2.	(A)	17.	(C)	32.	(B)	47.	(B)
3.	(C)	18.	(B)	33.	(E)	48.	(C)
4.	(B)	19.	(C)	34.	(E)	49.	(C)
5.	(A)	20.	(D)	35.	(B)	50.	(A)
6.	(D)	21.	(D)	36.	(C)	51.	(B)
7.	(A)	22.	(A)	37.	(A)	52.	(D)
8.	(B)	23.	(C)	38.	(E)	53.	(D)
9.	(E)	24.	(B)	39.	(B)	54.	(C)
10.	(D)	25.	(A)	40.	(C)	55.	(B)
11.	(C)	26.	(A)	41.	(E)	56.	(D)
12.	(D)	27.	(C)	42.	(C)	57.	(E)
13.	(B)	28.	(B)	43.	(B)	58.	(A)
14.	(C)	29.	(D)	44.	(D)	59.	(D)
15.	(D)	30.	(E)	45.	(A)	60.	(E)

DETAILED EXPLANATIONS OF ANSWERS

Part A: Essay

Sample Essays with Commentary

ESSAY I (Score: 5–6)

American youth are more interested in high paying jobs rather than a satisfying career because our culture is very materialistic, income is more impressive than a title to a job, and more money implies more power.

Our culture is very materialistic. A pair of faded, worn-out blue jeans costs close to $70.00, and seems to be a necessity for teenagers. It doesn't matter if your job is one that "sounds" good or makes you happy, as long as your income keeps you in step with the Joneses. Status symbols speak out for the high paying jobs. When people see you riding around in your new shiny Jaguar, they don't know if you're a garbage man or a lawyer, but what they do know is that you're making money, lots of it.

Income is more impressive than a title. If they can make more money running a junk yard than being a lawyer, the youth of today will become a junk dealer in a heartbeat. The question, "What is your average yearly income?" is just as popular now as the ancient question, "What do you do for a living?" Nobody really cares anymore what you do if you're making plenty of money.

The more money you have, the more power you have. You can easily impress your peers and people in lower social standing with your beliefs and ideas because they are all saying to themselves, "Well he must know what he's doing, or else how did he get all this money?" Money and power have always gone hand-in-hand and probably always will.

Income is more important to American youths than a satisfying career because this is a very materialistic culture we live in, income is far more impressive than a title, and more money implies more power. A satisfying career may satisfy you while you are at work, but a good income will satisfy you all of the time. With a high income, what job wouldn't be satisfying?

ANALYSIS

Essay I has a score range of 5-6. Even though it has some obvious flaws, its virtues of clear and concise organization, reasonable development with specific examples, and a clear conclusion help outweigh the problems. The quality of thought is clearly a bit superficial. The traditional three-part thesis which outlines the structure here serves almost as much as a mechanical formula as it does a guide map for the reader. The essay is unified about its thesis. Overall, word choice is not particularly sophisticated, cliches like "keep in step with the Joneses" detract from the effort. However, it is a reasonably good essay with few grammatical errors, given the 20-minute time limit.

ESSAY II (Score: 4–5)

Money has always been popular with the masses, but now it can be classified as an obsession. The worship of money has touched and corrupted many facets of our existence today. You see the corruption in the job market, in our social institutions, and, lastly, in government. Our youth have seen the light of the almighty dollar. It shows in almost every decision they make. I maintain, that we as adults need to get down to brass tacts and reeducate the youth of today on things that are important in life.

The colleges and universities of today are turning out doctors, lawyers, and businessmen and women in mass quantities. It is not that these particular fields of study are that attractive, or that they hold any great interest for these graduates. They are lured by the promise of big money. It is just common knowledge that anyone who wants to be rich should be a doctor. Young people of scholastic aptitude, therefore go through the motions, get a degree and hang out a shingle. This is all done without any consideration to what it means to practice medicine or law. These jobs are, or were, originally service oriented. They established themselves because there were people who could do these jobs and serve mankind.

Money is at the source of the corruption of our social attitudes. These attitudes often manifest themselves in the form of material possessions. The '80's phenomenon called Yuppie is a perfect example. The Yuppies will work themselves to death to wear the right clothes or drive the right car. They are so obsessed with the delights and happiness of material possessions. Money is also the motivation behind the rise in juvenile crime. Once where you had a group of teenagers shoplifting "penny-ante" merchandise, you now have well organized street gangs planning major heists. Often in our society people who obviously do not have money, by the way they dress or the kind of car they drive, are social outcasts. They are looked upon as inferiors.

The youth of today are taught the catechisms of money plus government equal corruption from a very young age. In history class we are taught, such and such ruler was very wealthy ergo very powerful, often without being told of the social ramifications.

ANALYSIS

Essay II has a score range of 4-5. The writer shows a bit more maturity of thought than that found in Essay I. Word choice and sentence structures also seem a bit more sophisticated. However, several errors (e.g., "brass tacts") hurt this essay's effectiveness. Internal paragraph unity is not as strong as it should be. The Yuppie example works, but it is almost a cliche by now. The main strength otherwise is a relatively interesting introductory paragraph and some very interesting thoughts at the end, which, however, need further development. Time probably caught up with the writer.

ESSAY III (Score: 3–4)

In my point of view, I would want both worlds, not just a high paying job which would give me all the luxuries that my parents and their parents before them dreamed of. Nor would I just want a job which would only reward me with happiness and self fulfillment. I think that there is a thin line between these two views, and our opinions on each of them sometimes depend on the past. Let us look at several examples.

One example which may sway over opinions to the high paying job would be the stories American youths hear about men and women who out of the midst of poverty, rose to power and ever since then tries to help people in the same fix. Young people may interpret this in two ways; "I want to be just like him!" and take the long road of hardship and pain in order to get that brass ring, or they will think, "That takes too long!" and decide to endeavor on get rich quick schemes. These schemes and plan "laid out by mice and men," do not pay off in the end, which results in the ever growing number of young people in crime.

Another example would be from the nearest source of information, the home. We as young people have heard the countless number of stories told to us by our fathers and grandfathers about how things were hard in the old days. You can think of the times which your father complains about the bills and all the sacrifices he's had to make. These scene will turn any youth's eyes to the land and lap of luxury.

This is the way I see the idea of to be rich or not to be rich. There is a thin line between these two subjects and its entirely up to our young adults to decide what to do.

ANALYSIS

Essay III has a score range of 3-4. It tries to achieve greater heights than it actually does. The essay sets forth a reasonably clear thesis and endeavors to develop it by example. Along the way, though, the language used and the awkward sentence structures cause breakdowns in the orderly progress of explanation. The first sentences of paragraphs two and four are examples of weak statements caused by a combination of poor word choice and awkward sentence structure. The examples are not at the specific level even though they are firmly clear. Several grammatical problems (e.g., sequence of verb tenses and subject-verb agreement) hurt.

ESSAY IV (Score: 1–2)

I agree with this. I wanted to work to get money for a car to drive to school. My first job was at Winn-Dixie. I was making money, money, money. I had it coming out of my ears. But when I got that car, the money began to disappear. I was buying gas and other things to dress up the car. My parents gave me more freedom. They told me that it better not interfear with my school work. At first it did, not, but after a semester, I began to put work in front of school. I wanted more money so I began to fail in school. After failing a quarter I realalized that I had to get my pryorities straight and I had lot of responsibility. I made myself work things out. Everything has turned out great and I am still employed.

Young Americans getting a job is good because it helps them learn responsibility and gives them money to save or spend for their own pleasure.

ANALYSIS

Essay IV has a score range of 1-2. The problems here are not just the obvious disarray and lack of overall organization. They also include unsophisticated sentence structure, missing thesis, apparent insecurity of the meaning of an essay, illogical statements ("I wanted more money so I began to fail in school.") and awkward misspellings ("interfear," "pryorities," and "realalized"). This writer seemed to want to tell a story rather than develop the idea in the expository essay form. The narrative leaves out huge gaps, particularly the most interesting part, the way he or she made "things work out."

Part B: Multiple-Choice

1. **(B)** Choice (A) raises questions of appropriate capitalization, but it is proper to capitalize this particular title, even without a name attached. Choice (C) might appear suspicious, but it is the correct spelling. Choice (D) is correct because "would" indicates a condition as suggested by the "If" at the beginning of the sentence. That leaves choices (E) and (B). One could argue that the Electoral College constitutes an oligarchy because of its smaller size (E), but the sharp student will recognize that the sentence poses a condition contrary to fact, requiring the subjunctive, "were," choice (B).

2. **(A)** Choices (B) and (C) could look incorrect, except that both are parallel and appropriately balance each other. Choice (D) does not even merit scrutiny; nothing is improper there. Again, either there is no error (E), or we must look to choice (A). Knowledgeable students will know that confusion exists between "flaunt" and "flout." "Flout" (to defy contemptuously) is correct in the context of the sentence; "flaunt" (to display arrogantly) is clearly incorrect.

3. **(C)** Choices (A) and (D) do not really require more than a cursory glance to show that they are acceptable. Choice (B) might require a second look because of the hyphen, but it is correct. Choice (C) is a clear example of faulty predication "reason . . . is because," and is incorrect.

4. **(B)** Reading the sentence, the student should be jarred by the inappropriate coordination of the verb phrases beginning "proposed" and "is." Changing "and" to "which" makes a much more euphonious and balanced sentence. That change would properly subordinate the definition of "induction." None of the other choices should raise concern, except, perhaps (C), but it is a correctly hyphenated word.

5. **(A)** Both (C) and (D) are possible choices, but (C) correctly uses the apostrophe to indicate plural. (Usage varies on this issue, but it is considered correct either with the apostrophe—1920s—or without—1920s). Choice (D) also correctly capitalizes "Indian," meaning American Indian. Nothing is amiss with choice (B) given the time noted and the subordinate clause verb "was." Choice (A), however, incorrectly uses "due to" to show causation with an active verb ("wrote"). "Because of" is the correct phrase.

6. **(D)** We have an illogical comparison in this sentence: "People from . . . " and "in the United States." Logical comparison demands that we compare like things to each other. In this case, the sentence compares people with the name of a nation. A logical comparison might read " . . . than people in the United States [do]." All other choices are correct: capitalized name of a geographical region (A), comparative adverb used with the active verb "stand" (B), appropriate subordinating adverb "when" (C).

7. **(A)** This one looks more difficult than it is. The sentence is a fragment because there is no verb except in the dependent clauses. Furthermore, one cannot correct the problem by eliminating the relative pronoun "that," choice (B), or by changing choices (C) or (D), "Because of" correctly modifies "cannot be explained away." By changing choice (A) to "claims," one completes the sentence and corrects the error.

8. **(B)** The problem should be spotted right away as a disagreement between the plural pronoun "their" and its singular antecedent "American," choice (B). "Asian-American"—choice (A)—is correctly hyphenated and capitalized. The phrase "and, therefore,"—choice (C)—is correctly punctuated because it links the compound verbs ("exists" and "has"). It is also precise (not wordy). The last choice, (D), is correctly spelled without a hyphen.

9. **(E)** One could quarrel with the use of the word "Curiously," but it is not a choice. Otherwise, the sentence is a perfectly balanced logical comparison between like things ("teachers of the English language" and "students of the Russian language"). Even though students and teachers are not precisely parallel, one can compare them in this context. There is no reason to suspect the other choices.

10. **(D)** The problem here is sequence of verb tenses. Every verb in the sentence except choice (D) is in the simple past tense, meaning occurrences in the finite past (not over a period of time). In the sentence context, "has" must be changed to "had." The only other possibility is choice (C). One could question the elegance of the repetition of "that," but it is both correct and necessary. The first two occurrences of "that" could be omitted, but they are not choices, and the sentence would not be any clearer than it is with them as stated.

11. **(C)** The phrase "refer back" is a textbook example of classic

wordiness. One neither refers "back" nor "ahead" ("forward"?); one simply refers "to" something without reference to time. Choice (A) correctly subordinates the following clause ("when" would be less precise here). Choice (B) is grammatically correct, if not particularly elegant. Again, the plural of "1600" formed by adding the apostrophe could be questioned, but it is acceptable.

12. **(D)**   Nonparallel structure is the key to this and many other test items. Because of the overwhelming importance of understanding balance and euphony in sentence structure, tests like this one emphasize parallel sentence structures. A noun phrase follows "not only," but a verb phrase follows "but also." The easiest way to balance the structure would be to omit the word "observed," choice (D). Choice (A) is correctly lowercase, and choices (B) and (C) arouse no suspicion.

13. **(B)**   "Who" should be "whom"; the objective case is needed. Choices (A) and (C) should not cause a second glance. Choice (D) is the correct prepositional phrase. "Who" versus "whom" is an important debate, well worth attention.

14. **(C)**   The use of "never" clearly causes a double negative (with "no" in the same sentence). Choice (A) could make you think, but it correctly suggests that Krutch feels regret that the familiar essay is hard to find. Choices (B) and (D) should not attract your attention unduly.

15. **(D)**   This is a case of needlessly shifting pronoun voice from third person ("... Americans have ... ") to first person (" ... we believe ... "). Choice (A) is correct, including the comma at the end of the interrupting phrase inside the quotation marks. Choice (B) is both spelled and used correctly. Choice (C) correctly uses "because" to show causation.

16. **(D)**   Whenever you see "imply" or "infer" as a choice, examine it carefully. Most likely, the usage will be in error, as it is here. An easy way to approach this pair of commonly confused words is to remember that generally only people "infer," but written material and people can "imply." In this case, the book cannot "infer." Choice (A) correctly shows "ownership" of the book. Choice (B) correctly suggests that over 80 years after the book's publication, it is important. Choice (C) correctly omits the hyphen in this word.

17. **(C)**   When you analyze the sentence for its fundamentals, you will

see the obvious subject-verb disagreement between the plural subject ("Filmmakers") and the singular verb ("helps"), choice (C). Choice (A) might warrant a brief look, but it correctly links the adjective clause with the person it modifies. Choices (B) and (D) do not merit attention beyond a cursory glance.

18. **(B)**   By examining choice (A), we see that the participial phrase correctly does not "dangle" and that "answering" is correct in context. Choice (C) is an appropriate relative pronoun used to introduce the subordinate clause. Choice (D) correctly uses the pronoun "it" to refer to its antecedent, "communism." However, choice (B) serves up the classic split infinitive, in which "exactly" awkwardly separates the two parts of the infinitive "to clarify."

19. **(C)**   This, too, is a classic error, the misplaced modifier. The phrase "travelling in a carriage" describes Mozart, but is so far away from the name in the sentence that it makes the sentence awkward. Choice (A) uses the correct verb. Choice (B) makes clear in the context that "composing" is different from "writing." Choice (D), although suspicious, correctly uses the subjunctive to suggest conditions contrary to normal facts. Choice (E) might look attractive, but (C) clearly is incorrect.

20. **(D)**   This is another misplaced modifier, in this case "Saying that . . . ," is the cause of the awkwardness in this sentence. However, you do not have the choice of the phrase to change. The next logical way to correct the sentence would be to move the noun being described ("Ernest Hemingway"), and that is a choice. Choice (A) is correctly spelled and used. Choice (B), though not the most elegant usage, is correct. Choice (C) parallels the earlier part of the clause and is correct.

21. **(D)**   The error here is noun agreement; "novels" is plural and requires the plural "classics." The only other choice that might arouse suspicion is (A), but "alike" is appropriate here.

22. **(A)**   The problem here is idiomatic word choice. We say "between [a number] and [another number]," not "between . . . to . . . " That idiom is "from . . . to . . . " Choice (C) merits a look, but we customarily capitalize "President" and its derivative, "Presidential," when they refer to the President of the United States.

23. **(B)**   Pronoun-antecedent is incorrect here. You will most certainly

hear people, educated and otherwise, say "everybody" or "everyone" and "their" together, but these forms are grammatically singular and require singular pronouns.

24. **(B)**   A not-so-simple case of subject-verb disagreement causes the error here. The whole phrase, "Reading . . . curriculum," is the singular subject of the correct verb "is." Nothing else merits a second glance.

25. **(A)**   Unless we change (A), we have no verb to complete the sentence. Substituting "suggest" for "suggesting" gives us a verb and completes the thought. You might question the use of quotes around "right-sized," but it is appropriate to indicate a questionable word choice.

26. **(A)**   This is an inappropriate use of "as far as" to substitute for the idiom "as for." "Crept" is the correct past tense of "creep," although one might prefer, incorrectly, "creeped."

27. **(C)**   The problem is either vague pronoun-antecedent reference ("they") or inappropriate comparison ("countries" do not have "salary increases"). Either way the word "they" is incorrect here. "The people in these countries" would be a good substitute for "they."

28. **(B)**   Context clues suggest the simple past tense verb "maintained" to be correct. "Has maintained" could also be used, but "maintains" is clearly incorrect.

29. **(D)**   "Lose" and "loose" are often confused by otherwise knowledgeable students.

30. **(E)**   Nothing really suggests itself as an error. You could question the use of the present tense verbs, but we customarily refer to written work as if we were reading it in the present.

31. **(C)**   The only concise (and clear in context) choice is (C). All the others, including the original, are wordy by comparison, except for choice (B). It does have one more word, even if it looks shorter than (C); and it fails to identify the antecedent of the pronouns.

32. **(B)**   The original awkwardly shifts pronoun voice from third person ("he") to second person ("you"). Choice (B) corrects the error and uses the appropriate present verb tense. Choice (C) repeats the initial error

and changes the tense to the past. Choice (D) corrects the voice shift but uses past tense. Choice (E) uses tense and is hopelessly wordy.

33. **(E)** The problem here is noun agreement. To be in agreement, the underlined phrase must be plural, since the noun subject is compound. Choice (B) does use the plural but adds an unnecessary word, and the plural word is not the best choice. Choice (C) is similar in both ways. Choice (D) looks better, but the best word here is "people," thus choice (E). Incidentally, an even better rephrasing—not a choice—is "to be free."

34. **(E)** Wordiness is again the major problem with the original sentence and choices (B) and (C). Choices (D) and (E) are the only sensible alternates, so you must decide which of the two is better. Choice (E) tops (D) is brevity (two words instead of four). It also retains the word "stereotype" (in a variant form) and, therefore, is closer to the original meaning than (D).

35. **(B)** Here, we have an incorrectly punctuated clause, which is unnecessary, and a redundancy (both "complex and complicated"). Obviously, choice (A) should be passed over. Choices (C) and (D) correct the punctuation and eliminate the redundancy, but they leave the unnecessary clause. Choice (E) corrects the punctuation and eliminates one word, but it does not solve the redundancy problem. Choice (B) correctly eliminates both the unnecessary clause (obviating the need for punctuation) and the redundancy. It is the most concise and best of the choices.

36. **(C)** Be alert for concise expression. Often that means looking for the shortest answer, but not always. In this case, the shortest answer is indeed the best one. (A) is wordy and has a vague pronoun "it" (unclear antecedent). Choice (B) uses an inappropriate colloquialism ("went to prove"). (D) is repetitious ("President") and unnecessarily wordy in differentiating the script from the pictures. (E) is repetitious like (D) and wordy toward the end.

37. **(A)** The choices are easy to discern in this sentence. The original sentence correctly uses present tense to discuss a published work. All of the other choices use some variation of past tense.

38. **(E)** The original sentence suffers from inadequate causal relationship and nonparallel structure. Choices (B) and (C) retain the problem with causation ("being" does not substitute for "because"), and (B) is

illogical. (D) is still not parallel, leaving choice (E) as the best one. It uses parallel structure and appropriate causation.

39. **(B)** The two problems with this sentence are improper coordination of ideas and inappropriate conversion of verbs to nouns. Choice (E) retains the coordination problem. Choice (C) and (D) keep the ungainly nouns. Choice (C) is repetitious ("myth"), and choice (D) is ambiguous ("it" could refer to "myth" or "belief").

40. **(C)** The original sentence presents an intriguing parallel or balanced structure problem. Choice (C) correctly balances the several elements of the sentence ("To claim . . . is to convey . . . is to make . . . as to claim . . . is to understand. . . . "). Each of the others fails to correct the initial non-parallel phrase ("The claim that . . . is").

41. **(E)** Initially, the problem is inappropriate causation ("being" for "because" or another alternate). Again, you should look for brevity. Choice (B) is wordy ("nevertheless a point of difference that") and has a vague pronoun ("it"). Choice (C) is both wordy ("Simply . . . in any way diminish the fact that") and a bit illogical. Choice (D) is repetitious ("grizzly").

42. **(C)** Originally, the sentence uses a comma to splice or run together two independent clauses without a coordinate conjunction. Choice (E) repeats the error, and choice (D) incorrectly changes the verb tense even though it does use the appropriate conjunction. Choice (B) correctly uses a semicolon but also changes the verb tense.

43. **(B)** "Being" is used poorly to indicate causation ("result being" is also wordy). Here, it is also repetitious because of "cause" in the last part of the sentence. Each of the choices except (B) repeats the use of "being." Choices (C) and (D) also use semicolons unnecessarily.

44. **(D)** The original gives us a classic case of nonparallel structure. The series begins with "provide new insights" (active voice verb phrase), which is not to change; so you must look for a choice which correctly completes the series with active voice verb phrases. Choice (D) is the only choice which passes the test. Choices (B) and (C) are both internally parallel, but not with the first part of the series. Choice (E) simply reverses the error of the original.

45. **(A)**   You should find the original acceptable from the start; and if you look at the alternates, it is the briefest one. Choices (C) and (D) incorrectly use "being that" [and choice (D) is wordy]. Choice (B) is repetitious ("prevailing rent at the time"). Choice (E) looks like a good possibility, but it does convert the verb to a noun, unnecessarily adding a word.

46. **(E)**   Simple awkward wordiness or even repetition mars all the choices except (E) and (C). In choices (A), (B), and (D), there is no need for the "in [a work] it" phrasing. (C) incorrectly splices independent clauses together with a comma. Therefore, choice (E) is the best answer.

47. **(B)**   The original involves a needless voice shift from first person to third person. Choice (B) correctly uses third person for both. Choices (C), (D), and (E) all retain the voice shift; each is awkwardly wordy as well.

48. **(C)**   A fine line separates this choice from the others, except for (E). Choice (E) is more concise, but it also is a dangling modifier. Each of the other choices adds unnecessary words. Choice (C) is both clear and concise.

49. **(C)**   The clause "a French composer" modifies Anton Ravel. In the original, it would appear to modify "the bolero." Choice (C) best corrects this ambiguity. Each of the other choices places the modifier in an incorrect place.

50. **(A)**   "This musical composition" should replace "it" in sentence 5, since the paragraph should not start off with a pronoun that lacks a clear antecedent. Choice (B) ("the folk dance") may look right, but since the rest of the passage concerns the music and not the dance, it would be inappropriate. Choices (C) and (D) are clearly the wrong antecedents for "it" in this sentence.

51. **(B)**   In the original, "clarinet, bassoon, and piccolo" would appear to modify "parts." Choice (B) best clears up this confusion by placing the clause so as to modify "instruments." Choices (A) and (C) are both technically correct, but are less clear in the structure of the sentence than choice (B). Choice (E) contains a misplaced modifier.

The word "beginning" in sentence 9 is in the present progressive tense. It should be changed to "begin" to accord with the present tense used in the rest of the sentence and throughout the passage.

53. **(D)** The word "relenting," in this context, is wrong; if the harmony remains in the same key for 15 to 17 minutes, this is surely "unrelenting."

54. **(C)** Choice (C) separates the temporal relation of the shift in key nicely with a single comma, where the unpunctuated original was too jumbled. Choices (A), (B), and (D) all use too many commas in awkward positions.

55. **(B)** The phrase "like in the movie *Orca*" not only disrupts the rhythm of the sentence, but the allusion itself is gratuitous and is not necessary to the author's point in this sentence, which is to ask rhetorically whether or not this particular killer whale should be released from captivity.

56. **(D)** "From her natural habitat" is clearly an error, because what is being debated in this letter is the fact that Dena does *not* live in her natural habitat. Therefore, "into" is the best substitution for "from." "Under" in choice (C) makes no sense in this context. Choice (A) changes the verb to the past tense, which is clearly wrong, since what is being discussed is surely that Dena presently deserves to be released. Choice (B) makes a quasi-poetical inversion, which is unnecessarily stylized for such a letter, and more importantly, the sentence retains the incorrect preposition "from."

57. **(E)** In the original, the modifier "Sea Habitat, Inc." was in the wrong position to be modifying "owners." Both choices (A) and (C) correct this in acceptable ways. Only choice (B) is incorrect; "Since" emphasizes the incidental fact that "Sea Habitat, Inc." are Dena's owners, and creates a misleading logical relation.

58. **(A)** Choice (A) best follows sentence 10, as it continues the theme of obstacles toward Dena's release. Choice (E) is the next best choice, but it would make sentence 11 sound redundant and repetitive. Choices (B) and (C) set up misleading logical relations with the phrases "As a matter of fact" and "As we all know," and would not follow well from sentence 10. Choice (D) is as gratuitous and unnecessary as the *Orca* allusion in sentence 4.

59. **(D)** "Holding" in sentence 7 should either be "holds" or "is holding"; "Stayed" in sentence 10 should be "stay" to agree with the present tense of the rest of the passage.

60. **(E)** Sentence 8 is simple in structure and direct in meaning, and is best with no punctuation. Choice (C) would also be a correct form, but does not improve the original any.

SAT II: Writing

Answer Sheets

Drill: Essay Writing

SAT II: Writing Test 1

Part A: Essay

SAT II: Writing Test 1

Part B: Multiple-Choice

1. Ⓐ Ⓑ Ⓒ Ⓓ Ⓔ
2. Ⓐ Ⓑ Ⓒ Ⓓ Ⓔ
3. Ⓐ Ⓑ Ⓒ Ⓓ Ⓔ
4. Ⓐ Ⓑ Ⓒ Ⓓ Ⓔ
5. Ⓐ Ⓑ Ⓒ Ⓓ Ⓔ
6. Ⓐ Ⓑ Ⓒ Ⓓ Ⓔ
7. Ⓐ Ⓑ Ⓒ Ⓓ Ⓔ
8. Ⓐ Ⓑ Ⓒ Ⓓ Ⓔ
9. Ⓐ Ⓑ Ⓒ Ⓓ Ⓔ
10. Ⓐ Ⓑ Ⓒ Ⓓ Ⓔ
11. Ⓐ Ⓑ Ⓒ Ⓓ Ⓔ
12. Ⓐ Ⓑ Ⓒ Ⓓ Ⓔ
13. Ⓐ Ⓑ Ⓒ Ⓓ Ⓔ
14. Ⓐ Ⓑ Ⓒ Ⓓ Ⓔ
15. Ⓐ Ⓑ Ⓒ Ⓓ Ⓔ
16. Ⓐ Ⓑ Ⓒ Ⓓ Ⓔ
17. Ⓐ Ⓑ Ⓒ Ⓓ Ⓔ
18. Ⓐ Ⓑ Ⓒ Ⓓ Ⓔ
19. Ⓐ Ⓑ Ⓒ Ⓓ Ⓔ
20. Ⓐ Ⓑ Ⓒ Ⓓ Ⓔ

21. Ⓐ Ⓑ Ⓒ Ⓓ Ⓔ
22. Ⓐ Ⓑ Ⓒ Ⓓ Ⓔ
23. Ⓐ Ⓑ Ⓒ Ⓓ Ⓔ
24. Ⓐ Ⓑ Ⓒ Ⓓ Ⓔ
25. Ⓐ Ⓑ Ⓒ Ⓓ Ⓔ
26. Ⓐ Ⓑ Ⓒ Ⓓ Ⓔ
27. Ⓐ Ⓑ Ⓒ Ⓓ Ⓔ
28. Ⓐ Ⓑ Ⓒ Ⓓ Ⓔ
29. Ⓐ Ⓑ Ⓒ Ⓓ Ⓔ
30. Ⓐ Ⓑ Ⓒ Ⓓ Ⓔ
31. Ⓐ Ⓑ Ⓒ Ⓓ Ⓔ
32. Ⓐ Ⓑ Ⓒ Ⓓ Ⓔ
33. Ⓐ Ⓑ Ⓒ Ⓓ Ⓔ
34. Ⓐ Ⓑ Ⓒ Ⓓ Ⓔ
35. Ⓐ Ⓑ Ⓒ Ⓓ Ⓔ
36. Ⓐ Ⓑ Ⓒ Ⓓ Ⓔ
37. Ⓐ Ⓑ Ⓒ Ⓓ Ⓔ
38. Ⓐ Ⓑ Ⓒ Ⓓ Ⓔ
39. Ⓐ Ⓑ Ⓒ Ⓓ Ⓔ
40. Ⓐ Ⓑ Ⓒ Ⓓ Ⓔ

41. Ⓐ Ⓑ Ⓒ Ⓓ Ⓔ
42. Ⓐ Ⓑ Ⓒ Ⓓ Ⓔ
43. Ⓐ Ⓑ Ⓒ Ⓓ Ⓔ
44. Ⓐ Ⓑ Ⓒ Ⓓ Ⓔ
45. Ⓐ Ⓑ Ⓒ Ⓓ Ⓔ
46. Ⓐ Ⓑ Ⓒ Ⓓ Ⓔ
47. Ⓐ Ⓑ Ⓒ Ⓓ Ⓔ
48. Ⓐ Ⓑ Ⓒ Ⓓ Ⓔ
49. Ⓐ Ⓑ Ⓒ Ⓓ Ⓔ
50. Ⓐ Ⓑ Ⓒ Ⓓ Ⓔ
51. Ⓐ Ⓑ Ⓒ Ⓓ Ⓔ
52. Ⓐ Ⓑ Ⓒ Ⓓ Ⓔ
53. Ⓐ Ⓑ Ⓒ Ⓓ Ⓔ
54. Ⓐ Ⓑ Ⓒ Ⓓ Ⓔ
55. Ⓐ Ⓑ Ⓒ Ⓓ Ⓔ
56. Ⓐ Ⓑ Ⓒ Ⓓ Ⓔ
57. Ⓐ Ⓑ Ⓒ Ⓓ Ⓔ
58. Ⓐ Ⓑ Ⓒ Ⓓ Ⓔ
59. Ⓐ Ⓑ Ⓒ Ⓓ Ⓔ
60. Ⓐ Ⓑ Ⓒ Ⓓ Ⓔ

SAT II: Writing Test 2

Part A: Essay

_____

_____

_____

_____

_____

_____

_____

_____

_____

_____

_____

_____

_____

_____

_____

_____

_____

_____

SAT II: Writing Test 2

Part B: Multiple-Choice

1. Ⓐ Ⓑ Ⓒ Ⓓ Ⓔ
2. Ⓐ Ⓑ Ⓒ Ⓓ Ⓔ
3. Ⓐ Ⓑ Ⓒ Ⓓ Ⓔ
4. Ⓐ Ⓑ Ⓒ Ⓓ Ⓔ
5. Ⓐ Ⓑ Ⓒ Ⓓ Ⓔ
6. Ⓐ Ⓑ Ⓒ Ⓓ Ⓔ
7. Ⓐ Ⓑ Ⓒ Ⓓ Ⓔ
8. Ⓐ Ⓑ Ⓒ Ⓓ Ⓔ
9. Ⓐ Ⓑ Ⓒ Ⓓ Ⓔ
10. Ⓐ Ⓑ Ⓒ Ⓓ Ⓔ
11. Ⓐ Ⓑ Ⓒ Ⓓ Ⓔ
12. Ⓐ Ⓑ Ⓒ Ⓓ Ⓔ
13. Ⓐ Ⓑ Ⓒ Ⓓ Ⓔ
14. Ⓐ Ⓑ Ⓒ Ⓓ Ⓔ
15. Ⓐ Ⓑ Ⓒ Ⓓ Ⓔ
16. Ⓐ Ⓑ Ⓒ Ⓓ Ⓔ
17. Ⓐ Ⓑ Ⓒ Ⓓ Ⓔ
18. Ⓐ Ⓑ Ⓒ Ⓓ Ⓔ
19. Ⓐ Ⓑ Ⓒ Ⓓ Ⓔ
20. Ⓐ Ⓑ Ⓒ Ⓓ Ⓔ

21. Ⓐ Ⓑ Ⓒ Ⓓ Ⓔ
22. Ⓐ Ⓑ Ⓒ Ⓓ Ⓔ
23. Ⓐ Ⓑ Ⓒ Ⓓ Ⓔ
24. Ⓐ Ⓑ Ⓒ Ⓓ Ⓔ
25. Ⓐ Ⓑ Ⓒ Ⓓ Ⓔ
26. Ⓐ Ⓑ Ⓒ Ⓓ Ⓔ
27. Ⓐ Ⓑ Ⓒ Ⓓ Ⓔ
28. Ⓐ Ⓑ Ⓒ Ⓓ Ⓔ
29. Ⓐ Ⓑ Ⓒ Ⓓ Ⓔ
30. Ⓐ Ⓑ Ⓒ Ⓓ Ⓔ
31. Ⓐ Ⓑ Ⓒ Ⓓ Ⓔ
32. Ⓐ Ⓑ Ⓒ Ⓓ Ⓔ
33. Ⓐ Ⓑ Ⓒ Ⓓ Ⓔ
34. Ⓐ Ⓑ Ⓒ Ⓓ Ⓔ
35. Ⓐ Ⓑ Ⓒ Ⓓ Ⓔ
36. Ⓐ Ⓑ Ⓒ Ⓓ Ⓔ
37. Ⓐ Ⓑ Ⓒ Ⓓ Ⓔ
38. Ⓐ Ⓑ Ⓒ Ⓓ Ⓔ
39. Ⓐ Ⓑ Ⓒ Ⓓ Ⓔ
40. Ⓐ Ⓑ Ⓒ Ⓓ Ⓔ

41. Ⓐ Ⓑ Ⓒ Ⓓ Ⓔ
42. Ⓐ Ⓑ Ⓒ Ⓓ Ⓔ
43. Ⓐ Ⓑ Ⓒ Ⓓ Ⓔ
44. Ⓐ Ⓑ Ⓒ Ⓓ Ⓔ
45. Ⓐ Ⓑ Ⓒ Ⓓ Ⓔ
46. Ⓐ Ⓑ Ⓒ Ⓓ Ⓔ
47. Ⓐ Ⓑ Ⓒ Ⓓ Ⓔ
48. Ⓐ Ⓑ Ⓒ Ⓓ Ⓔ
49. Ⓐ Ⓑ Ⓒ Ⓓ Ⓔ
50. Ⓐ Ⓑ Ⓒ Ⓓ Ⓔ
51. Ⓐ Ⓑ Ⓒ Ⓓ Ⓔ
52. Ⓐ Ⓑ Ⓒ Ⓓ Ⓔ
53. Ⓐ Ⓑ Ⓒ Ⓓ Ⓔ
54. Ⓐ Ⓑ Ⓒ Ⓓ Ⓔ
55. Ⓐ Ⓑ Ⓒ Ⓓ Ⓔ
56. Ⓐ Ⓑ Ⓒ Ⓓ Ⓔ
57. Ⓐ Ⓑ Ⓒ Ⓓ Ⓔ
58. Ⓐ Ⓑ Ⓒ Ⓓ Ⓔ
59. Ⓐ Ⓑ Ⓒ Ⓓ Ⓔ
60. Ⓐ Ⓑ Ⓒ Ⓓ Ⓔ

SAT II: Writing Test 3

Part A: Essay

_____

_____

_____

_____

_____

_____

_____

_____

_____

_____

_____

_____

_____

_____

_____

_____

_____

_____

SAT II: Writing Test 3

Part B: Multiple-Choice

1. Ⓐ Ⓑ Ⓒ Ⓓ Ⓔ
2. Ⓐ Ⓑ Ⓒ Ⓓ Ⓔ
3. Ⓐ Ⓑ Ⓒ Ⓓ Ⓔ
4. Ⓐ Ⓑ Ⓒ Ⓓ Ⓔ
5. Ⓐ Ⓑ Ⓒ Ⓓ Ⓔ
6. Ⓐ Ⓑ Ⓒ Ⓓ Ⓔ
7. Ⓐ Ⓑ Ⓒ Ⓓ Ⓔ
8. Ⓐ Ⓑ Ⓒ Ⓓ Ⓔ
9. Ⓐ Ⓑ Ⓒ Ⓓ Ⓔ
10. Ⓐ Ⓑ Ⓒ Ⓓ Ⓔ
11. Ⓐ Ⓑ Ⓒ Ⓓ Ⓔ
12. Ⓐ Ⓑ Ⓒ Ⓓ Ⓔ
13. Ⓐ Ⓑ Ⓒ Ⓓ Ⓔ
14. Ⓐ Ⓑ Ⓒ Ⓓ Ⓔ
15. Ⓐ Ⓑ Ⓒ Ⓓ Ⓔ
16. Ⓐ Ⓑ Ⓒ Ⓓ Ⓔ
17. Ⓐ Ⓑ Ⓒ Ⓓ Ⓔ
18. Ⓐ Ⓑ Ⓒ Ⓓ Ⓔ
19. Ⓐ Ⓑ Ⓒ Ⓓ Ⓔ
20. Ⓐ Ⓑ Ⓒ Ⓓ Ⓔ

21. Ⓐ Ⓑ Ⓒ Ⓓ Ⓔ
22. Ⓐ Ⓑ Ⓒ Ⓓ Ⓔ
23. Ⓐ Ⓑ Ⓒ Ⓓ Ⓔ
24. Ⓐ Ⓑ Ⓒ Ⓓ Ⓔ
25. Ⓐ Ⓑ Ⓒ Ⓓ Ⓔ
26. Ⓐ Ⓑ Ⓒ Ⓓ Ⓔ
27. Ⓐ Ⓑ Ⓒ Ⓓ Ⓔ
28. Ⓐ Ⓑ Ⓒ Ⓓ Ⓔ
29. Ⓐ Ⓑ Ⓒ Ⓓ Ⓔ
30. Ⓐ Ⓑ Ⓒ Ⓓ Ⓔ
31. Ⓐ Ⓑ Ⓒ Ⓓ Ⓔ
32. Ⓐ Ⓑ Ⓒ Ⓓ Ⓔ
33. Ⓐ Ⓑ Ⓒ Ⓓ Ⓔ
34. Ⓐ Ⓑ Ⓒ Ⓓ Ⓔ
35. Ⓐ Ⓑ Ⓒ Ⓓ Ⓔ
36. Ⓐ Ⓑ Ⓒ Ⓓ Ⓔ
37. Ⓐ Ⓑ Ⓒ Ⓓ Ⓔ
38. Ⓐ Ⓑ Ⓒ Ⓓ Ⓔ
39. Ⓐ Ⓑ Ⓒ Ⓓ Ⓔ
40. Ⓐ Ⓑ Ⓒ Ⓓ Ⓔ

41. Ⓐ Ⓑ Ⓒ Ⓓ Ⓔ
42. Ⓐ Ⓑ Ⓒ Ⓓ Ⓔ
43. Ⓐ Ⓑ Ⓒ Ⓓ Ⓔ
44. Ⓐ Ⓑ Ⓒ Ⓓ Ⓔ
45. Ⓐ Ⓑ Ⓒ Ⓓ Ⓔ
46. Ⓐ Ⓑ Ⓒ Ⓓ Ⓔ
47. Ⓐ Ⓑ Ⓒ Ⓓ Ⓔ
48. Ⓐ Ⓑ Ⓒ Ⓓ Ⓔ
49. Ⓐ Ⓑ Ⓒ Ⓓ Ⓔ
50. Ⓐ Ⓑ Ⓒ Ⓓ Ⓔ
51. Ⓐ Ⓑ Ⓒ Ⓓ Ⓔ
52. Ⓐ Ⓑ Ⓒ Ⓓ Ⓔ
53. Ⓐ Ⓑ Ⓒ Ⓓ Ⓔ
54. Ⓐ Ⓑ Ⓒ Ⓓ Ⓔ
55. Ⓐ Ⓑ Ⓒ Ⓓ Ⓔ
56. Ⓐ Ⓑ Ⓒ Ⓓ Ⓔ
57. Ⓐ Ⓑ Ⓒ Ⓓ Ⓔ
58. Ⓐ Ⓑ Ⓒ Ⓓ Ⓔ
59. Ⓐ Ⓑ Ⓒ Ⓓ Ⓔ
60. Ⓐ Ⓑ Ⓒ Ⓓ Ⓔ

SAT II: Writing Test 4

Part A: Essay

SAT II: Writing Test 4

Part B: Multiple-Choice

1. Ⓐ Ⓑ Ⓒ Ⓓ Ⓔ	21. Ⓐ Ⓑ Ⓒ Ⓓ Ⓔ	41. Ⓐ Ⓑ Ⓒ Ⓓ Ⓔ
2. Ⓐ Ⓑ Ⓒ Ⓓ Ⓔ	22. Ⓐ Ⓑ Ⓒ Ⓓ Ⓔ	42. Ⓐ Ⓑ Ⓒ Ⓓ Ⓔ
3. Ⓐ Ⓑ Ⓒ Ⓓ Ⓔ	23. Ⓐ Ⓑ Ⓒ Ⓓ Ⓔ	43. Ⓐ Ⓑ Ⓒ Ⓓ Ⓔ
4. Ⓐ Ⓑ Ⓒ Ⓓ Ⓔ	24. Ⓐ Ⓑ Ⓒ Ⓓ Ⓔ	44. Ⓐ Ⓑ Ⓒ Ⓓ Ⓔ
5. Ⓐ Ⓑ Ⓒ Ⓓ Ⓔ	25. Ⓐ Ⓑ Ⓒ Ⓓ Ⓔ	45. Ⓐ Ⓑ Ⓒ Ⓓ Ⓔ
6. Ⓐ Ⓑ Ⓒ Ⓓ Ⓔ	26. Ⓐ Ⓑ Ⓒ Ⓓ Ⓔ	46. Ⓐ Ⓑ Ⓒ Ⓓ Ⓔ
7. Ⓐ Ⓑ Ⓒ Ⓓ Ⓔ	27. Ⓐ Ⓑ Ⓒ Ⓓ Ⓔ	47. Ⓐ Ⓑ Ⓒ Ⓓ Ⓔ
8. Ⓐ Ⓑ Ⓒ Ⓓ Ⓔ	28. Ⓐ Ⓑ Ⓒ Ⓓ Ⓔ	48. Ⓐ Ⓑ Ⓒ Ⓓ Ⓔ
9. Ⓐ Ⓑ Ⓒ Ⓓ Ⓔ	29. Ⓐ Ⓑ Ⓒ Ⓓ Ⓔ	49. Ⓐ Ⓑ Ⓒ Ⓓ Ⓔ
10. Ⓐ Ⓑ Ⓒ Ⓓ Ⓔ	30. Ⓐ Ⓑ Ⓒ Ⓓ Ⓔ	50. Ⓐ Ⓑ Ⓒ Ⓓ Ⓔ
11. Ⓐ Ⓑ Ⓒ Ⓓ Ⓔ	31. Ⓐ Ⓑ Ⓒ Ⓓ Ⓔ	51. Ⓐ Ⓑ Ⓒ Ⓓ Ⓔ
12. Ⓐ Ⓑ Ⓒ Ⓓ Ⓔ	32. Ⓐ Ⓑ Ⓒ Ⓓ Ⓔ	52. Ⓐ Ⓑ Ⓒ Ⓓ Ⓔ
13. Ⓐ Ⓑ Ⓒ Ⓓ Ⓔ	33. Ⓐ Ⓑ Ⓒ Ⓓ Ⓔ	53. Ⓐ Ⓑ Ⓒ Ⓓ Ⓔ
14. Ⓐ Ⓑ Ⓒ Ⓓ Ⓔ	34. Ⓐ Ⓑ Ⓒ Ⓓ Ⓔ	54. Ⓐ Ⓑ Ⓒ Ⓓ Ⓔ
15. Ⓐ Ⓑ Ⓒ Ⓓ Ⓔ	35. Ⓐ Ⓑ Ⓒ Ⓓ Ⓔ	55. Ⓐ Ⓑ Ⓒ Ⓓ Ⓔ
16. Ⓐ Ⓑ Ⓒ Ⓓ Ⓔ	36. Ⓐ Ⓑ Ⓒ Ⓓ Ⓔ	56. Ⓐ Ⓑ Ⓒ Ⓓ Ⓔ
17. Ⓐ Ⓑ Ⓒ Ⓓ Ⓔ	37. Ⓐ Ⓑ Ⓒ Ⓓ Ⓔ	57. Ⓐ Ⓑ Ⓒ Ⓓ Ⓔ
18. Ⓐ Ⓑ Ⓒ Ⓓ Ⓔ	38. Ⓐ Ⓑ Ⓒ Ⓓ Ⓔ	58. Ⓐ Ⓑ Ⓒ Ⓓ Ⓔ
19. Ⓐ Ⓑ Ⓒ Ⓓ Ⓔ	39. Ⓐ Ⓑ Ⓒ Ⓓ Ⓔ	59. Ⓐ Ⓑ Ⓒ Ⓓ Ⓔ
20. Ⓐ Ⓑ Ⓒ Ⓓ Ⓔ	40. Ⓐ Ⓑ Ⓒ Ⓓ Ⓔ	60. Ⓐ Ⓑ Ⓒ Ⓓ Ⓔ

SAT II: Writing Test 5

Part A: Essay

_____

_____

_____

_____

_____

_____

_____

_____

_____

_____

_____

_____

_____

_____

_____

_____

_____

_____

_____

_____

SAT II: Writing Test 5

Part B: Multiple-Choice

1. Ⓐ Ⓑ Ⓒ Ⓓ Ⓔ	21. Ⓐ Ⓑ Ⓒ Ⓓ Ⓔ	41. Ⓐ Ⓑ Ⓒ Ⓓ Ⓔ
2. Ⓐ Ⓑ Ⓒ Ⓓ Ⓔ	22. Ⓐ Ⓑ Ⓒ Ⓓ Ⓔ	42. Ⓐ Ⓑ Ⓒ Ⓓ Ⓔ
3. Ⓐ Ⓑ Ⓒ Ⓓ Ⓔ	23. Ⓐ Ⓑ Ⓒ Ⓓ Ⓔ	43. Ⓐ Ⓑ Ⓒ Ⓓ Ⓔ
4. Ⓐ Ⓑ Ⓒ Ⓓ Ⓔ	24. Ⓐ Ⓑ Ⓒ Ⓓ Ⓔ	44. Ⓐ Ⓑ Ⓒ Ⓓ Ⓔ
5. Ⓐ Ⓑ Ⓒ Ⓓ Ⓔ	25. Ⓐ Ⓑ Ⓒ Ⓓ Ⓔ	45. Ⓐ Ⓑ Ⓒ Ⓓ Ⓔ
6. Ⓐ Ⓑ Ⓒ Ⓓ Ⓔ	26. Ⓐ Ⓑ Ⓒ Ⓓ Ⓔ	46. Ⓐ Ⓑ Ⓒ Ⓓ Ⓔ
7. Ⓐ Ⓑ Ⓒ Ⓓ Ⓔ	27. Ⓐ Ⓑ Ⓒ Ⓓ Ⓔ	47. Ⓐ Ⓑ Ⓒ Ⓓ Ⓔ
8. Ⓐ Ⓑ Ⓒ Ⓓ Ⓔ	28. Ⓐ Ⓑ Ⓒ Ⓓ Ⓔ	48. Ⓐ Ⓑ Ⓒ Ⓓ Ⓔ
9. Ⓐ Ⓑ Ⓒ Ⓓ Ⓔ	29. Ⓐ Ⓑ Ⓒ Ⓓ Ⓔ	49. Ⓐ Ⓑ Ⓒ Ⓓ Ⓔ
10. Ⓐ Ⓑ Ⓒ Ⓓ Ⓔ	30. Ⓐ Ⓑ Ⓒ Ⓓ Ⓔ	50. Ⓐ Ⓑ Ⓒ Ⓓ Ⓔ
11. Ⓐ Ⓑ Ⓒ Ⓓ Ⓔ	31. Ⓐ Ⓑ Ⓒ Ⓓ Ⓔ	51. Ⓐ Ⓑ Ⓒ Ⓓ Ⓔ
12. Ⓐ Ⓑ Ⓒ Ⓓ Ⓔ	32. Ⓐ Ⓑ Ⓒ Ⓓ Ⓔ	52. Ⓐ Ⓑ Ⓒ Ⓓ Ⓔ
13. Ⓐ Ⓑ Ⓒ Ⓓ Ⓔ	33. Ⓐ Ⓑ Ⓒ Ⓓ Ⓔ	53. Ⓐ Ⓑ Ⓒ Ⓓ Ⓔ
14. Ⓐ Ⓑ Ⓒ Ⓓ Ⓔ	34. Ⓐ Ⓑ Ⓒ Ⓓ Ⓔ	54. Ⓐ Ⓑ Ⓒ Ⓓ Ⓔ
15. Ⓐ Ⓑ Ⓒ Ⓓ Ⓔ	35. Ⓐ Ⓑ Ⓒ Ⓓ Ⓔ	55. Ⓐ Ⓑ Ⓒ Ⓓ Ⓔ
16. Ⓐ Ⓑ Ⓒ Ⓓ Ⓔ	36. Ⓐ Ⓑ Ⓒ Ⓓ Ⓔ	56. Ⓐ Ⓑ Ⓒ Ⓓ Ⓔ
17. Ⓐ Ⓑ Ⓒ Ⓓ Ⓔ	37. Ⓐ Ⓑ Ⓒ Ⓓ Ⓔ	57. Ⓐ Ⓑ Ⓒ Ⓓ Ⓔ
18. Ⓐ Ⓑ Ⓒ Ⓓ Ⓔ	38. Ⓐ Ⓑ Ⓒ Ⓓ Ⓔ	58. Ⓐ Ⓑ Ⓒ Ⓓ Ⓔ
19. Ⓐ Ⓑ Ⓒ Ⓓ Ⓔ	39. Ⓐ Ⓑ Ⓒ Ⓓ Ⓔ	59. Ⓐ Ⓑ Ⓒ Ⓓ Ⓔ
20. Ⓐ Ⓑ Ⓒ Ⓓ Ⓔ	40. Ⓐ Ⓑ Ⓒ Ⓓ Ⓔ	60. Ⓐ Ⓑ Ⓒ Ⓓ Ⓔ

SAT II: Writing Test 6

Part A: Essay

SAT II: Writing Test 6

Part B: Multiple-Choice

1. Ⓐ Ⓑ Ⓒ Ⓓ Ⓔ
2. Ⓐ Ⓑ Ⓒ Ⓓ Ⓔ
3. Ⓐ Ⓑ Ⓒ Ⓓ Ⓔ
4. Ⓐ Ⓑ Ⓒ Ⓓ Ⓔ
5. Ⓐ Ⓑ Ⓒ Ⓓ Ⓔ
6. Ⓐ Ⓑ Ⓒ Ⓓ Ⓔ
7. Ⓐ Ⓑ Ⓒ Ⓓ Ⓔ
8. Ⓐ Ⓑ Ⓒ Ⓓ Ⓔ
9. Ⓐ Ⓑ Ⓒ Ⓓ Ⓔ
10. Ⓐ Ⓑ Ⓒ Ⓓ Ⓔ
11. Ⓐ Ⓑ Ⓒ Ⓓ Ⓔ
12. Ⓐ Ⓑ Ⓒ Ⓓ Ⓔ
13. Ⓐ Ⓑ Ⓒ Ⓓ Ⓔ
14. Ⓐ Ⓑ Ⓒ Ⓓ Ⓔ
15. Ⓐ Ⓑ Ⓒ Ⓓ Ⓔ
16. Ⓐ Ⓑ Ⓒ Ⓓ Ⓔ
17. Ⓐ Ⓑ Ⓒ Ⓓ Ⓔ
18. Ⓐ Ⓑ Ⓒ Ⓓ Ⓔ
19. Ⓐ Ⓑ Ⓒ Ⓓ Ⓔ
20. Ⓐ Ⓑ Ⓒ Ⓓ Ⓔ

21. Ⓐ Ⓑ Ⓒ Ⓓ Ⓔ
22. Ⓐ Ⓑ Ⓒ Ⓓ Ⓔ
23. Ⓐ Ⓑ Ⓒ Ⓓ Ⓔ
24. Ⓐ Ⓑ Ⓒ Ⓓ Ⓔ
25. Ⓐ Ⓑ Ⓒ Ⓓ Ⓔ
26. Ⓐ Ⓑ Ⓒ Ⓓ Ⓔ
27. Ⓐ Ⓑ Ⓒ Ⓓ Ⓔ
28. Ⓐ Ⓑ Ⓒ Ⓓ Ⓔ
29. Ⓐ Ⓑ Ⓒ Ⓓ Ⓔ
30. Ⓐ Ⓑ Ⓒ Ⓓ Ⓔ
31. Ⓐ Ⓑ Ⓒ Ⓓ Ⓔ
32. Ⓐ Ⓑ Ⓒ Ⓓ Ⓔ
33. Ⓐ Ⓑ Ⓒ Ⓓ Ⓔ
34. Ⓐ Ⓑ Ⓒ Ⓓ Ⓔ
35. Ⓐ Ⓑ Ⓒ Ⓓ Ⓔ
36. Ⓐ Ⓑ Ⓒ Ⓓ Ⓔ
37. Ⓐ Ⓑ Ⓒ Ⓓ Ⓔ
38. Ⓐ Ⓑ Ⓒ Ⓓ Ⓔ
39. Ⓐ Ⓑ Ⓒ Ⓓ Ⓔ
40. Ⓐ Ⓑ Ⓒ Ⓓ Ⓔ

41. Ⓐ Ⓑ Ⓒ Ⓓ Ⓔ
42. Ⓐ Ⓑ Ⓒ Ⓓ Ⓔ
43. Ⓐ Ⓑ Ⓒ Ⓓ Ⓔ
44. Ⓐ Ⓑ Ⓒ Ⓓ Ⓔ
45. Ⓐ Ⓑ Ⓒ Ⓓ Ⓔ
46. Ⓐ Ⓑ Ⓒ Ⓓ Ⓔ
47. Ⓐ Ⓑ Ⓒ Ⓓ Ⓔ
48. Ⓐ Ⓑ Ⓒ Ⓓ Ⓔ
49. Ⓐ Ⓑ Ⓒ Ⓓ Ⓔ
50. Ⓐ Ⓑ Ⓒ Ⓓ Ⓔ
51. Ⓐ Ⓑ Ⓒ Ⓓ Ⓔ
52. Ⓐ Ⓑ Ⓒ Ⓓ Ⓔ
53. Ⓐ Ⓑ Ⓒ Ⓓ Ⓔ
54. Ⓐ Ⓑ Ⓒ Ⓓ Ⓔ
55. Ⓐ Ⓑ Ⓒ Ⓓ Ⓔ
56. Ⓐ Ⓑ Ⓒ Ⓓ Ⓔ
57. Ⓐ Ⓑ Ⓒ Ⓓ Ⓔ
58. Ⓐ Ⓑ Ⓒ Ⓓ Ⓔ
59. Ⓐ Ⓑ Ⓒ Ⓓ Ⓔ
60. Ⓐ Ⓑ Ⓒ Ⓓ Ⓔ